# The Invisible Hand of God at Work

## An Extraordinary God Experienced in an Ordinary Life

*To; Bob, Ingrid and Family, 7/22/16*

### Larry E. Burd

Foreword by Scott L. Weldon

*May you always be aware of the invisible hand of God at work in your lives. Joshua 4:24; Psalm 139: 9-10*

*Larry E. Burd,*

The Invisible Hand of God at Work

Copyright © 2016 Larry E. Burd
All rights reserved.

ISBN: 978-1-941733-77-6

Published by EA Books Publishing a division of
Living Parables of Central Florida, Inc. a 501c3
EABooksPublishing.com

# DEDICATION

.

### *To my family*

To my faithful wife Sharon, who has loved me for over forty-seven years despite my many faults.

To my four special children, Nathan, Amy, Evan, Lisa, and their spouses Mary, Darryl, Sarah and Gregg.

To my nine precious grandchildren, Madelyn, Chloe, Benjamin, Elliot, Liza, Everett, Jack, Owen, and Timothy.

### *To my Lord and Savior*

Without Jesus Christ in my life I would be nothing and would have nothing of value to write about. I praise Him for His invisible hand upon my life.

# ACKNOWLEDGMENTS

The problem I had with writing an acknowledgment was the concern that I would inadvertently fail to acknowledge someone I really wanted to thank. I apologize to you if you are that someone. I sincerely tried to include as many people as I could remember who contributed to this book in some way. The ideas for this book began to be birthed in my heart and mind fifteen years ago; there are many who have since helped and encouraged me.

First of all, there are those who challenged me to write a book someday. Those individuals include my son Evan Burd, my son-in-law Gregg Rader, my brother Dennis Burd, Eric Beattie, Beverly Matchette, Kara Barner, Joe Nestor, Sam Royer, Phil and Diane Mumau, Doris Julian, and Kelly Liberto.

I would like to thank Kris Hemphill for her excellent editorial assistance and the countless hours she spent helping me on this book. Kris knows me well, and her insights into what I was trying to write about were extremely helpful. I want to thank my wife, Sharon, for her loving help proofreading , but also for her willingness to allow me to include many details about our lives, our family and our ministries, many of which I am sure she wished I hadn't. Thanks to Jenn Lechliter from EA Publishing for her kind editorial assistance and to Cheri Cowell, owner of EA Books, a division of Living Parables of Central Florida, Inc., for allowing the invisible hand of God to guide her to enable my dream to come true to get my book published.

Special thanks to many who read portions of the book and shared their suggestions –Scott Weldon, Joe and Katie Kricks, Dr. Terry Zebulske, Dorene Krisovitch, Kevin Correll, Bill Oldham, Carla D'Addesi, Diane Mumau, Jessie Seneca, Brittany Barbera, Marco Lipperoni, Beverly Mattchette and Jack Tanis.

There are several people I want to thank for spending many hours typing the original manuscript. Thank you to Jill Schaffer and her daughters, Cayla and Elizabeth, as well as to Angela Spadafora.

Thanks to Brian and Andrea Hess as well as to Sue Cutlip for their computer assistance, which kept me from going insane at times.

Thanks to my closest friend on earth, after my wife and family, Scott Weldon, who wrote the foreword to the book.

Thanks to Kelly Vanek and Cassidy Communications for designing the cover and for being so excited about this project.

Thanks to the elders of Calvary Baptist Church who gave me the time to get started in writing.

Special appreciation and thanks to the countless number of brothers and sisters in Christ at Calvary Baptist Church and beyond who prayed for me to be able to complete this writing project.

My highest praise goes to my Lord and Savior Jesus Christ who gave me wisdom and strength and kept His invisible hand upon me, especially during the times when I wanted to quit writing, editing and re-editing and praying over this book. If anyone is encouraged by reading this book may they give Him the praise and glory for what He has done. "For it is God who works in you to will and to act according to His good purpose" (Philippians 2:13).

# TABLE OF CONTENTS

# FOREWORD

by Scott L. Weldon

Suppose you want to write a book. The excitement of the initial conception from months ago sparks with life. The ideas cascade and long-lost memories are awakened. The introduction to the life of this book is stated and you even decide on a name for it. The opening chapters flow. It begins to take on a life of its own. Somewhere in the process others begin to notice that something is alive in you. Joy radiates. There are tired days to be sure. Even total mental blocks. The book sleeps. But movement begins again and all energy is drawn inextricably toward the birth process. Finally your book is born. If you are husband and dad, you feel your first pangs of true empathy for what your wife went through!

Now you have just one more decision. It's called a foreword. How will you present your book to the world? You have met some well-known leaders with instant name recognition. And you have an unknown friend who has shared life and ministry with you for fifty years. You're best friends. Who will you choose? Pastor Burd chose the latter.

This book is a gift to us from the author's heart to ours. The invisible hand of a sovereign God becomes visible to us through his everyday discoveries interwoven with Scriptural insights and applications. This very personal and approachable man presents an approachable and personal God who delights in creating hundreds of "happy coincidences" and unexplainable moments to His children who trust Him. So go ahead. Meet my best friend and enter into conversation with him. He will introduce you to his Best Friend and help you to see things that are invisible to this world. You are about to meet a friend who will give you a "faith lift" and make you smile a lot. I know.

# PREFACE

For many years I have been intrigued by the numerous references in the Bible to "the hand of God" or "the hand of the Lord." I often thought that if I ever wrote a book, this would be an interesting subject to research and write about. So this book is about the invisible hand of God at work. But if "no one has ever seen God" (John 1:18), and God is a "Spirit" (John 4:24), then how can anyone know anything about the invisible hand of God at work? Although God's hand is unseen, it accomplishes great and mighty things as recorded in the Bible.

When God's people, the Israelites, crossed the Red Sea and the Jordan River on dry ground, it was because the invisible hand of God was at work performing miracles for His people. Joshua told the Israelites why God did these amazing miracles: "He did this so that all the peoples of the earth might know that the hand of the Lord is powerful and so that you might always fear the Lord your God" (Joshua 4:24).

When scores of people turned to the Lord in the book of Acts, it was because the invisible hand of God was at work. "The Lord's hand was with them, and a great number of people believed and turned to the Lord" (Acts 11:21).

Many of God's servants wrote about God's hand being upon them. David declared, "For day and night Your hand was heavy upon me" (Psalm 32:4). He also wrote about God's hand of guidance in his life. "If I rise on the wings of the dawn, if I settle on the far side of the sea, even there Your hand will guide me, Your right hand will hold me fast" (Psalm 139:9-10).

Ezekiel, the prophet, also wrote of the strong hand of the Lord being on him (Ezekiel 3:14,22).

Although the biblical references to "the hand of God" or "the hand of the Lord" were metaphorical, those who wrote about the invisible hand of God experienced His hand working amazing effects in their lives. And just as we cannot see the wind, but we can experience its effects, even so we cannot see God's hand at work, but we can experience the effects of God's hand upon our lives as His children.

I felt compelled to write this book. Psalm 145:4 declares, "One generation will commend Your works to another; they will tell of Your mighty acts." As Christians, we are to pass on to the next generation what we have experienced of the invisible hand of God at work in our lives. We are to declare His mighty acts to the next generation.

From an early age there were things that I observed in the lives of my grandparents and parents that made me wonder about the invisible God they loved and served. Then I observed amazing things that happened in my youth, marriage, years of raising a family and over the past forty-three years of pastoral ministry that can only be explained as the invisible hand of God at work. The Scriptures give numerous examples of how God's hand saves, guides, provides, heals and performs miracles, but always remains invisible to the human eye. This, to me, is a fascinating subject and one worthy of consideration.

Over the years, I have often shared with my family, friends and the people in the congregations where I have served what I experienced of the "mighty acts" of the invisible hand of God at work in my life. The response I received on numerous occasions was, "You ought to write a book and share these things." I thanked them for their kind words, but thought to myself, "When would I ever have time to write a book?" I'm the senior pastor of a large congregation and I host a weekly television program. I give oversight and encouragement to fifteen pastors and congregations as a part-time Regional Minister with the Atlantic Association of the North American Baptist Conference. I serve as Chairman of the Board of Share the Power, a ministry to pastors and Christian leaders in the Lehigh Valley of Pennsylvania. I travel occasionally to minister in other countries on mission fields. I'm a husband, father of four married children and grandfather of nine grandchildren—so I thought "forget the book writing idea. I'm far too busy to consider such a thing."

I am now in my forty-third year of ministry and will soon complete my thirty-third year at Calvary Baptist Church in

Easton, Pennsylvania. Three years ago the elders of my church asked me to share with them my thoughts about the future of my ministry. I told them I have no desire to retire. I want to continue to minister in one capacity or another as long as God gives me strength and wisdom. I shared with the elders that I had been earnestly praying about my future ministry. As I prayed, one of the things I believe God confirmed to me was that He wanted me to write a book and obey Psalm 145:4 to declare the "mighty acts" of what His invisible hand has done throughout my life.

I asked the elders of my church if they would give me the month of February 2013 as a sabbatical to begin writing a book. They said yes. Little did I realize then that I would be having major back surgery in January and would have a lengthy recovery. I concluded that the invisible hand of God opened a door for me to begin writing. During the four months of my recovery and sabbatical I was able to finish the first draft of this book.

To further confirm God's leading, I was reading Mark Batterson's amazing book, *The Circle Maker*. The author wrote, "The issue is never, 'Are you qualified?' The issue is always, 'Are you called?' I make this distinction between qualified and called with aspiring writers all the time. Too many authors worry about whether or not their book will get published. That isn't the question. The question is this: Are you called to write? That's the only question you need to answer. And if the answer is yes, then you need to write the book as an act of obedience. It doesn't matter whether anyone reads it or not." When I read these words I wrote in the margin of the book, "WRITE THE BOOK... OBEY GOD."

I want to thank my family, friends, the elders of Calvary Baptist Church, our congregation and people in our community who have encouraged me and have prayed for me as I wrote this book. God has heard and answered their prayers.

My daily prayer for many years has been, "Lord, use me for Your glory." Psalm 115:1 (KJV) has become one of my favorite verses of Scripture: "Not unto us, O Lord, not unto us, but unto Thy name give glory, for Thy mercy, and for Thy truth's sake."

Do you desire to experience more of the invisible hand of God at work in your life? As you seek to know, love and obey Him, be prepared. His hand will work in unexplainable ways and you will conclude that only God could have done these things and you will want to share with others what He did in your life.

It is my prayer that the next generation will experience the invisible hand of God at work in their lives as I have experienced His hand at work in my life. If that prayer is answered, then I will praise Him for His "mighty acts" which He has done not only in my life, but in the lives of countless multitudes throughout the ages. To God be the glory.

Larry E. Burd

CHAPTER 1

# THE INVISIBLE HAND OF GOD AT WORK IN MY GRANDPARENTS

*"Show the wonder of Your great love, You who save by Your right hand those who take refuge in You from their foes" (Psalm 17:7).*

"If you have that baby tonight, it's because you've eaten too many potato pancakes." That's what Grandpa Litke said to my mother, and within a few hours my parents were on their way to the hospital. Grandpa Litke was a loving man who had a bald head and a bushy mustache. He was a man of few words with a humorous personality, and when he spoke, I often laughed and knew he was right on target with what he said. Sure enough, his words came to pass, and on February 11, 1948, I was born in Philipsburg, Pennsylvania, a small town nestled in the center of the state. It was there that I began to learn many new things about life, including the joy of eating potato pancakes.

### The Influence Of My Godly Maternal Grandparents

Looking back on my early years, I believe the invisible hand of God was at work in the lives of my maternal and paternal grandparents. They were hardworking, godly people who lived what they believed. Their Christ-like character, compassion and concern had a powerful influence in my life.

Henry and Rosalie Litke, my maternal grandparents, were immigrants. Grandpa Litke emigrated from Poland to the United States at age twenty, on January 12, 1900. My grandmother, Rosalie, came from Russia, but had a brief stay in Brazil before arriving at Ellis Island in New York Harbor in 1892. After my grandparents were married, they settled in the little town of Forest, in central Pennsylvania. They had two sons, William (Bill)

1

and August (Gust), and four daughters, Alma, Martha, Bertha (my mother) and Amelia (Dolly). They were all raised in a Christian home and were members of the Forest Baptist Church, which was just across the street from the little farmhouse where they lived.

I had the privilege of observing the godly lives of Grandpa and Grandma Litke, almost on a daily basis. During the years before I went to college, my family lived in the small town of Munson, Pennsylvania, which was only two and a half miles from my grandparents' farm. Grandpa and Grandma raised a few milk cows and my dad made a daily trip to their farm to pick up two quarts of whole milk for our family. They didn't pasteurize in those days. It gave me a warm feeling inside just to experience the genuine love and kindness of my grandparents. They were such giving people. Whatever they had, they wanted to share with others.

## A Woman Of Faith

The apostle Paul wrote about Timothy's godly grandmother and mother in 2 Timothy 1:5, "I have been reminded of your sincere faith, which first lived in your grandmother Lois and in your mother Eunice and I am persuaded, now lives in you also." This verse of Scripture reminds me of Grandma Litke and my mother, as well. They were both women of sincere faith. They trusted God to meet their needs — no matter what those needs may have been for themselves, their families, or for others who they reached out to in the name of Jesus, their Savior and Lord.

I saw my grandmother's faith in action on numerous occasions when I was visiting in her home in my early years. Grandma loved people and enjoyed having them in her home for meals. Since she lived across the street from the church, she could observe people getting out of their cars to attend the Sunday morning worship services. If she spotted a new family, she kindly introduced herself and invited them to dinner at her house after the service. Many people accepted her warm invitation and enjoyed a delicious home-cooked Sunday dinner at Grandma's house.

On more than one occasion, I thought to myself, "How in the world is she going to pull this off? She has already invited a houseful of relatives for Sunday dinner, and now she's invited total strangers to join us." When I questioned her, "Grandma, do you think you'll have enough food for all these people?", she would reply by saying something like, "Sure, there will be enough food for everyone. I'll just throw in another potato or two. God will provide." And provide He did. I saw it with my own eyes.

Everyone enjoyed the meal, and there was even food left on the dining room table when we were all finished eating. The invisible hand of God was at work just as Psalm 145:15-16 declares, "The eyes of all look to You, and You give them their food at the proper time. You open Your hand and satisfy the desires of every living thing." Seeing my grandmother's faith in action increased my faith. If God could provide for Grandma Litke, He could provide for me. Still, I wrestled with the question: Would I be willing to trust this invisible God?

## A Woman Who Loved To Do Good And Have Fun

My grandmother taught me that there's greater joy in doing good than evil. Joy stems naturally from obedience. Jesus said, "If you obey My commands, you will remain in My love, just as I have obeyed My father's commands and remain in His love. I have told you this so that My joy may be in you and that your joy may be complete" (John 15:10-11). My grandmother's heart had been transformed by Christ living within her and His love overflowed in her life. Because of her close relationship with Christ, she desired to bless others rather than curse them. Psalm 34:14 says, "Turn from evil and do good." In Galatians 6:10, the Scripture puts it this way: "Therefore, as we have opportunity, let us do good to all people, especially to those who belong to the family of believers."

Across the fields and down a little hill from my grandma's farmhouse was a swampy area where cranberries grew. One day, she took me along with her and told me a story as we picked cranberries. "Many years ago," Grandma said, "a little girl and I came here to pick cranberries. When we arrived, we saw a pair of shoes that belonged to another little girl who was also picking cranberries. 'Let's fill her shoes with mud,' the girl with my grandma said. But my grandma replied, 'No, let's put a penny in her shoes and watch how happy she will be when she finds it.'" In sharing that simple story, my grandma taught me a profound, biblical truth that Christians are to "turn from evil and do good." Many of the lessons my grandma taught me as a child are still shaping my life today.

## A Woman With The Gift Of Hospitality

Grandma loved to bake, and if I smelled freshly baked rye or sweet bread when I opened the old backdoor to her house, I knew we would be taking some of that delicious bread home with us. I could hardly wait to get out of bed the next morning and taste that bread slathered in butter and strawberry jam. That was always a special treat that I will long remember.

The gift of hospitality was one of my grandma's strong suits. In I Peter 4:9 the Bible says, "Offer hospitality to one another without grumbling." Grandma's door was always open and people would often stop to visit with her and Grandpa. If she baked that day and people visited with them until late in the afternoon, Grandma would say, "Can you stay and have supper with us? We're having rye bread and coffee." Grandma didn't feel as though she had to prepare a five-course meal for her guests, she simply offered them whatever she had at the time. She was so gracious and many of her guests would accept her offer and stay longer to enjoy a simple meal together.

What was the source of my grandparents' genuine love, kindness, hospitality and graciousness? Why were they the kind of people they were? I was beginning to understand it was their humble relationship with God through faith in His Son, Jesus Christ, Who made them the way they were. The invisible hand of God was upon their lives and the visible fruit of the Holy Spirit was seen in how they lived and through the words they spoke. Galatians 5:22-23 was a daily vibrant experience for my grandparents: "But the fruit of the Spirit is love, joy, peace, patience, kindness, goodness, faithfulness, gentleness and self-control. Against such things there is no law." Their lives had a tremendous influence on my life.

## A Woman Who Served The Lord

Grandma Litke was the church clerk at Forest Baptist Church for over forty years. She took great delight in serving the Lord and His people faithfully. Jesus said, "Whoever serves Me must follow Me; and where I am, My servant also will be. My Father will honor the one who serves Me" (John 12:26). Grandma followed Jesus wherever He led her with His invisible hand. She also seemed to be guided by a "still, small voice" that no one else could hear, almost like Samuel who heard God's voice in I Samuel 3:1-10. *Was she really hearing the voice of Jesus? Was He the One who was speaking to her and guiding her to do the things she did?* Jesus said in John 10:27, "My sheep listen to My voice; I know them, and they follow Me." It was her willingness to listen and follow Jesus that brought such joy and vitality into her life. I observed this, and she made me want to have what she had. That I was aware of, she never forced her faith or way of life upon me or anyone else in our family, congregation or community. Grandma simply let her life be a natural witness and lovingly shared her faith with anyone who would listen to her.

## A Woman Of Bible Knowledge And Wisdom

My grandma was very knowledgeable about the Bible, but she also had much practical common sense and wisdom. I was anxious to visit her after I had completed my first six weeks at Houghton College, a Christian liberal arts college in Houghton, New York. I had just finished my first Bible course and Grandma had a question for me. She said, "I want to know what you have been learning at that college you've been attending. Can you tell me where in the Bible it says, 'Be still and know that I am God?'"

I couldn't believe she asked me that particular question. I was so excited, I felt like I could burst inside. There are over 31,000 verses in the entire Bible, and I had just memorized, in the past week, the one verse Grandma questioned me about. I was beaming with joy, and the buttons on my shirt were ready to pop as I said, "Grandma, that's Psalm 46:10." Grandma's jaw dropped. She never asked me another Bible question, and I never told her that that was the only verse I had memorized up to that point.

After this pleasant experience with my grandma, whom I loved and respected dearly, I thought I would ask her a question. By this time in my life I knew God had called me into the ministry and I needed some sound advice. "Grandma, what advice would you have for a young man going into the ministry?" My grandma knew many pastors, evangelists, and missionaries, and many of them had stayed in her home while ministering at the church across the street. She had learned much from them, and I am sure they learned much from her as well. She paused to think before she answered my question. She was wise and discerning and always chose her words well before she responded. She said, "I'll tell you two things about being in the ministry. Number one: When you are at the pulpit, speak up loudly and clearly. Nothing is more frustrating than to sit in church and not be able to hear what the speaker is saying, so speak up."

Grandma proceeded to give me her second word of advice about the ministry. "As a pastor, you must be like a duck." "Be like a duck?" As an eighteen-year-old teenager, I certainly didn't know much about the ministry, and I had no clue as to what being like a duck was all about. I asked her, "Grandma, what do you mean when you say a pastor must be like a duck?" She said, "A lot of what you hear you must let it roll off your back like the water rolls off the back of a duck." What wise advice my grandma had just given me. Her two points of advice have been rehearsed in my mind many times over the past forty-three years of being a pastor. Her discerning, practical, and sound advice has helped me greatly in my ministry so that even today I project my voice when I am preaching. I have also learned to let negative words roll off my back.

Proverbs 9:9-10 declares, "Instruct a wise man and he will be wiser still; teach a righteous man and he will add to his learning. The fear of the Lord is the beginning of wisdom, and knowledge of the Holy One is understanding." I greatly valued the instruction and teaching received from my godly grandma.

About a month before my grandma died, I had a dream about her. In my dream I was in her dining room, which had been converted into her bedroom. She was lying in a hospital bed, close to death. Although it was light outside in my dream, it suddenly got dark, like we were having an eclipse. I went to the window beside my grandma's bed to see what was taking place outside. As I looked up into the dark sky I saw two very large but beautiful hands that were motioning like they wanted someone to come to them.

Were those beautiful hands motioning for my grandma to come because it was time for her to leave this life and go to heaven? This dream was very meaningful to me and in reality it came to pass. Within four weeks, Grandma Litke died and we celebrated her life and coronation day with her family and friends. The invisible hand of God had been at work throughout her ninety-two years, and now she was received into the strong and gentle hands of Jesus Christ, her wonderful Lord and Savior.

## The Influence Of My Godly Paternal Grandparents

Just as the invisible hand of God was at work in my maternal grandparents, even so it was the same with my paternal grandparents. The Bible says, "The gracious hand of our God is on everyone who looks to Him, but His great anger is against all who forsake Him" (Ezra 8:22).

Grandpa and Grandma Burd, Lawrence Frank and Bertha, were also godly people. They experienced the gracious hand of God upon their lives because they looked to God as the source of all their needs. Isaiah 45:22 (KJV) says, "Look unto Me, and be saved, all the ends of the earth; for I am God, and there is none else."

My grandparents looked to God and were "saved" or rescued from the penalty and power of sin. Romans 6:23 tells us, "For the wages of sin is death, but the gift of God is eternal life in Christ Jesus our Lord." Because we have all sinned before a holy and righteous God, we all deserve to die, but God offers us salvation through faith in His only Son, Jesus Christ.

God gave a dramatic and graphic picture of His plan to rescue people in Numbers 21:4-9.

> "They traveled from Mount Hor along the route to the Red Sea, to go around Edom. But the people grew impatient on the way; they spoke against God and against Moses, and said, 'Why have you brought us up out of Egypt to die in the desert? There is no bread! There is no water! And we detest this miserable food!' Then the Lord sent venomous snakes among them; they bit the people and many Israelites died. The people came to Moses and said, 'We sinned when we spoke against the Lord and against you. Pray that the Lord will take the snakes away from us.' So Moses prayed for the people. The Lord said to Moses, 'Make a snake and put it up on a pole; anyone who is bitten can look at it and live.' So Moses made a bronze snake and put it up on a pole. Then when anyone was bitten by a snake and looked at the bronze snake he lived."

Interestingly, the snake on a pole is the same symbol the medical profession often uses.

Jesus referred to this story in the book of Numbers. In John 3:14-15 Jesus said, "Just as Moses lifted up the snake in the desert, so the Son of Man must be lifted up, that anyone who believes in Him may have eternal life." Jesus was lifted up on the cross when He died for the sins of the world, and anyone who looks to Jesus to be saved will have eternal life, just as He promised.

My grandparents looked to Jesus, and He gave them the gift of eternal life. Jesus touched them with His invisible hand, and their lives were changed forever.

Bill Gaither wrote the words to the song, "He Touched Me": "Shackled by a heavy burden, 'neath a load of guilt and shame; then the hand of Jesus touched me, and now I am no longer the same. He touched me, O, He touched me, and O the joy that floods my soul; Something happened and now I know, He touched me and made me whole."[1]

---

[1] The Hymnal for Worship and Celebration, (Word Music: Waco, 1963), 504.

My grandpa Burd once told me there were times in his life when he got so happy in Jesus that he "commenced to shoutin'." My grandparents lived on a farm in Newport, Pennsylvania, which was about twenty-five miles from Harrisburg, the capital of the state. It was over 100 miles from where we lived in Munson, so I didn't get to see my paternal grandparents very often. But when I did, they were just like my maternal grandparents, a powerful influence in my life.

Grandpa and Grandma Burd had five sons: Denton, Charles, Kenneth, Galen, and Leroy, who was my father. They also had three daughters: Mildred, Catherine, and Eleanor. They all grew up on the farm and were hardworking, godly people. Each one had their daily chores to do. My dad must have spent considerable time in the kitchen because he often spoke about cooking for a family of ten. When my parents got married, my dad wanted to cook. After some frustrating experiences that my mother spoke about, she finally gave in and said, "Leroy, you do the cooking; I'll do the cleaning and ironing." And that's the way it was in our house all through the years of my childhood and youth.

### A Man Of Prayer

Grandpa Burd was a man of prayer. He was about five feet seven inches tall—but what he didn't have in height, he certainly made up for in spiritual power. Not only did he spend time in prayer privately, but I can never remember a time when he didn't pray with me personally or with us as a family before we left his house. I could feel the power of God intensifying as he prayed.

Grandpa loved the book of Revelation in the Bible, and he often referred to it in his prayers. As he prayed, I could picture a panorama of many of the events in the book unfolding before my eyes. He prayed with such spiritual power that I could feel my spirit being lifted into the heavenly realm; I sensed God's presence and love clearly. His prayers impacted me in many positive ways.

I have one of my grandpa's well-worn Bibles that was passed down to me when he died. In the opening pages of his Bible he had written several prayer requests. He prayed three very specific prayers for me. One, that God would save me; two, that God would call me into the ministry; and the last request was that God would use me in what Grandpa called "His evangelistic field." He prayed that God would use me as an evangelist.

I am so thrilled that God allowed my grandfather to live long enough to see the answers to all three of his requests. God did save me. He called me into the ministry. He opened doors for me to preach the Gospel in many churches and do the work of an evangelist in seeking to lead lost people to a saving knowledge of Jesus Christ. These three life-changing events have all come to pass as a result of my grandfather's humble, godly, powerful prayers.

Thank God for godly grandparents who pray for their grandchildren. I cherish his old Bible, and I want it — as well as several of my Bibles — to be passed on to my children when I die and then to my grandchildren as well. What a great treasure there is to be found in an old, tattered Bible. Someone once said, "If your Bible is falling apart, your life probably isn't."

## A Man Called To Preach

Grandpa Burd was a man called of God to preach the gospel. The power of God was upon him and worked through him as he preached. The invisible hand of God was at work in his life and in my grandmother's life as well. Isaiah 51:14 says, "I have put My words in your mouth and covered you with the shadow of My hand." This is what I experienced in the life of my grandpa Burd. God put His words in Grandpa's mouth and covered him with the shadow of His hand. This is the only explanation that made sense to me as I observed my grandpa's life and heard him preach God's Word with anointed power.

Although my grandpa was ordained to the ministry, he never pastored a church. He often filled the pulpit when a church needed a guest speaker. He preached at camp meetings, revival meetings and evangelistic meetings. He was always ready to preach, pray, or die at any moment. His Bibles were filled with notes, quotes, and anecdotes that he collected through the years.

## A Man With A Love For Souls

Grandpa Burd was a man with a love for souls. He believed Proverbs 11:30, "He that wins souls is wise," and Daniel 12:3, which states, "Those who are wise will shine like the brightness of the heavens, and those who lead many to righteousness, like the stars for ever and ever." Grandpa believed according to the Bible that everyone had a soul, and that the soul was eternal and would live on forever in a real heaven or hell. Grandpa wanted to do everything he could to lead people to a saving knowledge of Jesus Christ before it was eternally too late.

Even in Grandpa's late eighties when his health was failing, he was still praying for souls. If he couldn't get out to share Jesus Christ with people directly, he would pray that God would lead people to his house where he could talk with them. I remember visiting him one day, and he was so excited about sharing the good news of his faith with everyone or anyone who would listen to him. With great joy and enthusiasm (which in the Greek language means "God within") and a big smile on his face he said, "Larry, a lady got stuck in the snow in front of our house. She came to the door and asked if she could use our telephone to call for help...and I led her to Christ right here in the living room." His passion for souls influenced my life tremendously. Today, I feel the same passion welling up in my soul for the souls of lost people who need Jesus in their lives.

### "A Passion for Souls"
Herbert G. Tovey [2]

Give me a passion for souls, dear Lord,
A passion to save the lost;
O that Thy love were by all adored,
And welcomed at any cost.

Though there are dangers untold and stern,
Confronting me in the way,

---

[2] Herbert G. Tovey, Revival Hymns and Choruses, ( Public Domain Cyber hymnal)

Willingly still would I go, nor turn,
But trust Thee for grace each day.

How shall this passion for souls be mine?
Lord, make Thou the answer clear;
Help me to throw out the old Lifeline
To those who are struggling near.


Jesus, I long, I long to be winning
Men who are lost, and constantly sinning;
O may this hour be one of beginning
The story of pardon to tell.

### A Man Ready To Meet His Creator And Lord

Grandpa Burd was a man who longed for the day—especially when his body became frail in his late eighties—when Jesus would call him home to his mansion in heaven. In John 14:1-3 (KJV) Jesus said, "Let not your heart be troubled; you believe in God, believe also in Me. In My Father's house are many mansions; if it were not so, I would have told you. And if I go and prepare a place for you, I will come again, and receive you unto Myself, that where I am, there you may be also."

The word "mansions" in the King James Version of the Bible is translated "rooms" in the New International Version. I would much prefer living in a mansion for all eternity, rather than just in a room. I think I'll stick with the King James Version on this particular verse.

In addition to Grandpa's love for the book of Revelation, he also often referred to I Thessalonians 4:13-18. Many Bible scholars speak of this passage of God's Word as "the rapture." The word rapture literally means "snatched away" or "caught up." In Latin, the phrase "caught up" is "rapturo," from which comes the English word "rapture."

The apostle Paul wrote those words in I Thessalonians 4:13-18 to help prepare believers, those who had repented of their sins and trusted in Jesus Christ alone for salvation, for heaven. They were anxiously awaiting the return of Jesus Christ who would take them with Him back to heaven:

> "Brothers, we do not want you to be ignorant about those who fall asleep (have died), or to grieve like the rest of men, who have no hope. We believe that Jesus died and rose again, and so we believe that God will bring with Jesus those who have fallen asleep (have died) in Him. According to the Lord's own word, we tell you that we who are still alive, who are left till the coming of the Lord, will certainly not precede those who have fallen asleep (have died). For the Lord Himself will come down from heaven, with a loud command, with the voice of the archangel and with the trumpet of God, and the dead in Christ will rise first. After that, we who are still alive and are left will be caught up (raptured, snatched away) together with them in the clouds to meet the Lord in the air. And so we will be with the Lord forever. Therefore, encourage each other with these words."

Scriptures about the return of Christ are also sometimes called "The Blessed Hope" (Titus 2:13). These divinely inspired words were recorded by the apostle Paul. They are filled with great hope, assurance and comfort. These were the words that my grandfather treasured in his heart and mind as he was anxiously waiting for Jesus Christ to return and take him to heaven.

On August 29, 1978, I was on my knees in my church office praying. At that time, I was the pastor of Bethel Baptist Church in Getzville, New York. I had a very unusual and startling experience that morning. As I was praying, I saw myself preaching at my grandpa's funeral. In this experience, vision, or whatever it may be called, I was standing beside my grandpa's casket preaching his funeral message. I was pleading with my relatives and others in the audience to turn from their sins and to invite Jesus Christ into their lives by faith, as their Savior and Lord, if they hadn't done that before. Many relatives in the audience were in tears. This experience troubled me deeply. It seemed so real that I immediately got up from my kneeling position and recorded what had happened in my prayer journal.

As I pondered what I experienced, I found myself in an internal struggle with my thoughts. *Was this real?* Did I just imagine this or could it have been a vision from God? Was God trying to prepare me ahead of time for my beloved grandpa's death? Why would I be asked to preach at his funeral service? Yes, I am his grandson, and we had a close relationship, but Grandpa had his own pastor at the Methodist church in Newport where he was actively involved when he was physically able to attend church services and other special events. Maybe I would be asked to read a passage of Scripture or offer a prayer someday at his funeral, but it didn't seem likely that I'd be asked to preach the funeral message.

This internal struggle went on for several days. I remember driving my car in Buffalo to one of the major hospitals where people from our church or community would go for medical care, and I found myself thinking, "What am I going to preach about at Grandpa's funeral? He loved the book of Revelation and the Scriptures about the rapture in I Thessalonians chapter four. I think that's what I'll preach about." Then I would catch myself thinking these thoughts and I'd say, "No, no, no, I'm not going to be preaching at Grandpa's funeral. Just get those thoughts out of your mind."

About a week after my unusual experience, my dad called. "Larry, Grandpa Burd has had a stroke and he's in the hospital." I never said a word to my dad about the experience I had had in prayer. Other than sharing what was happening with one of our deacons at our church, I kept it to myself. It was too unusual, sacred, and confusing. It's even difficult for me to write about it many years later.

Another week passed by, and on a Wednesday night, I was about to begin leading our weekly prayer meeting when the telephone rang in the hallway at the church. Someone came to me and said, "Your father is on the phone. He wants to talk to you." I wondered if the call was about Grandpa's condition. When I picked up the telephone receiver my dad said, "Larry, your grandpa died." I expressed my love and concern to my dad on the death of Grandpa, his dad. Then my dad said something that I was not expecting to hear. He said, "Larry, the family has discussed this, and we want you to preach at Grandpa's funeral." I said, "Dad, I've known that for two weeks."

My internal struggle was over. I concluded that only God could have given me that vision two weeks before as I knelt in prayer in my office. God was preparing me for what would soon happen.

Perhaps this unusual, but very real, experience was what Peter was speaking about in Acts 2:17-18. "In the last days, God says, I will pour out my Spirit on all people. Your sons and daughters will prophesy, your young men (I was only 30 when this happened) will see visions, your old men will dream dreams. Even on my servants, both men and women, I will pour out my Spirit in those days, and they will prophesy."

On Saturday, September 16, 1978, I preached the gospel at my grandpa's funeral service as I stood beside his casket. Many of my relatives were in tears. I pleaded with them to turn from their sins and to invite Jesus Christ into their lives, by faith, as their Savior and Lord, if they hadn't done that before. The vision that God placed in my heart eighteen days earlier had come to pass exactly as He had revealed it to me that day as I knelt in prayer in my office. Psalm 32:8 says "I will instruct you and teach you in the way you should go; I will counsel you and watch over you." In the New Testament the Bible says, "Those who are led by the Spirit of God are sons of God" (Romans 8:14).

I did not seek this unusual experience, but neither can I deny that it happened. God is sovereign. God is in control. God can reveal Himself in any way He chooses. God is so gracious and merciful to sometimes give His children glimpses of the things to come.

Experiences like this have helped me to be open to the leading of the Holy Spirit. When something unusual happens, I have learned to commit the situation to God in prayer. I have turned to His Word to see if there were similar experiences that may have happened in the lives of His people in the past. I have often asked God to confirm what I was experiencing through reading His holy Word, by seeking to be led by His Holy Spirit, observing circumstances around me, or listening to what God may be saying through other people who cross my path. God does not lead His children astray. When we are surrendered to do His will for His glory, we can expect God to make His will clear to us.

I am so thankful to God for my godly maternal and paternal grandparents. The invisible hand of God was at work in their lives. They taught me by their actions and words. I miss them, but the Christian legacy they left for their family and friends continues to live on. They influenced my life greatly, and I am eternally grateful and blessed for the privilege I had to get to know my grandparents. Proverbs 10:7 says, "The memory of the righteous will be a blessing..."

## Think About It

- Did you have the privilege of having godly grandparents?
- How did their lives influence you?
- If you did not have godly grandparents, what have you learned from them that you want to apply or not apply in your life?
- If your grandparents are still living, try to visit, email or call them. Let them know the positive ways they have influenced your life.

CHAPTER 2

# THE INVISIBLE HAND OF GOD AT WORK IN MY PARENTS

*"Surely it is You who love the people; all the holy ones are in Your hand. At Your feet they all bow down, and from You receive instruction" (Deuteronomy 33:3).*

## God Has A Purpose For Every Life

In his book, *The Purpose Driven Life,* pastor and author Rick Warren wrote that God has a purpose for everyone's life. "You must begin with God, your Creator. You exist only because God wills that you exist. You were made by God and for God- and until you understand that, life will never make sense. It is only in God that we discover our origin, our identity, our meaning, our purpose, our significance, and our destiny. Every other path leads to a dead end."[3] I found this to be true in my life before I became a Christian.

The very first verse in the Bible, Genesis 1:1, declares, "In the beginning God created the heavens and the earth." The earth didn't just happen; God created it. God created the sun, moon, stars, animals, plant life, and all the creatures of the sea, land, and air.

Abraham Lincoln believed in a Creator God. He said, "I can see how it might be possible for a man to look down upon the earth and be an atheist, but I cannot conceive how a man could look up into the heavens and say there is no God."[4] Psalm 19:1 says, "The heavens declare the glory of God, and the skies proclaim the work of His hands."

---

[3] Warren, Rick. *The Purpose Driven Life.* (Grand Rapids: Zondervan, 2002), 18
[4] www.goodreads.com/quotes/131220-I-can-see-how-it-might-be-possible

On the sixth day of creation, God created the most intelligent form of life. In Genesis 1:27-28, the Bible says, "So God created man in His own image, in the image of God He created him; male and female He created them. God blessed them and said to them, 'Be fruitful and increase in number; fill the earth and subdue it. Rule over the fish of the sea and the birds of the air and over every living creature that moves on the ground."

God created the first man, Adam, and his wife, Eve. A Sunday school teacher was trying to explain to her third grade students how God created Adam and Eve. She asked the students, "What do you think God said after he created Adam?" A little girl replied, "I think God looked at Adam and said, 'I can do better than that,' so He created Eve."

The Bible says in Job 12:10, "In His hand is the life of every creature and the breath of all mankind." God created us with His own hands. "Then the LORD God formed a man from the dust of the ground and breathed into his nostrils the breath of life, and the man became a living being" (Genesis 2:7).

When God called Jeremiah to be a prophet, He said to him, "Before I formed you in the womb I knew you, before you were born I set you apart; I appointed you as a prophet to the nations." God had a plan and purpose for Jeremiah's life, and He has a plan for every life He created.

God had a plan and purpose for the lives of my parents. Perhaps the first evidence of the invisible hand of God at work in my father's life happened when he was eighteen months old. His life could have quickly been taken from him, but God spared him.

Dad's early years were spent on a farm in Thompson, Iowa. One day, as an eighteen-month-old toddler, he wandered into the barn and pulled the tail of a newborn colt. The colt reared its back leg and kicked him in the face. By God's grace and mercy, he wasn't killed, but did have a large gash from the corner of his right eye that opened his cheek and required many stitches. The country doctor came to the house, and at the kitchen table sewed up the wound. The scar on his face was a continual reminder that the invisible hand of God had spared his life. The Bible says in Isaiah 41:10, "So do not fear, for I am with you; do not be dismayed, for I am your God. I will strengthen you and help you;

I will uphold you with My righteous right hand." Without God's invisible righteous right hand upholding my father, or anyone else, no one could live and fulfill His purpose for their life. Our lives are in His hands.

### "Your Hands"
### by JJ Heller

I have unanswered prayers
I have trouble I wish wasn't there
And I have asked a thousand ways
That you would take my pain away
You would take my pain away
I am trying to understand
How to walk this weary land
Make straight the paths that crooked lie
Oh Lord, before these feet of mine
Oh Lord, before these feet of mine
When my world is shaking, heaven stands
When my heart is breaking
I never leave your hands
When you walked upon the earth
You healed the broken, lost and hurt
I know you hate to see me cry
One day you will set all things right
Yeah, one day you will set all things right

When my world is shaking, heaven stands
When my heart is breaking
I never leave your hands

Your hands that shaped the world
Are holding me
They hold me still[5]

My dad became a Christian at age seven. Jesus said, "Let the little children come to me and do not hinder them, for the

---

[5] Heller, JJ. *Your Hands*. Stone Table Records. CD. 2009.

kingdom of God belongs to such as these" (Mark 10:14). Dad's family had moved from the farm in Iowa to a farm in Newport, Pennsylvania. One night in East Newport when his dad, Reverend Lawrence Frank Burd, was preaching the good news about Jesus Christ and His plan of salvation, Dad realized during that service that he had sinned before God. He asked God to forgive his sins, and invited Jesus Christ to come into his life and be his Savior and Lord. He believed Jesus died on the cross for his sins and was raised from the dead so he could have eternal life. Jesus said in John 1:12, "Yet to all who received Him, to those who believed in His name, He gave the right to become children of God." Dad was not only one of his parents' eight children, but he was now a child of God. He had begun a new life in Christ.

After graduating from Newport High School, Dad worked for the railroad. One day while he was in Harrisburg, Pennsylvania, God arranged for a divine appointment, and he met a young secretary who worked for the Pennsylvania State Police. Her name was Bertha Litke. After a short engagement, they married and moved to Tucumcari, New Mexico, where Dad was transferred with the railroad. My brother Dennis, who is two years older than me, was born in New Mexico. Their stay in New Mexico was brief, and soon they moved back to Pennsylvania and settled in the town of Munson, only two and a half miles from my mother's parents in Forest, Pennsylvania.

My parents both had a godly legacy passed on to them from their parents, and it was their desire to pass the same on to their three children.

The invisible hand of God was at work in the transfer of their legacy. Many of the godly qualities I observed in my grandparents, I also observed in my parents. I have never done extensive research on my family background beyond my grandparents. Often what we discover about our family's past history, even those experiences that may have been painful and even now may be difficult to think about, are sometimes what God uses to conform us into His likeness. In reality, many of us may not want to look at our past for fear of what we may find.

I heard of a man who once paid a friend seventy dollars to research his family tree. When the research was completed, he paid his friend an additional seventy dollars to keep him quiet.

## A Family Founded On Faith

My parents were both committed Christians when they got married. God established the marriage relationship when He created Adam and Eve. God said, "It is not good for the man to be alone. I will make a helper suitable for him" (Genesis 2:18).

God had assigned work for Adam in the Garden of Eden. Not only was he to till the soil and care for the beautiful garden in which God placed him, but he was also to name the animals, birds, and creatures which God had created. Adam perhaps felt left out when he noticed all the creatures in the garden had mates. God created them male and female and wanted them to be fruitful and multiply. God knew Adam needed a mate as well. God met Adam's need when He created Eve to be his wife.

Genesis 2:21-24 says, "So the Lord God caused the man to fall into a deep sleep," (some wives think their husbands are still in a deep sleep), "and while he was sleeping He took one of the man's ribs and closed up the place with flesh. Then the Lord made a woman from the rib He had taken out of the man, and He brought her to the man. The man said, 'This is now bone of my bones and flesh of my flesh; she shall be called woman, for she was taken out of man.' For this reason, a man will leave his father and mother and be united to his wife, and they will become one flesh."

The 'one flesh' relationship is more than simply a physical relationship. God intended for husbands and wives to experience physical, emotional, and spiritual oneness in their marriage.

According to Genesis 2:24, there should be leaving, cleaving, and weaving in a marriage relationship. First, there should be leaving; "For this reason, a man will leave his father and mother." Second, there should be a cleaving to one another in a new family relationship. And third, there should occur a weaving or uniting together to become one flesh.

The kind of physical, emotional, and spiritual oneness God desires in a marriage can only be experienced when both the husband and wife are in the family of faith and have a personal relationship with Jesus Christ that binds them together like layers of plywood glued together.

When the Israelites were preparing to enter the Promised Land, God warned them not to intermarry with the unbelieving people in the nation all around them. God said, "Do not intermarry with them. Do not give your daughters to their sons or take their daughters for your sons, for they will turn your sons away from following me to serve other gods, and the Lord's anger will burn against you and will quickly destroy you" (Deuteronomy 7:3-4).

In the New Testament, II Corinthians 6:14 declares, "Do not be yoked together with unbelievers. For what do righteousness and wickedness have in common? Or what fellowship can light have with darkness?"

Through the years of my ministry, I have tried diligently to counsel couples on what a Christian marriage is, according to the Bible. If one of them was not a Christian, and if after patiently explaining, over a period of several weeks, what it means to be a Christian, if that person had not yet trusted Christ as their Savior and Lord, then I would delay performing their marriage ceremony. If I performed their ceremony, knowing that they were not being equally joined together as God intended according to II Corinthians 6:14, then I believe I would be disobeying God's Word and violating my conscience.

Some couples have become angry with me because of my commitment to the biblical stance, "do not be yoked together with unbelievers." I am committed to obeying God's Word even if people are upset with me as a result.

A man named Paul was such a person. I saw him a couple years ago and he said, "Pastor Burd, do you remember me?" I didn't recognize him at first, for it had been many years since we had seen one another. He said, "Eighteen years ago you refused to perform our wedding ceremony, and I was very angry at you. I have since become a Christian and I want you to know you did the right thing in not performing our wedding." I was delighted to hear that Paul had become a Christian and now understands God's plan and purpose for marriage.

Some Christians justify dating unbelievers by calling it "missionary dating." They believe they can lead the one they love to Christ, but what often happens is that the unbeliever leads the Christian astray. If God says, "Do not be yoked together with unbelievers" it would be best to obey God even while dating. If Christians do not date unbelievers they will not need to be concerned about marrying an unbeliever. God's plan is always best.

Marriages that are going to last through the years must be built on a solid, biblical foundation of faith in God and His Word. My parents were married for forty-seven years and were committed to doing just that. By faith they believed Psalm 127:1, "Unless the Lord builds the house, its builders labor in vain. Unless the Lord watches over the city, the watchmen stand guard in vain."

In Psalm 11:3, David asked this question: "When the foundations are being destroyed, what can the righteous do?" Many marriages are being destroyed today because they are not built on a solid, spiritual foundation. Jesus Christ is that foundation. The apostle Paul said in I Corinthians 3:11, "For no one can lay any foundation other than the one already laid, which is Jesus Christ."

Jesus spoke about a wise man and a foolish man. They both built a house, but on two different foundations. This is what Jesus said about these two men: "Therefore, anyone who hears these words of Mine and puts them into practice is like a wise man who built his house on the rock. The rain came down, the streams rose, and the winds blew and beat against that house; yet it did not fall, because it had its foundation on the rock. But everyone who hears these words of mine and does not put them into practice is like a foolish man who built his house on sand. The rain came down, the streams rose, and the winds blew and beat against that house, and it fell with a great crash" (Matthew 7:24-27). Marriages that are not built on a solid rock foundation will not be able to withstand the storms of life.

All marriages and families will face the storms and winds of life. My parents had their share of struggles raising and disciplining three children. They both worked full-time to provide for their family and also cared for my sister who had rheumatic fever.

Every couple and family will experience various trials, tribulations, and temptations at one time or another. The question is: How will they weather these storms and difficulties in life? Is their marriage and family built on a solid rock foundation—Jesus Christ and His Word—or are they building on sinking sand?

Hundreds of years ago, the prophet Micah wrote about families that were facing strife and disunity: "For a son dishonors his father, a daughter rises up against her mother, a daughter-in-law against her mother-in-law, a man's enemies are the members of his own household" (7:6). That certainly sounds like a family feud. What could anyone do to change these circumstances in a family? In the very next verse, Micah 7:7, the prophet tells God's people how to deal with family dysfunction: "But as for me, I watch in hope for the Lord, I wait for God my Savior; my God will hear me."

Micah's hope for change was in the Lord. Micah did not see the situation as a hopeless end, rather an endless hope. Micah was willing to wait for God and for His answer to the problems in families. He prayed and put the dysfunctional situation in God's hands. Prayer should always be our first response, not our last resort. He was confident God would hear and answer his prayers. Micah was a man of faith. Families that pray together have a greater probability of staying together.

I believe the invisible hand of God was at work in helping my parents build their marriage and family on the solid rock of Jesus Christ and by placing their faith in Him and the teaching of His Word.

## A Family Founded On Unconditional Love

My parents loved one another and their three children unconditionally. They were not hesitant to hold hands, hug and kiss one another, or say "I love you" in the presence of their children. Their outward affection was but a glimpse of the inward love that they had for one another. Ephesians 5:25 says, "Husbands, love your wives, just as Christ loved the church and gave Himself up for her." That's the kind of self-sacrificing, unconditional love I saw in my parents. I felt secure and stable knowing how much they loved one another. In our home, my parents continually said "I love you" to my brother, sister, and me. I never felt as though their love for me was based on my performance, behavior, or attitude. I certainly disappointed and disobeyed them many times, but they never withheld their love from me.

When I was probably about five years old, just a few days before Christmas, my older brother Dennis and I were running through the house playing horsey. We were pretending we were riding a horse, but actually we were riding a broom handle.

Suddenly the 'horse' backed up and the broom handle went through the large picture window in the living room. The window was smashed into hundreds of pieces. After cleaning up the mess, my parents covered the window with cardboard because it couldn't be replaced until after Christmas. It was an embarrassing sight when family and friends came to visit on Christmas day. My parents were sad, mad, and frustrated that they had to replace the window when funds were low, especially at Christmas time.

I can't remember how my brother and I were disciplined for breaking the window, but based on my parents' approach to discipline I'm sure we were disciplined in one way or another. As sad as this event was in my childhood, I never felt loved any less than if the window had never been broken. I experienced unconditional love from my parents, and I never feared the loss of their love because of anything I did or did not do. The apostle John wrote about unconditional love in I John 4:7-12:

> "Dear friends, let us love one another, for love comes from God. Everyone who loves has been born of God and knows God. Whoever does not love does not know God, because God is love. This is how God showed His love among us: He sent His one and only Son into the world that we might live through Him. This is love: not that we loved God, but that He loved us and sent His Son as an atoning sacrifice for our sins. Dear friends, since God so loved us, we also ought to love one another. No one has

ever seen God; but if we love one another, God lives in us and His love is made complete in us!"

Where did my parents get unconditional love for each other and for their children? How were they able to express genuine love, not only for their family, but for many people around them in their neighborhood, church, and where they worked? God was the source of their unconditional love. They trusted Him to fill them with His love. The Bible says in Romans 5:5, "God has poured out His love into our hearts by the Holy Spirit, whom He has given us." The invisible hand of God was at work in my parents' lives and I was a recipient of His blessing and unconditional love through them.

### A Family Founded On The Word Of God And Prayer

My parents loved the Word of God, the Bible. They believed it was divinely inspired by God and had practical applications for their personal lives, marriage, and family. II Timothy 3:16-17 declares, "All Scripture is God-breathed and is useful for teaching, rebuking, correcting, and training in righteousness, so that the man of God may be thoroughly equipped for every good work."

Both of my parents were Sunday school teachers at Forest Baptist Church, where we attended as a family. Dad taught adults and my mother taught children. They took their teaching responsibilities seriously and spent quality time in preparing to teach their classes.

My dad was also the Sunday school superintendent in our small congregation. Each Sunday, he presented a well-researched devotional to all who were in attendance, before we separated into various Sunday school classes. My mother helped my dad with his research to find illustrations, stories, quotes, etc., but he always taught something from the Bible. The Bible was the most important book in his life and in our home.

When I saw my dad standing in front of our church sanctuary teaching about the Bible, he seemed like a pastor to me. In fact, when I was very young, I thought my dad was a pastor. He was always a friend to our pastors and tried to help make their pastoral load lighter.

Dad was also a deacon in our church. He was not only a spiritual leader in the church, but the director of a community-wide vacation Bible school, and the spiritual leader of our home. He loved children and often took neighborhood children with us to Sunday school and church services.

My parents taught the Word of God at home. Having family devotions with their children was important to them. After finishing an evening meal, while sitting at the table, my parents would read the Bible or a devotional book to us. Like Joshua, in Joshua 24:15, Dad believed "as for me and my house, we will serve the Lord."

Moses instructed parents to teach their children God's Word as recorded in Deuteronomy 6:6-7. "These commandments that I give you today are to be upon your hearts. Impress them on your children. Talk about them when you sit at home and when you walk along the road, when you lie down and when you get up." In this verse Moses instructed God's people to teach their children His commandments. When were they to do this? When the children were sitting at home, going for a walk, and when they were lying down and getting up. These are strategic times to teach children spiritual truth.

Proverbs 22:6 declares, "Train a child in the way he should go, and when he is old he will not turn from it." The apostle Paul also said, "Fathers, do not exasperate your children; instead, bring them up in the training and instruction of the Lord" (Ephesians 6:4).

Our time of family devotions was not long or exasperating. Someone said, "When having family devotionals, remember K.I.S.S.; Keep It Short and Simple." That's what my parents tried to do in teaching us the Word of God.

One of my fondest memories of our devotional times around the kitchen table was the night when my sister Rosalie, who was eight years old, prayed that Jesus would forgive her sins and come into her life to be her Savior and Lord. That simple prayer changed her life and she was given the gift of eternal life.

My parents believed in the power of prayer. One of my favorite quotes about prayer is by an unknown author: "When we work, we work, but when we pray, God works." The Bible says, "Call to Me and I will answer you and tell you great and unsearchable things you do not know" (Jeremiah 33:3). Jesus said, "If you remain in Me and My words remain in you, ask whatever you wish, and it will be given to you. This is my Father's glory, that you bear much fruit showing yourselves to be My disciples" (John 15:7-8).

My parents trusted God to meet their needs regardless of how small or large those needs may have been. I remember a time when my parents needed thirty dollars to pick up a pair of new glasses for my mother. They didn't have the money, but they knew how to pray and trusted God to provide for them. At that time, my dad was a mail carrier at Penn State University in State College, Pennsylvania. He went in and out of dozens of university buildings each day. One day, he was in a university building and he opened the door of an elevator. There on the floor was thirty dollars. If he had gone down the hallways asking if anyone had lost some money, someone would have probably said, "If it's green on one side and grey on the other, then it's mine." Dad concluded the Lord had answered prayer and met their need.

My dad and mother prayed and trusted God to supply thousands of dollars to remodel our house, provide for cars, meet our family needs, and have money for tuition to enable three children to go to college. My parents not only believed in the Word of God and prayer, but they were willing to sacrifice whatever was necessary to meet the needs of their family and to generously support their church with tithes and offerings.

The subject of tithing, giving a tenth of one's income to the Lord's work, was not always a pleasant subject with my dad. I can still picture Dad sitting at his desk in the living room, writing out checks to pay bills. I could hear him grumbling and complaining, "Oh no, how are we ever going to pay all these bills?"

I remember my mother lovingly and gently asking Dad, "Leroy, are we tithing?" Dad would say something like, "No, we're not tithing. How can we tithe when we have all these bills?"

My mother replied, "Just write out the tithe check first. God will supply our needs." It took some time for Dad to trust God and discover the joy of tithing, but when he learned this valuable biblical lesson he became a faithful, generous tither. When he began to tithe on a regular basis, God did what He promised in Malachi 3:10: "'Bring the whole tithe into the storehouse, that there may be food in My house. Test Me in this,' says the Lord Almighty, 'and see if I will not throw open the floodgates of heaven and pour out so much blessing that you will not have room enough for it.'"

The principle of honoring God with one's wealth was something I learned from my parents at an early age. When Dad was writing out checks and paying bills without grumbling and complaining, I concluded he must be tithing and God must be providing for our needs. This experience impacted my life–yet another example of the invisible hand of God at work.

Just as God supplied the needs of Ezra the scribe, I learned to trust Him to meet my needs as well. The Bible says in Ezra 7:6, "The king had granted him everything he asked, for the hand of the Lord his God was on him." Even though Ezra could not see God's invisible hand, he knew His hand was upon him and would meet his needs.

An elderly lady shared these words with me many years ago: "Yesterday, He helped me. Today, He did the same. How long shall this continue? Forever praise His name!"

## A Family Founded On The Promises Of Eternal Life

My parents believed in God's promises of eternal life. They believed what Jesus said in the Bible. In John 11:25-26, Jesus said, "I am the resurrection and the life. He who believes in Me will live, even though he dies; and whoever lives and believes in Me will never die." Do you believe this?"

Jesus promised eternal life to all who would believe in Him. When He said, "whoever lives and believes in Me will never die," He was not talking about physical death, but spiritual death. As human beings, we will all die someday, unless Jesus returns in the rapture (I Thessalonians 4:13-18), and takes us into Heaven as believers in Him without facing death. How amazing that some Christians, those who are alive when Jesus returns, will never face physical death. Jesus said, "Because I live, you also will live" (John 19:14).

When the apostle Paul wrote about the promises of eternal life, he said, "For to me, to live is Christ and to die is gain" (Philippians 1:21). Paul taught that, because Jesus was raised from the dead, He would give eternal life to all who believed in Him. In Romans 8:11, the Bible says, "And if the Spirit of Him who raised Jesus from the dead is living in you, He who raised Christ from the dead will also give life to your mortal bodies through His Spirit, who lives in you."

The French philosopher Voltaire was an unbeliever and wanted nothing to do with Jesus Christ. On his deathbed, he said to his doctor, "I am abandoned by God and man. I will give you half of what I am worth if you give me six months life."

The doctor replied, "Sir, you cannot live six weeks." Voltaire responded, "Then I shall go to hell and you will go with me."[6] Soon after, Voltaire died. He had no hope of eternal life. For him, life was a hopeless end.

What a contrast between Voltaire and evangelist D.L. Moody. Moody had a personal relationship with Jesus Christ and faced death unafraid. "A few hours before entering the 'Homeland,' Dwight L. Moody caught a glimpse of the glory awaiting him. Awakening from a sleep, he said, 'Earth recedes. Heaven opens before me. If this is death, it is sweet! There is no valley here. God is calling me, and I must go.' His son, who was standing by his bedside, said, 'No, no, father, you are dreaming.'

"'No,' said Mr. Moody, 'I am not dreaming; I have been within the gates; I have seen the children's faces.' A short time elapsed and then, following what seemed to the family to be the death struggle, he spoke again. 'This is my triumph; this is my coronation day. It is glorious!'"[7]

Heaven and hell are both an eternal reality according to the clear teaching of the Bible. Jesus warned people about hell. He

---

[6] Tan, Paul Lee, Encyclopedia of 7700 Illustrations (Rockville: Assurance Publishers, 1979), 313
[7] Ibid, 313

spoke more about hell than He did about heaven. In Mark 9:48, Jesus described hell as a place where the "worm does not die, and the fire is not quenched." The writer of the book of Hebrews said, "It is a dreadful thing to fall into the hands of the living God" (Hebrews 10:31).

Heaven is a prepared place for a prepared people. Heaven is the land of the living; earth is the land of the dying. We are all in the process of dying. Comedian Woody Allen once said, "I'm not afraid to die, I just don't want to be there when it happens." [8]

I have a pastor friend, Jake Leverette. Jake and his wife, Peggy, lost two of their sons in tragic accidents. One son died in a car accident at age eighteen, and the other son died in a tobogganing accident at age twenty-six. On a number of occasions, I heard Jake quote these words: "Life is short. Death is sure. Sin the cause. Christ the cure." I have used these twelve words numerous times during the years of my ministry because they are easily remembered and convey deep biblical truth.

Jesus Christ, through His death on the cross, paid the ultimate sacrifice for the sins of the world. When He rose from the grave victoriously, He proved that He was the Son of God and had conquered death. In Romans 6:23, the Bible says, "For the wages of sin is death, but the gift of God is eternal life in Christ Jesus our Lord." Anyone who trusts in Christ alone for salvation will receive eternal life the moment he or she puts personal faith in Him.

## An Unforgettable Experience

When the time came for my parents to leave this life and go to heaven, they were ready. They looked forward to meeting their Savior and Lord, Jesus Christ. Of course, they would be missed by their family and friends, but they knew that the best was yet to come for them. They spoke freely about heaven and their desire to be there whenever the Lord was ready for them.

My mother died on July 22, 1992, at the age of seventy-three. She died from lung cancer. She never smoked a day in her life, but she worked for many years as a secretary in an office where others

---

[8] Thinkexist.com/quotation/I-am-not-afraid-of-death-I-just-don-t

smoked. Did she develop cancer because of breathing second hand smoke day after day? I will never know the answer to that question, but it is a known fact, thousands of people die every year because of the effects of smoking.

Four months before my mother died, she was in intensive care in the hospital. One day, the doctor who was taking care of her told us she wouldn't live through the night. We said our goodbyes to her as a family. We prayed for her and told her how much we loved her. We told her she could go to heaven to be with Jesus. We expected her to die very soon, but God had a different plan. She lived through the night and began to improve each day.

Her doctor said, "I don't know what you people are doing for her, but keep it up." We were simply loving her and praying for her. The doctor was amazed at her sudden improvement, and after a week she was transferred to a rehabilitation facility. After another week, the doctor sent her home and we enjoyed having her with us four more months.

I will never forget what I experienced three days before my mother died. My parents lived in Mechanicsburg, Pennsylvania, at the time, and I lived with my family in Bethlehem, Pennsylvania. It was a two hour drive between the two cities, about 100 miles. When my dad called to say my mother was perhaps near death, we quickly drove to their house to be with them.

My mother was not responding. It was like she was in a coma. But suddenly, she became alert. She opened her eyes and began to speak. Our family members were all gathered around her bed. She looked at each member of her family. She told us how much she loved us. But what caught my attention was the beautiful smile she had on her face. She was radiant. Psalm 34:5 says, "Those who look to Him (to the Lord) are radiant; their faces are never covered with shame."

There is no doubt in my mind that the radiance I saw on her face was because she was looking to the Lord, ready to meet Him. This amazing experience reminded me of what the Bible says about Stephen just before he was stoned to death: "All who were sitting in the Sanhedrin looked intently at Stephen, and they saw that his face was like the face of an angel" (Acts 6:15). After those brief, memorable moments, my mother closed her eyes again. She lived for three more days before the invisible hands of Jesus received her into heaven.

When the beggar Lazarus died, "the angels carried him to Abraham's side"(Luke 16:22). Abraham was in heaven. Matthew 8:11 tells us clearly: "I say to you that many will come from the east and the west, and will take their places at the feast with Abraham, Isaac and Jacob in the kingdom of heaven." What a wonderful picture this is of being in heaven some day and sitting down at a feast with the patriarchs of the Old Testament and the New Testament as well. But the best part about heaven is that Jesus Christ will be there to welcome those who know Him and love Him. They will have fellowship with Him and all other believers for all eternity.

Thirteen months after my mother died, my dad remarried. God brought a wonderful Christian lady into his life, Gladys Snyder. I had the joy of performing their wedding ceremony. God gave them seven and a half delightful years together. They spent about half their time in Pennsylvania and the other half in Florida.

Shortly after returning from Florida in April 2001, Gladys died suddenly at age eighty-three. Eight months later, December 12, 2001 at age eighty, my dad died while living at Messiah Village in Mechanicsburg. While Dad was slowly deteriorating from cancer and then finally near death, he asked me several times, "Why is this taking so long?" He wanted to depart and be with his Savior and Lord. He loved Jesus Christ and served Him faithfully.

Shortly before he died, I heard him speak about the bright lights and beautiful flowers he was seeing. There were no bright lights in his dimly-lit nursing home room, and there were certainly no flowers blooming outside his window in December. Was Dad catching a glimpse of the beauty and majesty of heaven? I mentioned this to one of the nurses in the nursing home, and she said she had heard similar comments from a number of Christian patients when they were close to death.

My parents believed in the promises of God regarding eternal life. They were not perfect, but they were forgiven. They trusted in Jesus Christ for the forgiveness of their sins, and they received the gift of eternal life. The godly legacy they lived and left for their children and grandchildren continues to influence our lives today.

The invisible hand of God was at work in their lives. That's why they were such special people, not only to their family, but to many people who knew them and loved them.

*Dear God, I thank You for the godly parents You gave to me as well as to my brother and sister. I thank You for their unconditional love, training, and discipline. Thank You for the many ways my parents sacrificed for their children. Most of all I thank You for their faith in Jesus Christ and the Christ-like example they tried to live each day. I will always be grateful to You for my Christian parents and the impact they have had in my life.*

## Think About It

- Have you discovered God's purpose for your life? Are you seeking to follow His purpose? If you do not know His purpose for your life, ask God to reveal it to you.
- Do you sense the invisible hand of God upon you?
- Have you experienced unconditional love? Do you love others unconditionally?
- Is your life founded on the Word of God and prayer?
- If you are married and have a family, are you building your marriage and family on the solid rock of Jesus Christ?
- Do you believe in the promises of eternal life as recorded in the Bible?
- If you were to die today, would your soul go to heaven or hell?

CHAPTER 3

# *THE INVISIBLE HAND OF GOD AT WORK IN MY YOUTH*

*"Reach down Your hand from on high; deliver me and rescue me from the mighty waters..." (Psalm 144:7).*

## A Rescue In Time Of Great Danger

The invisible hand of God was at work throughout my childhood. As I look back upon my life, I now realize how merciful and gracious God has been to me. When David reflected on God's mercy, he prayed, "Have mercy on me, O God, have mercy on me, for in You my soul takes refuge. I will take refuge in the shadow of your wings until the disaster has passed," (Psalm 57:1).

God rescued me in a time of great danger when I was about six years old. My Uncle Gust and Aunt Effie lived on a farm near Doylestown, Pennsylvania. During the summertime we went on a family vacation to visit them and their three children. One day we had a picnic next to a stream where we went swimming. I enjoyed being in the cool water, but I had not yet learned how to swim. My brother Dennis and my cousin Skip decided to wade out further into the stream, where a tree had fallen into the water. Despite the fact that they were both older and taller than me, I decided to follow them, but apparently I took a slightly different path and fell into a deep hole in the middle of the stream and went underwater. I remember thrashing my arms frantically and bobbing to the surface a couple of times. I was drowning. Perhaps in a few more seconds I would have died. But God had a plan and purpose for my life, and it was not to end in the deep water of that stream. God showed great mercy to me that day.

Uncle Gust spotted me thrashing in the water and realized I was drowning. He raced into the stream and rescued me. I was terrified by this near-death experience. Was the invisible hand of God at work in my life at that moment? Was the invisible hand also upon my uncle when he saved me from drowning? I believe that is what happened. I am more aware of that now than I was at age six. Perhaps what David prayed in Psalm 144:7 was what I had experienced that day: "Reach down Your hand from on high; deliver me and rescue me from the mighty waters..." Isaiah the prophet said, "When you pass through the waters, I will be with you; and when you pass through the rivers, they will not sweep over you. When you walk through the fire, you will not be burned; the flames will not set you ablaze" (Isaiah 43:2). God reached down His hand from on high and delivered me and rescued me from the mighty waters. He showed me His great mercy and spared my life when I was only six years old.

## A Rebellious Nature

I was born with a rebellious, sinful nature. According to Genesis chapter three, Adam and Eve sinned and ate the forbidden fruit in the Garden of Eden, and then became afraid and tried to hide from God. Satan deceived Eve, and she began to doubt, which led to their disobedience of God. God had given the beautiful Garden of Eden to Adam and Eve. There were many trees in the garden for them to enjoy, but God told them not to eat from the tree in the middle of the garden. If they ate from that tree or even touched it, they would die. Adam and Eve were not satisfied with all God gave them. They still wanted more; they wanted fruit from the forbidden tree. In Genesis 3:6-13, the Word of the Lord describes how Adam and Eve disobeyed God and got into serious trouble with him:

> "When the woman saw that the fruit of the tree
> was good for food and pleasing to the eye, and also
> desirable for giving wisdom, she took some and ate
> it. Then the eyes of both of them were opened, and
> they realized that they were naked; so they sewed

fig leaves together and made coverings for themselves. Then the man and his wife heard the sound of the Lord God as he was walking in the garden in the cool of the day, and they hid from the Lord God among the trees of the garden. But the Lord God called to the man, 'Where are you?' He answered, 'I heard you in the garden and was afraid because I was naked; so I hid,' And He said, 'Who told you that you were naked? Have you eaten from the tree that I commanded you not to eat from?' The man said, 'The woman you put here with me-she gave me some fruit from the tree, and I ate it.' Then the Lord said to the woman, 'What is this that you have done?' The woman said, 'The serpent deceived me, and I ate.'"

In this passage of scripture, we discover how Adam and Eve refused to take responsibility for their sin and tried to pass the buck to someone else. Eve blamed the serpent. Adam blamed Eve, but God held them all accountable for their sin. This sinful rebellious nature that started with Adam and Eve has been passed on to every person in history. When Adam and Eve had children, they passed down their sinful nature to them. Their act of disobedience affected the lives of every person who has ever been born, including my life. The Bible says, "Therefore, just as sin entered the world through one man, and death through sin, and in this way death came to all men, because all sinned," (Romans 5:12). The apostle Paul also said, "There is no one righteous, not even one; there is no one who understands, no one who seeks God. All have turned away, they have together become worthless; there is no one who does good, not even one," (Romans 3:10). The Bible makes it very clear that the entire human race has sinned before God. In a briefer statement we read, "For all have sinned and fall short of the glory of God" (Romans 3:23). When the Bible says we all have sinned it literally means all. All means all and that is all that all means. Sin means we have fallen short of God's standard or we have missed the mark. Sin is also breaking God's laws which He established for our good.

Sin is extremely deceptive. Sin sees the bait, but not the hook. Sin will take us farther than we want to go. It will keep us longer than we want to stay. It will cost us more than we want to pay. Billy Sunday once said, "One reason sin flourishes is that it is treated like a cream puff instead of a rattlesnake."[9]

When I was a child I didn't understand what the Bible taught about original sin or that I had a sinful, rebellious nature. What I did know was that I could and did disobey my parents. I was rebellious, deceptive, and did many foolish things in my childhood. The Bible says, "Folly (or foolishness) is bound up in the heart of a child, but the rod of discipline will drive it far from him" (Proverbs 22:15). I experienced the rod of discipline on numerous occasions. Proverbs 13:24 says, "He who spares the rod hates his son, but he who loves him is careful to discipline him." There is certainly a difference between abusive and appropriate discipline. God disciplines us out of love and we must do the same with our children.

I remember being at my grandparents' farm, and having done something worthy of a good spanking. I don't remember what I did, but I certainly remember the consequence that resulted. I can still picture my dad carrying me across the yard and behind grandpa's barn where the painful punishment was to take place. As Dad carried me, he said it was because he loved me that he was going to discipline me. That didn't make a bit of sense to me at the time. I tried to convince him to find a better way to express his love for me. When we got behind the barn I "felt" dad's love for me on my backside, but I also felt his love when he hugged me as tears streamed down my cheeks.

In Hebrews 12:5-6 we read, "My son, do not make light of the Lord's discipline, and do not lose heart when he rebukes you, because the Lord disciplines those he loves, and he punishes everyone he accepts as a son." Uncle Gust also must have loved me because I remember a spanking he gave me. I know my Grandpa Litke loved me, but he didn't get the opportunity to express his love the way my dad and uncle did. Even though he was furious as he chased me and climbed the ladder to the hayloft in the barn, I hid under the hay and he couldn't find me.

---

[9] www.goodreads. Com/quotes/190656-one-reason-sin-flourishes-is-that

For the first eight grades of my education I attended a country four-room school in Munson, Pennsylvania. There were two grades in each classroom and a large pot-bellied stove in the corner of each room. One of the fun things the boys got to do was go outside to the coal shed and bring in buckets of coal for the stove. I have many fond memories of my days at the Munson School, but I can also recall at least three times when I went home after school with a sore backside. Teachers were permitted to paddle students, with real paddles, in those days.

My first paddling took place in second grade. I had just learned how to whistle. When a young student teacher entered our classroom to teach music, I whistled at her as loudly as I could. My classroom teacher didn't appreciate my newly acquired talent, but she did express her love by giving me a paddling. When I told my parents that night what had happened at school, my dad, like my teacher, also expressed his love to me. Someone said, "Children are like canoes. They'll go straight when paddled from the rear."

My defiant nature got me into trouble when I attended a community-wide Vacation Bible School. What made things worse was that my dad was the chairman of the team of pastors and leaders that planned the Bible school program. My bad behavior was a secret to no one. I will only mention a few of the mischievous "fun things" I did.

I caught a green snake (yes, it was alive), put it in a little plastic container, and took it to Bible School. I would ask the girls if they wanted to see my pet. When I opened the container, they screamed and went running in many directions. Of course, the adult teacher soon found out why the girls were screaming and I got in trouble. I would also hide behind the stage in the school where the Bible School was held and turn the lights on and off. But there was one occasion of my misbehavior that infuriated the teachers. I climbed up the chain link cage around the baseball backstop, laid down and refused to come down.

Why was I disobedient to my parents? Why did I get into so much trouble at school, Vacation Bible School and Sunday school? Why did I fight with my older, stronger brother? Why did I steal two erasers from a five and ten cent store? The invisible hand of

God was at work in my life because I felt guilty and my conscience troubled me greatly. Like the apostle Paul in Romans 7:15 I was learning that "I do not understand what I do. For what I want to do I do not do, but what I hate I do."

When David sinned before God he felt the hand of God upon him. In Psalm 32:4 he said, "For day and night Your hand was heavy upon me; my strength was sapped as in the heat of the summer." God's unseen hand was so heavy upon me that when my parents went shopping the following week I sneaked back into the five and ten cent store and returned the erasers from where I had stolen them. I sighed with relief that no one saw me and that I didn't have to face jail time. God was merciful to me.

Through the years I have filled out many health questionnaires. One of the questions that is often asked is, "Do you smoke?" I did smoke, but I quit when I was eleven. An older boy in our neighborhood smoked. When I asked him for some cigarettes, he gave them to me. I nearly choked to death trying to smoke them, but what I didn't realize was that my brother saw me smoking. One night, as my family was eating dinner, my brother Dennis and I got into an argument. I squealed on him for something he had done. He was thirteen at the time. When my dad had finished spanking my brother, through his tears, my brother looked at me and said, "Yeah, and he's been smoking." Dad said, "Larry, have you been smoking?" I said "yes" and got a spanking that was so memorable. Dad really showed his love that night, and I never smoked again. I concluded that the pain on my backside was far worse than any pleasure I could experience by choking on cigarette smoke.

There were times during my rebellious childhood when I felt like I couldn't control my behavior. It was almost like an unseen evil presence was inside me controlling me. *What was wrong with me?*

In Ephesians 2:1-3 the apostle Paul explained why my rebellious nature controlled me: "As for you, you were dead in your transgressions and sins, in which you used to live when you followed the ways of this world and of the rulers of the kingdom of the air, the spirit who is now at work in those who are disobedient. All of us also lived among them at one time, gratifying the cravings of our sinful nature and following its desires and thoughts. Like the rest, we were by nature objects of wrath."

I was born with a sinful, rebellious nature. There was an evil spirit of disobedience in me. Only Jesus Christ, through his death on the cross and his victorious resurrection from the dead, could change me and give me a new nature. I wasn't ready for that change just yet.

## A Dangerous Nature

God's invisible hand must have been at work in my life during my early teen years or I could have been seriously injured or even lost my life. The Bible says, "You give me Your shield of victory, and Your right hand sustains me." (Psalm 18:35). Only God's right hand could have sustained me through some of the crazy and dangerous things I did in my early teenage years.

Uncle Charles, my dad's brother, lived on a turkey farm in Newport, Pennsylvania, just across the field from where my grandparents lived. He was a big, strong farmer. I once watched him eat four quarts of home-made ice cream at one time. Uncle Charles and Aunt Lena had one son, Jimmy, who was several years older than me. He wasn't around much during my visit with my aunt and uncle. I visited them for a couple of weeks during the summer. I was probably about fourteen or fifteen years old at the time.

I loved my uncle and had fun pulling tricks on him. He had a large pole barn where he raised thousands of turkeys. The barn was divided into numerous sections to separate the turkeys. At the one end of the pole barn was a dimly-lit and very dusty feed-room. There was a telephone in the feed room. Uncle Charles often received important calls from people wanting to order turkeys. One day, I went into the feed room and taped the telephone receiver to the telephone. When my uncle was near the opposite end of the pole barn feeding turkeys, I ran to another building and dialed the number for the feed room. The phone rang and rang. Uncle Charles wanted me to run and answer it but I told him I wanted to stay and feed the turkeys. Watching him run from one section of the pole barn to another, opening the door of each section, and chasing back the turkeys from the door was a hilarious sight to see. Meanwhile, the phone continued to ring.

I followed my uncle at a distance. I wanted to see his reaction to what I had done. Uncle Charles was out of breath when he reached the feed room. As he reached for the receiver, he picked up the entire telephone. When he realized the telephone was taped to the receiver, he was madder than hornets chased out of their nest. The phone continued to ring as he angrily pulled the tape off. When he finally said, "hello?" there was no answer. Uncle Charles never hit me, although he came very close.

I usually rode along with my uncle in his truck when he went to Shiremanstown to pick up feed for the turkeys. One day, I decided to not go with him, but instead to stay on the farm. He would be returning mid-afternoon and would eat lunch when he returned. My aunt and uncle kept the window shades closed in the kitchen so it would be cooler on hot summer days. The kitchen table was covered with an over-sized table cloth that drooped over the sides of the table. In the dimly-lit kitchen it was a perfect hiding place. When I saw my uncle's truck coming down the lane to the farm, I hid under the table. When he sat at the table eating lunch, I remained silent. After about fifteen minutes I made my move. I grabbed tightly onto his ankles and made a loud noise like an Indian war signal. I nearly scared him to death. He could have had a heart attack. He still didn't hit me, but he sure was angry.

These were harmless practical jokes; at least they were harmless to me. But what I did next was extremely dangerous. I can hardly believe I did this, but I did.

On this particular afternoon, Uncle Charles had to go for feed again. He wanted me to go with him so he could keep a close eye on me, but I again convinced him to let me stay on the farm. Actually, I would be in the back of the truck, but he wouldn't know it. My uncle's truck was not an eighteen-wheeler, but it was a big truck, with a large wooden frame box that had a roof over it behind the cab. Inside this part of the truck was a tarp. My uncle used the tarp to protect the feed if it began to rain. When he was ready to leave, he hollered for me. I never answered him, because I was already in my hiding place under the tarp. He had no idea where I was, but he needed to go for the feed so he left without me; so he thought.

My uncle was driving on Route 322, at probably sixty-five miles per hour, along the Susquehanna River to Shiremanstown. That's when I did the most dangerous thing I have ever done. I decided it was time to visit Uncle Charles in the cab of the truck. Surely this adventure would scare him more than any of the other tricks I had pulled on him. Why I was not afraid to do this, I do not know. Looking back now, one little slip of my foot or one quick turn while my uncle was driving, and I could have been killed.

So what did I do that was so dangerous? I climbed outside the wooden-framed box of the truck and slowly walked along the narrow edge toward the cab of the truck on the driver's side, while holding tightly to the two-by-fours that were about three feet apart on the outside of the wooden box. Traffic zoomed by, but no one blew their horn lest they frighten me and I lose my balance and fall. I inched my way along until I reached the cab. Uncle Charles hadn't seen me yet. My next extremely dangerous act was to lurch forward and grab onto the large mirror on the front door of the truck with my left hand, while holding onto a two by four with my right hand. As I lurched forward, I shouted into the open window of the cab, "Hey Uncle Charles, how are you doing?" He didn't slam on the brakes for fear I would fall to the pavement and be killed. He slowed down as quickly as he could and pulled over to the side of the highway to stop the truck. He got me into the cab of the truck and gave me one of the sternest lectures I've ever had. He didn't have a heart attack. He didn't hit me, although this time he came extremely close. This incident must have occurred close to the end of my visit at my uncle's farm, or he would have called my parents to come and get me or else put me on the next bus back home.

Uncle Charles and I rehearsed these stories many times over the years. We laughed as we recalled them. But now I realize that it was only God's mercy that spared my life. Surely God's invisible hand was upholding and protecting me, or I would have fallen from the truck to my death. Psalm 89:13 says, "Your arm is endued with power; Your hand is strong, Your right hand exalted." Even though God's hands are invisible, they are strong and powerful. God's invisible hand was at work in my life in far more ways than I will ever know. The Bible says, "Keep me, O Lord my God; save me in accordance with Your love. Let them know that it is Your hand, that you, O Lord, have done it," (Psalm 109:26-27). God spared my life on numerous occasions. I praise Him, glorify Him, and give Him all the honor due to His holy name. "Ascribe to the Lord the glory due His name; worship the Lord in the splendor of His holiness" (Psalm 29:2).

I am so thankful to God for the privilege of being able to record some of the mighty acts that He has done in my life. I want Him to be exalted in this book. It's all about Him; it's not about me. I am only an ordinary person, but I have come to know and experience an extraordinary God. "Not to us, O Lord, not to us but to Your name be the glory, because of Your love and faithfulness." John the Baptist recognized he was only a humble servant God chose to use for His glory. John said, "He [speaking of Jesus] must become greater; I must become less" (John 3:30).

One of the reasons for writing this book is to pass on to the next generation what I have experienced of the greatness of God in my life. I want my family, friends, and anyone who reads this book to become more aware of the invisible hand of God at work in their lives—even if they do not realize it at this time. Psalm 145:4 compels me to write what I am writing: "One generation will commend your works to another; they will tell of Your mighty acts."

Even though I did some crazy and dangerous things in my youth, God's invisible hand was upon me to uphold, sustain and preserve me, so I could come to know Him and His purpose for my life. God said to His people Israel, "Listen to me, O house of Jacob, all you who remain of the house of Israel, you whom I have upheld since you were conceived, and have carried since your birth. Even to your old age and gray hairs I am He, I am He who will sustain you. I made you and I will carry you; I will sustain you and I will rescue you" (Isaiah 46:3-4).

## The Joy Of Selling Whatever Could Be Sold

In Mark 10:17-22 Jesus told the story of the rich young ruler:

> "As Jesus started on his way, a man ran up to him and fell on his knees before him. 'Good teacher,' he said, 'What must I do to inherit eternal life?'
>
> 'Why do you call me good?' Jesus answered, 'No one is good except God alone. You know the commandments: do not murder, do not commit adultery, do not steal, do not give false testimony, do not defraud, and honor your father and mother.'
>
> 'Teacher,' he declared, 'All of these I have kept since I was a boy.' Jesus looked at him and loved him. 'One thing you lack,' He said, 'Go, sell everything you have and give to the poor, and you will have treasure in heaven. Then come follow me.' At this the man's face fell. He went away sad, because he had great wealth."

This young man thought he had to do something to inherit eternal life. Surely his good works would save him. He didn't understand that salvation was by grace through faith and not by doing good works. "For it is by grace you have been saved, through faith; and this is not for yourselves, it is the gift of God; not by works, so that nobody can boast" (Ephesians 2:8-9). If anyone could save themselves by doing good works then they wouldn't need Jesus. His death on the cross and resurrection from the grave was not necessary, if they could save themselves.

Even if this young man could keep all the commandments all the time, which he couldn't possibly do, he still couldn't be saved by keeping the commandments. Romans 3:20 declares, "Therefore no one will be declared righteous in His sight by observing the law; rather through the law we become conscious of sin." The law does not save us, it simply shows us that we need to be saved.

Jesus loved the rich young ruler. He knew everything about him and he knew what the man loved most: his wealth. His wealth was more important to him than having eternal life, God's way. His wealth was more important to him than knowing Jesus personally and following Him as Lord of his life. Psalm 62:10 says, "Though your riches increase, do not set your heart on them." Solomon was the wisest man who ever lived, other than Jesus, and he said, "Whoever loves money never has money enough; whoever loves wealth is never satisfied with his income. This too is meaningless" (Ecclesiastes 5:10).

The rich young ruler was unwilling to sell whatever he had and give it to the poor and follow Jesus. Because he loved his wealth more than Jesus he lost the greatest treasure of all: eternal life in heaven with Jesus. He never discovered the joy of selling what he had and giving to others.

Wealth can be a subtle trap and lead to many problems. "People who want to get rich fall into temptations and a trap and into many foolish and harmful desires that plunge men into ruin and destruction. For the love of money is a root of all kinds of evil. Some people, eager for money have wandered from the faith and pierced themselves with many griefs" (I Timothy 5:10).

The apostle Paul gave a clear warning to those who were rich and proud of their wealth: "Command those who are rich in this present world not to be arrogant nor to put their hope in wealth, which is so uncertain, but to put their hope in God, Who richly provides us with everything for our enjoyment. Command them to do good, to be rich in good deeds, and to be generous and willing to share" (I Timothy 5:17-18).

There is nothing wrong with having wealth if it has been obtained honestly and is used for God's glory. There were many people in the Bible who were wealthy; like Abraham, David, Solomon, and Joseph of Aramethea. God blessed them because they used His wealth for His purposes. They saw themselves as stewards and not owners of the wealth. It all belonged to Him. "The silver is Mine and the gold is Mine; declares the Lord Almighty" (Haggai 2:8).

During my childhood and youth, I discovered the joy of selling whatever I could to make money. I had never heard of the word "entrepreneur"–one who organizes, operates, and assumes the risks of a business venture—but I guess that's what I was as a young boy.

I sold fishing worms. I liked to go fishing, and I dug my own earthworms from our garden. I had more worms than I needed, so I decided to make a sign and put it in our yard near the country road where we lived. The sign read: "Worms for Sale." It was a simple sign, but it caught the attention of people as they drove by. Before long, I had customers and I was earning money.

Then my brother and I got into the rabbit sales business. We built rabbit pens. Rabbits multiply quickly and so did our sales. I did have one customer who got mad at me. He wanted a buck and a doe (a male and a female rabbit), but I sold him two bucks. I soon became more accurate at distinguishing bucks from does. Years later, my unhappy customer still kidded me about the two bucks I sold him.

My parents knew a man who sold various items for the Fuller Brush Company. He asked me if I wanted to sell costume jewelry for him. Since the worms and rabbits were selling mostly to men, I figured the jewelry would be something I could sell to the ladies of the community. On Saturdays I took a jewelry box with fold-out drawers, and found many customers as I went door to door. Most items sold for between one and two dollars, and I believe my commission was twenty-five percent of whatever I sold. I wasn't making millions, but I was off to a good start. I also sold greeting cards, home-made fudge that I made, TV Guides, a national newspaper called the Grit, and sweet corn on the cob when it was in season.

During the summer when I was a young teenager, I mowed lawns and also picked wild huckleberries. One summer, a friend and I picked three-hundred quarts and sold them for a dollar a quart to the Nittany Lion Inn in State College, Pennsylvania. We made good money that summer. The joy of selling whatever I could sell seemed to come naturally to me. I'll write more later about selling during my college years.

God created each person with His divine plan in mind. He created each of us with various talents and abilities. When we become a Christian we begin to have a personal relationship with Jesus Christ by faith. He then gives us special spiritual gifts to be used for His glory. In I Corinthians 12:4-7 the Bible says, "There are different kinds of gifts, but the same Spirit. There are different kinds of service, but the same Lord. There are different types of working, but the same God works all of them in all men. Now to each one the manifestation of the Spirit is given for the common good." We will never have more joy and fulfillment than when we discover God's purpose for our lives and give ourselves to fulfilling His purpose for His glory. Until we discover God's purpose, we will be like round pegs trying to fit into square holes. They just don't fit, and we won't fit into life as God planned until we discover and follow His plan.

Russell Kelfer wrote the following poem:

### "You Are Who You Are For A Reason"

You are who you are for a reason.
You're part of an intricate plan.

You're a precious and perfect unique design.
Called God's special woman or man.

You look like you look for a reason.
Our God made no mistake.
He knit you together within the womb,
You're just what he wanted to make.

The parents you had were the ones he chose,
And no matter how you may feel,
They were custom-designed with God's plan in mind,
And they bear the Master's seal.

No, that trauma you faced was not easy.
And God wept that it hurt you so;
But it was allowed to shape your heart
So that into his likeness you'd grow.

You are who you are for a reason,
You've been formed by the Master's rod.

You are who you are, beloved,
Because there is a God! [10]

During my childhood and youth, God's invisible hand was at work in my life, although most of the time I wasn't aware of it. He rescued me in times of danger. He put godly grandparents, parents, and many other people in my life to teach me His truth and to discipline me when I needed it. He gave me life experiences, and allowed me to get to know many people by name as I sold various things. These experiences would be invaluable for what God had planned for my future.

My life was about to change. I would soon make the most important decision I had ever made. This decision would be the turning point of my life. It would set me on a path that I never wanted to be on. I was about to experience the invisible hand of God at work in my life in ways I could never had dreamed possible.

## Think About It

- Have there been times in your life when God rescued you from great danger?
- Are there characteristics of a rebellious nature in you?
- Do you recognize how fragile life is and that God has shown great mercy to you?
- Are you using the special talents, abilities and gifts God has given to you?

_____

[10] Quote3z.blogspot.com/2015/01/russell_kelfer

CHAPTER 4

# THE INVISIBLE HAND OF GOD AT WORK IN MY CONVERSION AND CALL TO MINISTRY

*"The Lord's hand was with them, and a great number of people believed and turned to the Lord" (Acts 11:21)*

## Something Was Missing In My Life

Mickey Mantle was one of the greatest professional baseball players of all time. The Hall of Famer played for eighteen years with the New York Yankees. During his career, he had 536 home runs, 1,509 RBI's, a .298 career batting average, seven world championships, and three MVP awards. In 1956, he won the Triple Crown: a .353 batting average, 52 home runs, and 130 RBI's.

Mickey's father, Mutt Mantle, died of Hodgkin's disease at age forty. His grandfather and two uncles also died of the same disease before they turned forty. Mickey lived every day with the thought that the same fate awaited him. He decided that he would dedicate his life to baseball, but he had a serious problem. He was addicted to alcohol.

Ed Cheek, in the brief pamphlet, "Mickey Mantle: His Final Inning," wrote: "Convinced an early funeral was his inevitable fate, though often joking about it, he played hard and partied even harder. For him, there was no tomorrow. Tragically, this attitude led to a forty year bout with alcohol that caused his body to grow old before its time and clouded his mind. Many criticized his self-destructive lifestyle, saying that it sabotaged the greatest combination of power and speed that the game had ever seen. In the autumn of his life, Mantle came to agree with those critics, admitting that his drug of choice, alcohol, kept him from reaching his full potential as a player and as a person. He had learned the hard lesson that a man reaps what he sows."[11]

Something was missing in Mickey Mantle's life. There was an emptiness that his career, fame, and fortune could not fill. In 1994, he checked himself into the Betty Ford Center to get help for his addiction. He was making progress, but in 1995 doctors discovered that cancer had destroyed his liver. He was facing death and he was afraid.

One of Mickey's teammates with the Yankees was Bobby Richardson, who played second base. Bobby was a Christian, and through the years he had tried to share with Mickey the good news of God's love and the offer of forgiveness and eternal life, but Mickey wasn't interested.

Mickey wanted to live his life his own way. But now he was facing the final inning of his life and he realized that a relationship with his Creator and God was missing in his life. The guilt of his sins troubled him greatly. He knew he was separated from God and one day, he turned to God and asked for forgiveness of his sins and by faith invited Jesus Christ into his life as his Savior and Lord.

Mickey decided to call his friend Bobby Richardson and ask him to pray for him. Bobby prayed for Mickey and went to visit him in the hospital. Bobby looked directly into his friend's eyes and said, "Mickey, I love you, and I want you to spend eternity in heaven with me."

Mickey smiled and said, "Bobby, I've been wanting to tell you that I have trusted Jesus Christ as my Savior." Bobby was overjoyed to hear Mickey confess his faith in Jesus Christ.

Bobby Richardson was asked to speak at Mickey's funeral service. Before the audience of 2,000 who attended the service and a national TV audience, Bobby said, "There are only two groups of people: those who say 'yes' to Christ, and those who say 'no.'" He added that, "since none of us knows when we will face our own final inning, saying 'maybe' is really saying 'no.'"[12] The Bible says, "Whoever believes in the Son has eternal life, but whoever rejects the Son will not see life, for God's wrath remains on him" (John 3:36).

---

[11] Mickey Mantle: His Final Inning, Gospel Tract by Ed Cheek, American Tract Society (Garland, Texas, 1998)

[12] Ibid.

Just as there was something missing in Mickey Mantle's life, there was something missing in my life as well. Even though I had the wonderful privilege of having godly grandparents on both sides of my family and growing up in a Christian home, that did not make me a Christian. The Bible says, "So then, each of us will give an account of himself to God" (Romans 14:12). We must individually and personally trust Christ as our Savior and Lord if we want to have forgiveness of our sins and receive the gift of eternal life.

Through the invisible hand of God at work in my childhood and youth, I was exposed to the truth of the gospel. I knew that there was a God who created the sun, moon, and stars, and that they didn't just come about by random chance.

I had a fear of God and knew I was accountable to Him. I remember saying a bad word while riding my bicycle when I was about ten years old. I suddenly became so fearful of God's wrath and thought I might fall off my bike, so I got off of it and walked beside it.

My parents, grandparents, and Sunday school teachers taught me that God loved me, that Jesus died on the cross for my sins, and that I needed Him in my life. I knew I needed to repent and turn from my sinful ways and become a Christian, but I didn't want to. I wanted to live my life the way I wanted to live it.

When I was eleven years old an evangelist spoke in our church each night for about a week. He preached about Jesus and how we could have a personal relationship with Him. My parents, grandparents, and Sunday school teachers all wanted me and the other young people in our church to become Christians. My dad even arranged for me to have an appointment with the evangelist so he could explain the gospel message to me personally. I felt like I was under pressure to do what other people wanted me to do.

One night, at the close of the church service, the evangelist asked if anyone would like to become a Christian and invite Jesus Christ into their life. He invited those who would like to make this decision to come forward to the front of the sanctuary.

Several of my friends went forward. I felt like I was under peer pressure to do what they were doing. I didn't want to disappoint them or my parents or other people who wanted me to become a

Christian. I am not sure I really wanted to know God at that time, but I followed my friends to the front of the sanctuary.

I do not remember anyone praying with me or explaining anything to me about becoming a Christian, but now, in the minds of other people who attended that service, I supposedly was a Christian because I went forward at a public church service.

Was I really a Christian, or had I just gone forward in that service because I thought that was expected of me? Did my heart truly desire to know Jesus Christ as my Savior and Lord at that time?

As I look back upon this experience I cannot say with any degree of certainty that I truly trusted Jesus Christ that night to forgive me of my sins and to come into my life. But there was now an expectation from my family and people in our church that I was to begin living like a Christian. The problem was that my attitudes, actions, and desires had not changed.

For the next several years, I lived the life of a phony. I began to pretend I was a Christian. The Bible speaks of those who have "a form of godliness but deny its power" (II Timothy 3:5). I lived like a chameleon, a lizard which can change the color of its skin to blend in with its surroundings. When I was with my Christian friends, I tried to act like a Christian should act. But when I was with my non-Christian friends, I lived the way they lived.

My attitudes, actions, language, and desires were just like theirs. I could swear, tell dirty jokes, and say inappropriate things about people just like my non-Christian friends had been doing. But then I could quickly flip flop and not do any of those things when I was with my Christian friends. I was simply deceiving myself and those around me by pretending to be a Christian, but felt terrible guilt inside knowing I was living a double life. God knew how I was living my life, and I feared that my parents and other people would discover my phoniness. Living a double life became challenging and stressful.

John Newton worked on a slave trade ship before he became a Christian in 1748. As a result of a violent storm at sea he cried out to God for mercy, and the Lord saved him, not only physically from the storm, but his life was changed spiritually as well. After becoming a Christian, Newton said, "In evil long I took delight, unawed by shame or fear, till a new object struck my sight, and stopped my wild career."[13]

The new object that captured Newton's attention was Jesus Christ. He became a minister in the Church of England and became best known as the author of the hymn "Amazing Grace."

## A Defining Moment

When I was almost seventeen, someone captured my attention and I discovered the answer to what was missing in my life. The emptiness, fear, guilt, and loneliness were suddenly gone and I was a changed person. How did this dramatic change happen in my life?

When I was in eleventh grade at West Branch Area High School in Allport, Pennsylvania, I was struggling through the fall months with a continuous sore throat. I went to a doctor, who said, "I want you in the hospital the day after Thanksgiving. You must have your tonsils removed."

I quickly objected. "There's no way I can be in the hospital over Thanksgiving vacation! Deer season starts the Monday after Thanksgiving and I want to go hunting." I grew up in the country—and my dad, brother, friends, and nearly everyone I knew went deer hunting. I couldn't possibly risk missing the first day of the season. The doctor replied, "Then I want you in the hospital the day after Christmas. Removing your tonsils is a simple procedure, and you'll probably go home the same day or the next day."

Having a person's tonsils removed may be a simple procedure for some people, but it wasn't for me. In 1965, the anesthesiologist used ether to put me to sleep before the surgery. Because the surgery took longer than expected, I was given another drug, sodium pentothal, to keep me asleep until the surgery was completed.

Apparently, I had an allergic reaction to the combination of these two drugs, and I became very sick. I couldn't eat anything but Jell-O and ice chips for several days. I felt like I had swallowed a baseball and it was lodged in my stomach. I was

---

[13] www.hymnary.org/text/in_evil_long_I_took_delight

losing weight rapidly: twenty-four pounds in about two weeks. The doctor couldn't figure out exactly what was happening to me. The puzzled looks on my parents' faces as they visited me in the hospital made me think I was in serious condition.

During the nine days when I was in the hospital, I did some very serious thinking. *Why was I so sick? Was God trying to get my attention? Was I going to live or die? If I did die, where would I go after my death? Would I go to heaven or hell? Was there really a heaven and hell that I would face after death, or was that just a myth or a fanciful story in the Bible?*

I had been taught by my parents and Sunday school teachers that heaven and hell were real, but I didn't know what I believed personally. I had no assurance or peace in my mind or heart that if I died I would go to heaven.

I was deeply troubled by my sins—plagued with guilt and remorse for my rebellious behavior in my childhood and youth, and for the many things that I had done against a holy and righteous God. The Bible says, "It is a dreadful thing to fall into the hands of the living God" (Hebrews 10:31). I knew I wasn't ready to face God. Hebrews 9:27 says, "Man is destined to die once, and after that to face judgment."

It was at this time in my life that I believe the invisible hand of God was at work in drawing me into a personal relationship with Him. In Psalm 32:3-4, David said, "When I kept silent, my bones wasted away through my groaning all day long. For day and night Your hand was heavy upon me; my strength was sapped as in the heat of summer." I felt as if the heavy hand of God was upon me.

In God's divine providence and mercy, a man came to visit me in the hospital. Albert Zinz was a chemistry teacher in my high school and a Sunday school teacher in my church. He was concerned about me and gave me a book entitled *Let's Play Ball*. The book contained the stories of professional athletes who were Christians. The story that captured my attention most was about Bobby Richardson, Mickey Mantle's friend, who played second baseman for the New York Yankees from 1955 through 1966.

Bobby Richardson had a great baseball career. He was the only World Series MVP (Most Valuable Player) to be selected from the losing team. He had fame and fortune, good health, a great family, and everything he ever wanted in life.

He made a statement that Jesus Christ meant more to him than baseball or anything else in his life. Jesus Christ was Lord of his life, and he was not ashamed to tell others about Him.

When I first read this story, I thought Bobby Richardson was a religious fanatic, and I didn't want to read any more. I put the book down on the nightstand in the hospital room.

Several more days passed as I laid in my hospital bed. I wasn't getting any better physically, and I was greatly troubled spiritually. I decided to pick up the book and read it again. *What was there about Jesus Christ that was so important to Bobby Richardson?*

*Wasn't Jesus just a great religious leader like Buddha, Mohammed, or Confucius?* I had read about these religious leaders, which raised the question in my mind: How was Jesus any different from them? Didn't they all basically teach morals, values, and good works? What did any of them do for me personally? Then this penetrating thought came into my mind: Jesus Christ was the only one who loved me enough to die for me.

Buddha, Mohammed, and Confucius didn't die for me. The Bible says, "But God demonstrates His own love for us in this: While we were still sinners, Christ died for us" (Romans 5:8). "For God so loved the world that He gave His one and only Son, that whoever believes in Him shall not perish but have eternal life" (John 3:16).

God's great love for me—even though I had disobeyed, disgraced, and rebelled against Him—began to grip and soften my hardened heart. *How could He love me so much?* I felt so unworthy of His love. *What had I ever done for Him? How could He let Himself be crucified on a cross and have nails driven through His hands and feet for me?*

Isaiah the prophet said, "Surely He took up our infirmities and carried our sorrows, yet we considered Him stricken by God, smitten by Him and afflicted. But He was pierced for our transgressions, He was crushed for our iniquities; the punishment that brought us peace was upon Him, and by His wounds we are healed. We all, like sheep, have gone astray, each of us has turned to his own way; and the Lord has laid on Him the iniquity of us all" (Isaiah 53:4-6). These verses captured my attention that Jesus would suffer such pain for me, even though I had been straying away from Him and His unconditional love for me. I had been going my own way and not responding to His great love.

That day, lying in a hospital bed in Philipsburg, Pennsylvania, I realized how much God loved me; enough to let His sinless Son die on a cruel cross and shed His precious blood for me so I could be forgiven of my sins. I John 1:7 declares, "But if we walk in the light, as He is in the light, we have fellowship with one another, and the blood of Jesus, His Son, purifies us from all sin."

I recognized I was a sinner and needed His forgiveness. I knew I couldn't save myself: "For it is by grace you have been saved, through faith-- and this is not from yourselves, it is the gift of God-- not by works, so that no one can boast" (Ephesians 2:8-9). No amount of good works that I could ever do would secure salvation for me.

In fact, if I could save myself by doing good works, then I did not need Jesus. I truly believed Jesus rose from the dead to give me eternal life. "That if you confess with your mouth, 'Jesus is Lord,' and believe in your heart that God raised Him from the dead, you will be saved" (Romans 10:9). I was ready to confess Jesus Christ as Lord of my life. I was ready to ask Him to forgive me of all of my sins and to come into my life and save me.

Finally, I had my answer! Jesus Christ was the One who was missing in my life. I now saw clearly my need for Him to become the Lord and Savior of my life. The moment of my true conversion and surrender to Jesus Christ had come.

On that cold, bedridden day in January 1965, I prayed a very simple prayer that changed my life forever. I don't remember the exact words I prayed, but my sincere prayer was something like this: "Jesus, if You are really up there in heaven, and if it's true that You died on the cross for my sins, then I ask You to forgive me for all my sins. I am willing to repent and turn away from sin. I invite You into my life as my Savior and Lord. Thank You for giving me the gift of eternal life. Please change me because I know I can't change myself. In Jesus' name I pray, Amen."

God used the powerful testimony of Bobby Richardson to show me my need of a personal relationship with Jesus Christ, and to open my heart and mind to the truth of the gospel message which is the best "good news" I had ever heard in my life.

I prayed for many years that someday I could meet Bobby Richardson and thank him personally for the amazing influence he had in my life and how his testimony was used by God to lead me to a saving knowledge of Jesus Christ.

God heard and answered my prayer. In John 15:7 Jesus said, "If you remain in Me and My words remain in you, ask what you wish, and it will be given you." On May 8, 1998 I had the wonderful privilege of meeting Bobby Richardson at Faith Church in Allentown, Pennsylvania, when he was the guest speaker at a banquet. I had the overwhelming joy of sitting beside him and talking with him at the banquet before he spoke to several hundred men. He gave me an autographed baseball which I have treasured through the years. What a thrill it was for me to actually meet Bobby Richardson, the man who was so influential in helping me meet Jesus Christ, the Lord of my life.

## How My Life Began To Change

Receiving Jesus Christ into my life by faith, to be my Savior and Lord, was the most significant decision I have ever made. Jesus said, "To all who received Him, to those who believed in His name, He gave the right to become children of God" (John 1:12). By placing my faith in Jesus Christ alone for salvation, I became a child of God. I was no longer just God's creation; I was now His child.

One of the Bible verses Bobby Richardson mentioned in his story was II Corinthians 5:17: "Therefore, if anyone is in Christ, he is a new creation; the old has gone, the new has come!" When I read this verse of scripture, it was almost like the invisible hand of God had lifted it off the page of the book and magnified it with bold print. I suddenly got so excited to think that this verse from God's Word could actually be true in my life. Because I was "in Christ" and "Christ was in me," I was no longer the same person.

I was now a new creation. Colossians 1:27 says, "Christ in you, the hope of glory."

Could the old things in my life really be gone? Could I begin to experience new things? This is exactly what began to happen in my life. Old things were beginning to pass away and no longer were important to me. New things began to happen in my life.

One of the first new things I began to experience was a hunger and thirst for the Word of God. In Matthew 5:6 Jesus said, "Blessed are those who hunger and thirst for righteousness, for they will be filled." My intense hunger and thirst for His Word soon led to a hunger and thirst for His righteousness. I wanted to learn all I could about God, His righteousness, and how I could live a new life in Christ in a way that would truly please Him.

No one told me to read the Bible. I wanted to read it and apply the truth of God's Word in my life. I soon discovered that the Bible was a very practical book and that it revealed how God wanted His people to live. The more I read the scriptures, the more I began to love Jesus and His powerful Word. "Oh, how I love Your law! I meditate on it all day long" (Psalm 119:97).

After I became a Christian, I began to pray and take God's promises seriously concerning prayer. In Jeremiah 33:3 the Lord said, "Call to Me and I will answer you and tell you great and unsearchable things you do not know." There were many things I did not know, especially about God and His plan for my life. God was hearing and answering my prayers and I was thrilled. I got so excited about experiencing answers to prayer. Too many things were happening in my life that were not just coincidences. God was actively at work answering my prayers and changing my life.

One of the old things that began to change in my life was my vocabulary. There were some words I used that were not pleasing to God. God was beginning to convict me about the swear words I had been using. Now that the Spirit of God was living inside of me, whenever one of those words slipped out of my mouth, it was like someone took a sledgehammer and hit the Liberty Bell in Philadelphia. I heard the word ringing in my mind and I knew that word must be removed from my vocabulary if I was to honor the Lord with my words. Someone once said, "Jesus Christ is the Savior of humanity, not a word of profanity." All words of profanity had to be downloaded from the computer of my heart and deleted.

Jesus said in Matthew 12:36-37," But I tell you that men will have to give account on the day of judgment for every careless word they have spoken. For by your words you will be acquitted, and by your words you will be condemned." I realized that God would hold me accountable for my words, and as my language began to change, I felt a new power at work within me. These changes didn't all happen overnight, but within a few weeks I knew I was a new person and that the "old has gone, the new has come" just as II Corinthians 5:17 said it would.

I previously mentioned that the man who gave me the book about Bobby Richardson, and other Christian athletes, was Albert Zinz. He was also the play director of our junior and senior class plays. I enjoyed drama and had roles in plays when I was in high school and also when I was in college.

## A Confirming Conversation

Something happened at play practice one afternoon about a month after I had become a Christian. A friend, Maryann, asked me a question: "Larry, what has happened to you?" Her question surprised me, and I asked, "What do you mean?" She replied, "You seem so different to me." Now I was really intrigued.

"Maryann, how am I different? What do you see in me that has changed? Are the changes you see positive or negative?"

She said something like, "You just seem different to me. I've noticed that you're studying more and participating in class. You seem happier and you're talking about your faith. It's almost like you're the same person on the outside, but you're different on the inside. It's like you've been born again as a new person."

Wow! I could hardly believe what I had just heard. I'm not sure Maryann was familiar with the biblical words "born again," but I responded, "Maryann, I think that that's exactly what has happened to me."

My friend saw something of the new life I had been experiencing since I invited Jesus Christ into my life. I didn't know where in the Bible it was written about being "born again," but when I got home from school that day I was determined to read the Bible until I found the Scripture. I found it in John chapter three where Jesus said to a very religious man Nicodemus, "I tell you the truth, no one can see the kingdom of God unless he is born again" (John 3:3). I discovered that being born again was another way of explaining what it means to repent of sin, believe the good news that Jesus died on the cross for my sins and was raised again from the dead, and to receive Christ into my life as my Savior and Lord. After I read John 3:1-8, I knew for certain I had been born again.

I had the assurance of my salvation, and I believed I had received the gift of eternal life as Jesus said in John 10:27-30: "My sheep listen to My voice; I know them, and they follow Me. I give them eternal life, and they shall never perish; no one can snatch them out of My hand. My Father, who has given them to Me is greater than all; no one can snatch them out of My Father's hand. I and My Father are one."

I often wondered, through the years since I was in high school, if perhaps God put the words into my friend Maryann's mouth at play practice that day. The positive changes my friend said she saw in me confirmed in my heart and mind that what I had experienced in Christ was real, and that He was the One who was changing me and giving me a new life.

## Four Specific Changes I Experienced

When I became a Christian, God gave me a new heart. I had a spiritual heart transplant. Ezekiel the prophet spoke about God's people having a new heart. "I will sprinkle clean water on you, and you will be clean; I will cleanse you from all your impurities and from all your idols. I will give you a new heart and put a new spirit in you; I will remove from you your heart of stone and give you a heart of flesh. And I will put My Spirit in you and move you to follow My decrees and be careful to keep My laws" (Ezekiel 36:25-27). When God gave me a new heart, I began to experience pardon, power, peace, and purpose.

## *Pardon*

God granted me a pardon from the penalty of my sins. Romans 6:23 declares, "For the wages of sin is death, but the gift of God is eternal life in Christ Jesus our Lord." God lifted the death penalty, the sentence of death that I deserved because of my sins, the moment I asked Him to forgive me of my sins and trusted that Jesus Christ paid for my pardon when He died on the cross for me.

God gave me the assurance that my pardon was a reality, although I was so unworthy of this gift. "Therefore, there is now no condemnation for those who are in Christ Jesus, because through Christ Jesus the law of the Spirit of life set me free from the law of sin and death" (Romans 8:1-2).

A man wrote to a pastor, "What does it mean that God forgave you?" In this computer age, the pastor wrote back, "It means that all your files were deleted."

To have all the files of my sins deleted left me feeling as clean as newly fallen snow on a beautiful winter day. Isaiah 1:18 is a description of how I felt when God pardoned me: "Come now, let us reason together," says the Lord. "Though your sins are like scarlet, they shall be as white as snow; though they are red as crimson, they shall be like wool."

## *Power*

A new power for living came into my life the day Jesus Christ became my Lord and Savior. The apostle Paul said, "I want to know Christ and the power of His resurrection..." (Philippians 3:10). Paul experienced the dynamic power of Jesus Christ working in his life after his conversion on the road to Damascus as recorded in Acts 9:1-19.

The same power that raised Jesus Christ from the dead lives in every born-again believer. Romans 8:10-11 makes this fact very clear: "But if Christ is in you, your body is dead because of sin, yet your spirit is alive, because of righteousness. And if the Spirit of Him who raised Jesus from the dead is living in you, He who raised Christ from the dead will also give life to your mortal bodies through His Spirit, who lives in you."

The Apostles experienced the power of the Holy Spirit in their lives even when they were being persecuted. "After they prayed, the place where they were meeting was shaken. And they were all filled with the Holy Spirit and spoke the Word of God boldly" (Acts 4:31).

The Apostles demonstrated a new power in their lives that enabled them to have unembarrassed freedom of speech to be witnesses for Christ. I began to experience this new power in my life. God's power helped me to live the Christian life, be a witness for Christ, and overcome the temptations and trials of life.

## *Peace*

My new life in Christ enabled me to experience amazing peace in my heart and mind that I couldn't explain, but it was real. "Therefore, since we have been justified through faith, we have peace with God through our Lord Jesus Christ" (Romans 5:1). The peace of God in my heart is still there over fifty-one years later.

When I invited Jesus Christ into my life in 1965, the United States was engaged in the Vietnam War. More than 58,000 U.S. soldiers were killed in that war, including several of my high school friends. Although the war was raging in Vietnam, there had been a war raging in my heart as well. The powers of darkness were fighting against God to keep me from coming to Christ.

God won the battle for my soul. Immediately after I prayed and surrendered my life to Christ that day in the hospital, I began to sense peace in my soul. It was almost like a nurse rushed into my room and announced that she just heard on the news that the Vietnam War was over. The troops were coming home and a peace treaty had been signed.

Jesus promised His peace to all who would follow Him. Shortly before He went to the cross to suffer for the sins of the world, He said, "Peace I leave with you; My peace I give you. I do not give you as the world gives. Do not let your hearts be troubled and do not be afraid" (John 14:27).

I was at peace with God, with myself, and with others as much as possible. I had peace and assurance that if I were to die, I would go to heaven not because of anything good I had done, but because I believed what Jesus had done for me in dying on the cross in my place and in being raised from the dead.

## *Purpose*

I had a new purpose for living. I no longer wanted to live for myself, but for Him who loved me and gave Himself for me. The motto for my life became: "He died for me, I'll live for Him." God said to His people, "For I know the plans I have for you," declares the Lord, "plans to prosper you and not to harm you, plans to give you hope and a future" (Jeremiah 29:11).

God had a purpose for my life. He was changing me day by day. I began to experience pardon, power, peace, and purpose like never before. The invisible hand of God was at work in my life, and I was elated about the future. I wanted to know what His purpose was for my life.

Eric Liddell, the Olympic runner in the movie *Chariots of Fire*, believed God had a purpose for his life. He said, "I believe God made me for a purpose, but He also made me fast, and when I run, I feel God's pleasure."[14] I began to feel the pleasure of God in my life as I daily surrendered to Jesus Christ and asked Him to reveal His purpose to me.

## How God Called Me Into the Ministry

If there was one thing I never wanted to be, it was a pastor. If someone had asked me at the beginning of my senior year in high school to make a list of 100 occupations that I may be interested in, I would never have put the ministry on the list. I hated the thought of being in the ministry.

When I was in my childhood and youth, our family attended a very small Baptist church. The congregation could only afford to pay the pastor a meager salary. He was poor and lived in a little

---

[14] www.imdf.com/title/tt0082158/quotes Chariots of Fire (1981)

parsonage that always seemed in need of repair. By this world's standards, he had very little material wealth.

I wanted to be in a good-paying profession, and not be poor like my pastor. I heard the story of a little boy who shook hands with his pastor after the morning worship service.

He said, "Pastor, when I grow up and get a good job, I'm going to give you money."

The pastor was puzzled by the little boy's comment, and he asked, "Why would you want to give me money?"

The boy replied, "Because my daddy says you're the poorest pastor we have ever had."

Some pastors are poor materially, and some are poor for other reasons. One poor pastor had hoped to get a discount from a tailor. As he was being fitted for a new suit he said to the tailor, "I'm a poor preacher."

The tailor quickly replied, "I know, I've heard you preach."

I didn't want to be a poor pastor, no matter how the word "poor" was defined.

When I was about fourteen, I was visiting my grandparents who lived across the street from our church. Our pastor stopped for a visit while I was there. During the conversation, the pastor made a comment to my grandmother that I think he wanted me to hear.

He said, "Larry's going to be a pastor someday." I didn't respond to his comment, but inside I was boiling over with anger because of what he had said. I didn't want to be a pastor, and I also didn't want to be a missionary and live in a little mud hut in Africa or some other country.

I wanted to be a lawyer when I grew up. I admired my Uncle Bill, who was a lawyer and later became a judge. I wanted to be like him. He was very successful in his career. He was wealthy, could travel anywhere, and always drove a Cadillac. He lived in what I thought was a mansion in State College, Pennsylvania. I can't remember if his house had seven bedrooms and five fireplaces, or five bedrooms and seven fireplaces. But it was a big house, very big.

Perry Mason became an idol to me. I knew God didn't like idols, so I'll say I was fascinated with the television lawyer. Every day after school, I wanted to watch his program. I remember thinking, "That's what I want to be someday. I want to be a lawyer and put criminals behind bars." That was my plan and purpose for my life. But that was not what God had planned for me.

My decision to become a true follower of Christ took place in January 1965. It was exciting to experience the invisible hand of God at work in my life. Psalm 45:4 says, "In Your majesty, ride forth victoriously on behalf of truth, humility, and righteousness; let Your right hand display awesome deeds." I began to experience some awesome deeds that God was doing.

I had a great desire to share my faith with anyone who would listen to me. There were times when I found myself saying things I believe God put in my mouth. God said, "I have put My words in your mouth and covered you with the shadow of My hand — I Who set the heavens in place, Who laid the foundations of the earth, and Who say to Zion, 'You are My people'" (Isaiah 51:16). There was no doubt in my mind that God had His invisible hand upon my life and there were times when I knew He filled my mouth with His words. Jeremiah 5:14 was a verse that encouraged me greatly as I trusted in Him to speak through me. God said to Jeremiah: "I will make My words in your mouth fire and these people the wood it consumes."

On New Year's Eve 1965, I spent several hours seeking God in prayer and Bible reading. God said in Jeremiah 29:12-13, "Then you will call upon Me and come and pray to Me, and I will listen to you. You will seek Me and find Me when you seek Me with all your heart."

I was seeking God that night with all my heart. I wanted Him to speak to me through His Word and through His Holy Spirit. Just as the Holy Spirit spoke to Philip in Acts 8:29 and told him, "Go to that chariot and stay near it," when He wanted Philip to share Christ with the Ethiopian eunuch, so I wanted the Holy Spirit to speak to me.

This was a holy moment in my life. As I continued to seek God, the words of a poem began to form in my mind. As I sat at the kitchen table, I took a piece of paper and began to write. The words seemed to flow effortlessly. I finished writing these words at 5:00 a.m. on January 1st, 1966.

### "Think About It"

Have you ever thought what Christ means to you,
Or have you been busy with sinful things to do?
Have you ever talked with the Savior above,
Have you ever asked Him to show you His love?

In this world with its sorrows, griefs, and cares,
We wonder how long Christ will us spare.

So I ask you now while you are still here,
To talk with the Master and He'll make it clear.

Why did Christ die for a sinner like me?
Why was He willing to set me free?
You ask me why He loves me so much,
You will never know until you've been touched.

The touch of the Master's Hand can be,
The greatest power that could set you free.
He'll lift you up from your worldly sin,
He'll cleanse your heart and give you peace within.

The line in the poem, "We wonder how long Christ will us spare," seemed almost surreal because later that day a twenty year old young man from my church who was in the military died when his parachute failed to open. Within a few days his funeral service was held. I Corinthians 7:29 reminds us that "the time is short." There is an expiration date on everyone's life. God used this event to get my attention and to cause me to seek His will for my life even more earnestly.

God led me to write a gospel tract with the poem as the theme. I went to a printer and had several hundred copies made. God put a burning desire in my heart to tell people about Jesus Christ and how they could have a personal relationship with Him. That God would use this tract for His glory was my prayer.

Jesus said to His disciples, "But you will receive power when the Holy Spirit comes on you; and you will be My witnesses in Jerusalem, and in all Judea and Samaria, and to the ends of the earth" (Acts 1:8). I felt God's power working in my life, and I wanted to be a witness for Him. I wanted my friends and people in our community to discover the joy, peace, forgiveness, and assurance of eternal life that I had experienced.

Bill Bright, founder of Campus Crusade for Christ, said: "Success in witnessing is simply taking the initiative to share Christ in the power of the Holy Spirit, and leaving the results up to God."[15] I had no power to save anyone, but Jesus did and I wanted to introduce people to Him.

As I shared the life-transforming message of Jesus Christ, I began to hear comments like, "You should go into the ministry for your career. You should become a pastor."

I would respond by saying, "I want to be a lawyer. I can still share my faith as a Christian lawyer. I can teach a Sunday school class and be actively involved in my church. I don't have to be a pastor to be a witness for Christ. I don't want to be a pastor."

If God wanted me to be a pastor or be involved in some form of ministry, He would have to make it very clear to me. I was not about to choose the ministry as a profession. If God called me into the ministry, I would know it and would not be fulfilled in doing anything else.

Jesus said to His apostles, "'You did not choose Me, but I chose you and appointed you to go and bear fruit—fruit that will last. Then the Father will give you whatever you ask in My name" (John 15:16).

The apostles were chosen by Jesus for their ministry. They didn't choose to be apostles, they were chosen. Ephesians 4:11-12 says, "It was He who gave some to be apostles, some to be prophets, some to be evangelists, and some to be pastors and teachers to prepare God's people for works of service, so that the body of Christ might be built up."

---

[15] www.cru.org/.../transferable-concepts/be-a-fruitful-witness.6htm/

## A Turning Point

How did God make it known to me that He was calling me into the ministry? I didn't want to be in the ministry. I had negative feelings about the ministry even from my youth. Why couldn't I be a Christian lawyer and serve God in other ways?

Even though I loved Jesus and wanted to serve Him, I still wanted my will for my life. As I persisted in going my own way, I noticed I was losing my joy and enthusiasm in the Christian life. Instead of having peace and fulfillment, I felt frustrated. Proverbs 28:26 says, "He who trusts in himself is a fool, but he who walks in wisdom is kept safe." The more I trusted in myself and what I wanted to do in life, the more foolish I became. I was experiencing an internal struggle between my will and God's will.

Through two very unusual experiences, God captured my attention and made His will known to me about His plan and purpose for my life. In the first unusual experience, God showed me great mercy and taught me the value of obeying His still, small voice.

During a time of great discouragement in the prophet Elijah's life, the Lord made His will known to him. According to I Kings 19:11-12, the Lord was not in the wind, an earthquake, or a fire. God communicated to Elijah in "a gentle whisper" or "still small voice" as the King James Version of the Bible describes it. God also spoke to His people saying, "Whether you turn to the right or to the left, your ears will hear a voice behind you saying, 'This is the way; walk in it'" (Isaiah 30:21).

Mary Smith was one of my customers when I sold the weekly newspaper, the *Grit*. I delivered my newspapers on Friday nights and Saturday mornings. I rode my bicycle to the homes of my customers until I learned how to drive. During my senior year in high school, I worked on Saturdays as a window washer at the Nittany Lion Inn, so I didn't deliver my newspapers until Saturday night.

Mary Smith's house was the first stop on my newspaper route. Her house was located near a sharp curve on a country road. Since I arrived at her house about the same time each week, she was ready with the money for the newspaper and I would quickly hand it to her and get back into my car. I parked the car at the same spot every Saturday night, not far from the curve. It was a dangerous place to park, but it only took a minute or two to run to her house and back to the car, so I took the risk of parking there.

One Saturday night it was raining and I was already later than my normal time to stop at Mary's house. I had a date that night with the girl who would one day become my wife, and I didn't want to be late. As I drove toward Mary's house, a still small voice seemed to be saying to me, "Don't park there." As I got closer to her house, the voice said again, "Don't park there." I thought I must be just imagining that I was hearing a voice. It was raining. I was running late. I always parked in that same spot. I would get soaked in the rain if I didn't park near her house.

*Was God speaking to me?* As unusual as it seemed, I decided not to park where I usually did, but in a parking area perhaps seventy-five yards from Mary's house. I grabbed a newspaper and started running in the rain. As I ran on the road toward Mary's house, I could hear the sound of a speeding car heading directly toward the curve in the road. I thought, "that car is never going to make it around the curve; it's going to crash." I quickly ran up a few stair steps from the road to Mary's house.

As I stood in the rain, I watched as a drunken man crashed his car into the guardrail that was around the edge of the curve and swerved wildly on the road in the exact spot where my car would normally have been parked. If I had parked there that night and had been getting out of my car or crossing the road, I could have been killed. Only seconds before the crash I had been running on the road to Mary's house. Realizing what could have happened had I not listened to the still small voice within me, I looked up into the sky and said, "Oh God, you have a plan for my life." This was an unforgettable moment when I was very aware of the invisible hand of God at work. "Save us and help us with Your right hand, that those who love You may be delivered" (Psalm 60:5). God saved my life and delivered me that night. I was convinced He had a plan for my life, and I now wanted to know His plan and faithfully follow it, even if He was calling me into the ministry. This was truly a turning point in my life.

## Another Unusual Experience

In the spring of 1966, I was only a few months from graduating from high school. Many questions were unanswered, and I was wrestling with them in my mind. *What college was I going to attend? What was I going to major in?* I didn't want to spend four years of my life majoring in courses I wasn't interested in studying. The main question in my mind was, "What does God want me to do with my life? What is His will?" I came to the conclusion, whatever God's will was for my life, that it would be the best life possible. He created me with talents, abilities, and spiritual gifts. He knew what would bring the greatest fulfillment and joy into my life. Psalm 40:8 declares, "I desire to do Your will, O my God; Your law is within my heart."

Martin Luther said, "God created out of nothing. Therefore, until a man is nothing, God can make nothing out of him."[16] John the Baptist said, "He (Jesus) must become greater; I must become less" (John 3:30). What God began to teach me was that I needed to become nothing, and Jesus Christ needed to become everything in my life. I needed to surrender fully and completely to His will. I finally came to the place where I said, "Lord, I am willing to do Your will no matter what it is, even if You want me in the ministry, but please make it very clear to me."

The second unusual experience God used to call me into the ministry happened on March 22nd, 1966. During the evening hours of March 22nd, I decided to spend an extended time reading the Bible and praying about God's will for my life. It was a warm night for the month of March, so I sat outside on our back porch. I couldn't find a flashlight, but I did find a candle and began reading the Bible by candlelight.

Psalm 62:8 describes how David poured out his heart to the Lord, and that was what I was doing as well: "Trust in Him at all times, O people; pour out your hearts to Him, for God is our refuge."

As I sat on the porch meditating, dark clouds began to fill the sky as if an early spring thunderstorm was approaching. As I looked at the clouds, I saw something that seemed strange to me.

---

[16] Azquotes.com/quote/849334

There was one area where the clouds would not cover what appeared to be a hole in the sky. The clouds would come to the edge of the hole, but then seemed to back away. What happened next is difficult for me to describe. Some people may say that it was a vision from God, while others may say it was just an interesting experience. While I gazed at the hole in the sky, I thought about the return of Jesus Christ as described in I Thessalonians 4:16-17. "For the Lord Himself will come down from heaven, with a loud command, with the voice of the archangel and with the trumpet call of God, and the dead in Christ will rise first. After that, we who are still alive and are left will be caught up together with them in the clouds to meet the Lord in the air. And so we will be with the Lord forever."

Was God giving me a glimpse of what it will be like when Jesus Christ returns for His bride (all true believers), at the moment they meet Him in the clouds to return with Him to heaven? I began to picture thousands of Christians being caught up in the clouds and passing through that hole in the sky into heaven to be with Jesus forever and ever. As my total attention was focused on what I was envisioning, a falling star fell through the hole in the sky. At that moment, I felt enveloped in the presence of God; it was unlike any experience I had ever had before. It was as if I was sitting on the lap of Jesus and He gave me the strongest bear hug I could imagine.

What about the falling star? To me, this star represented a person who did not make it into heaven. Who was that person? Was this someone I could have shared Christ with, but didn't?

Thoughts came into my mind that startled me. "Someone is going to die? Who is going to die? Am I going to die? Is my father, mother, brother, or sister going to die?" These were not just random thoughts; they came into my mind with solemn conviction. I was absolutely certain someone was going to die.

The invisible hand of God was at work in my life. God said to His people, "So do not fear, for I am with you; do not be dismayed, for I am your God. I will strengthen you and help you. I will uphold you with My righteous right hand" (Isaiah 41:10). If God was calling me into the ministry He would be with me, and would strengthen me and help me. He would uphold me with His righteous right hand just as He promised.

While I was reflecting on what I had experienced, the words of a poem were again forming in my mind much like I had experienced almost three months before. I began to write...

### "What He Did For Me"

As I sat on the porch with my pen in hand,
I asked the Lord if He would understand.
If I prayed to Him with an earnest heart,
Would He take my life and never depart?

Could He use a soul with a life like mine?
Could He make my face forever to shine?
Had He a place in this world for me?
Would I be willing to readily see?

Christ had the answer, He loved me so much.
He took all my sin, and He left me the touch.
The touch that I have, will never depart.
It's here to stay, and it's deep in my heart.

Now what could He do with a life like mine?
Yes, I am willing to readily climb.
The steps are before me, the past is behind.
**My Jesus, forever, You'll always be mine.**

The next morning, I was getting ready to go to school. As I was in the bathroom shaving, I was singing the words of a hymn entitled, "I'll Go Where You Want Me to Go," by Mary Brown. The words of the chorus caught my attention. "I'll go where You want me to go, dear Lord, o're mountains, or plains or sea; I'll say what You want me to say, dear Lord, I'll be what You want me to be." When I sang those words, "I'll be what you want me to be," I felt like a hypocrite. It seemed as if God was making me look at myself in the mirror. *Would I really go where He wanted me to go? Would I really say what He wanted me to say? Would I really be what*

*He wanted me to be?* As tears streamed down my cheeks, I prayed, "Yes, Lord, I will be what You want me to be. If You want me to be in the ministry, I'm willing. If You send me to a Podunk (any small or insignificant town or village) in Maine, I'll go. If You want me to live in a mud hut in Africa, I'll do it." This was my moment of truth with God. I fully surrendered myself to His will. All I needed was to be sure that He was calling me. I was committed to following Him.

I got on the school bus and soon arrived at West Branch Area High School in Allport, Pennsylvania. As I was getting off the bus, a girl came running up to me and said, "Larry, did you hear about Jimmy Clark?" I said, "No, what happened to him?" She replied, "He was killed last night." I will never forget what I blurted out. "Oh God, the star, the star." As I entered the school and walked down the hallway, I was overwhelmed with the assurance that God was calling me into the ministry. It hadn't been thirty minutes since I surrendered myself to do God's will. I now had the assurance I desired. God called, and I answered His call.

God used the death of sixteen-year-old Jimmy Clark to break my heart and give me the desire to share Jesus Christ and His wonderful love, forgiveness, grace, mercy, and eternal life with anyone who would be willing to listen. Jimmy had been walking on the street the night before, near his house in Munson, not far from where I lived. His neighbor, Butchy Coble, bumped him with his bicycle. Jimmy fell and hit his head on the street and died. I do not know if Jimmy had a personal relationship with Jesus Christ, but I hope he did. Jimmy's death took place as I was sitting on the porch seeking God's plan and purpose for my life.

To further confirm God's call to the ministry, on the afternoon of the day I heard of Jimmy's death I received my acceptance letter to Houghton College. That night, my parents asked me what I was going to major in at Houghton. With tears in my eyes, I replied, "God has called me into the ministry."

## Think About It

- Do you sense there is something missing in your life?
- Have you repented (turned away) from your sins and received Jesus Christ into your life as your Savior and Lord?
- If you have not received Jesus Christ into your life would you like to do that right now? Pray this prayer from your heart and Jesus Christ will come into your life: *"Jesus, I recognize that You love me and that I need You. I am truly sorry for the sins I have committed against You and I ask You to forgive me. Thank You for dying on the cross for my sins and for shedding Your blood so I could be cleansed from all uncleanness. I believe You were resurrected from the dead to give me eternal life. I open the door of my heart and receive You into my life as my Savior and Lord. Please change me and help me live my life for You. In Jesus' name I pray. Amen."*
- If you have received Christ into your life at some point in the past, what changes have you experienced since coming to know Him?
- Have you discovered God's calling and plan for your life?
- Are you willing to surrender your life to His will?

CHAPTER 5

# *THE INVISIBLE HAND OF GOD AT WORK IN MY MARRIAGE*

*"You have made known to me the path of life; You will fill me with joy in Your presence, with eternal pleasures at Your right hand" (Psalm 16:11).*

### Knowing The Will Of God

Nothing in life could be better than knowing and doing the will of God. Psalm 40:8 declares, "I desire to do Your will, O my God; Your law is within my heart." When we desire to do God's will and are committed to obeying Him, He makes His will known to us.

Jesus said, "My teaching is not My own. It comes from Him who sent Me. If anyone chooses to do God's will, he will find out whether My teaching comes from God or whether I speak on My own. He who speaks on his own does so to gain honor for himself, but he who works for the honor of the one who sent him is a man of truth; there is nothing false about him" (John 7:16-18). Anyone who wants to know God's will must be committed to do His will. Sometimes we want to know God's will first and then we will decide if we want to do it or not. God does not work that way. He only reveals His will as we choose to do His will.

God delights to guide His children on the path of life. David declared, "You have made known to me the path of life" (Psalm 16:11) and also prayed, "Show me Your ways, O Lord, teach me Your paths; guide me in Your truth and teach me, for You are God my Savior, and my hope is in You all day long" (Psalm 25:4,5). As we place our hope in the Lord He shows us His path in life.

Could God's invisible hand lead me to a life partner if it was in His will that He wanted me to be married? Yes, He could lead me, and He did. God promises to guide us with His hand even though His hand is invisible. "If I rise on the wings of the dawn, if I settle on the far side of the sea, even there Your hand will guide me, Your right hand will hold me fast" (Psalm 139:9-10).

## How I Met My Wife-To-Be

When I turned to God in sincere faith He began to reveal Himself to me. His hand was at work in my life drawing me to Himself. After I turned to the Lord and believed in Him, I began to pray that He would lead me to a Christian girl who would one day become my wife.

When I was in the hospital to have my tonsils removed, I met a girl who worked at the hospital as a nurse's aide. She had beautiful dark hair, brown eyes, and a smile that could melt the heart of a seventeen-year-old boy. I really liked her, but there was a problem. I was seventeen and she was twenty-one. She caught my attention, but I don't think I caught hers. My sadness turned to excitement, however, when she told me she had a seventeen-year-old sister.

I thought that if her younger sister was anything like she was then I would like to meet her. She went to Philipsburg-Osceola High School while I was a student at West Branch Area High School. I knew a girl who attended her school and through her I arranged to have a blind date. The night I met her I had another problem. I had the opposite experience that I had had with her older sister. This time, she did not capture my attention, but apparently I captured hers.

A few weeks after we met she called my house. I was not home, but she spoke to my mother and said she wanted to invite me to go with her to her junior-senior prom. When my mother told me she had called I put off calling her back because I didn't want to go to the prom with her.

One day my mother firmly told me, "You have to call that girl and tell her you'll go with her to the prom."

I protested, "I don't want to go with her to the prom."

My mother replied, "You've waited too long to call her. She'll never get a date this close to the prom. You're going to take her."

My mother was not usually that stern. I knew she felt sorry for the girl, especially since I did not call her back, but while she was very nice, I was not interested in going out with her again. I reluctantly obeyed my mother and made plans to go to the prom.

Perhaps the invisible hand of God was guiding my mother to encourage me to go to the prom even though I did not want to go. According to Romans 8:28 God does turn things around for the good of those who love Him. "And we know that in all things God works for the good of those who love Him, who have been called according to His purpose."

I loved God and wanted His purpose for my life, but I certainly did not believe that attending a prom with a girl I did not want to go out with had any good or divine purpose for my life. Looking back on this event I now believe it was in God's divine purpose for me to attend. God's purpose and my purpose concerning the prom were very different, but God was teaching me to trust Him and to realize that His ways are always best. "To everything there is a season, and a time to every purpose under the heaven" (Ecclesiastes 3:1). This was a valuable lesson I needed to learn and soon I would discover that attending the prom proved to be one of the greatest events in my life.

My closest friend in my high school was Fred. Fred had been dating a girl named Sharon who also attended Philipsburg-Osceola High School. I had never met Sharon, so I had no idea what she looked like. Fred and I decided we would double-date the night of the prom. Being with my close friend Fred and his date eased my discomfort about being at the prom.

The night of the prom my date and I arrived at her high school before Fred and Sharon. When Fred and Sharon arrived and walked across the gymnasium floor toward us, I was immediately attracted to Sharon. Her beautiful blonde hair, cute smile and gorgeous prom dress were stunning. She captured my heart unlike any girl I had ever seen before. When our eyes met, I experienced something inside I had never experienced before. I felt like I was about to meet the girl of my dreams and the answer to my prayers.

When we were introduced to each other, suddenly a scene from the movie *West Side Story* flashed through my mind. It was the scene when Tony saw Maria for the first time and he excitedly began to sing, "Maria, Maria, I just met a girl named Maria." Well, I had just met a girl named Sharon and I was now excited about being at the prom.

I didn't want to ignore my date, but I sure did enjoy talking to Sharon. The four of us sat together at a small table that was covered with an overlapping table cloth. Fred and I decided to get some punch for the four of us. When we returned, I accidently bumped Sharon's shoe under the table when I pulled in my chair. I couldn't believe what happened next. Sharon bumped my shoe under the table, and I am certain it was not by accident.

All evening at the prom we couldn't stop smiling at one another. I did not get to dance with Sharon, but as she danced with Fred and I danced with my date we smiled at each other over the shoulder of our partners.

Without a doubt there was a spark between us. But now I faced yet another problem. Fred was my best friend and I couldn't just call Sharon the day after the prom and ask her for a date. That was far too risky. I could lose a friend and gain a black eye at the same time.

*What should I do?* I was anxious to see Sharon again, but how could that come about? I really liked her and I sensed she liked me as well. *Would I ever be able to have a date with her? Would she be willing to go out with me? What about Fred? How serious was he about dating Sharon? Would she forget about me if I did not have contact with her before long?* I had many questions swirling around in my mind. I needed answers and so I turned to God for His help.

I had recently discovered that the best thing to do when I didn't know what to do was to pray. I began to pray and trust God that if He wanted Sharon and me to see each other again, then He would work it out.

I began to claim God's promises as I prayed. "Call to Me and I will answer you and tell you great and unsearchable things you do not know" (Jeremiah 33:3). "Have faith in God," Jesus answered. "I tell you the truth, if anyone says to this mountain, 'Go, throw yourself into the sea; and does not doubt in his heart but believes that what he says will happen, it will be done for him. Therefore I tell you, whatever you ask for in prayer, believe that you have received it, and it will be yours'" (Mark 11:22-24). God's promises were so encouraging to me; they filled me with renewed faith and hope.

I was faced with a problem that was like a huge mountain before me. I believed God was a mountain-moving God and He could move this mountain in answer to my prayers. I needed a miracle, and fortunately, I had met the miracle-working God just a few months before.

The words of an old song lifted my spirit as I prayed. "Got any rivers you think are uncrossable? Got any mountains you can't tunnel through? God specializes in things thought impossible. He can do just what no other can do."[17]

Did God hear and answer my prayers? He certainly did. Someone said, "When we work we work, but when we pray God works." I was discovering that prayer should be my first response and not my last resort. The invisible hand of God was at work and soon I was to meet Sharon again.

### How We Met Again

I lived in Munson and Sharon lived in Osceola Mills. They were both small towns in central Pennsylvania about ten miles apart. The largest town in our area was Philipsburg and that's where many people in our area went shopping.

On a Friday night, about a month after the prom, my prayers were answered. I was walking alone on the street in Philipsburg and suddenly there she was, walking toward me with her mother. She introduced me to her mother, who then walked away so Sharon and I could talk.

I was so excited to see Sharon. My heart began to flutter, my palms began to perspire, and I felt nervousness welling up inside of me. *What do I say?* I thought to myself. *Don't say anything stupid.*

After greeting one another, I could tell by her cute smile that she was as happy to see me as I was to see her.

During our brief conversation I asked Sharon, "Have you seen Fred lately?" It was a risky question, but I had to ask it. *What if my intuition was wrong? What would I say if she said she was still dating*

---

[17] www.traditionalmusic.co.uk./gospel_songs_chords/got_any_rivers.htm

*Fred?* My mind was racing and my pulse increasing as I waited for her answer.

She replied, "No, I haven't seen Fred for several weeks. I think he's interested in another girl."

Wow, that news thrilled me more than a cold drink on a very hot day.

Then Sharon said she had to get back to work where she was employed as a secretary in a hardware store. I now realized we only had a few more seconds to talk, so I asked, "How did you like the prom?"

Sharon was a soft-spoken, shy girl, and what she said next shocked me. I was totally unprepared for her response.

With a twinkle in her eye and a coy smile on her face she said, "I enjoyed the prom, but I think I would have had more fun if I had been with you."

When Sharon said those unforgettable words, I felt like my whole body went limp. The ten pennies I had been nervously jiggling in my right hand suddenly all fell to the sidewalk, some rolling on the street.

I couldn't believe what I had just heard. I was overcome with joy and I knew that this was the moment I needed to communicate my feelings to her and ask her for a date.

I said, "I think I would have had more fun if I had been with you at the prom."

As we smiled at each other, we knew there was something special about what we had just said to one another. This was a defining moment in our relationship and the beginning of our romance.

I was now ready to ask her for a date. So before she rushed back to her job at the hardware store, I said to Sharon, "I have a motor scooter and I like to go for a ride on Sunday afternoons. If I happened to be on your street around two-thirty on Sunday afternoon, would you like to go for a motor scooter ride with me?"

Without any hesitation and with a joyful glee in her voice she said, "Yes," as she rushed off quickly to go back to work at the hardware store.

God had graciously answered my prayers in bringing Sharon and me together that memorable Friday night on the street in Philipsburg, and we just sealed plans for our first date.

Why God ever put Saturday before Sunday, I'll never know, but Sunday couldn't come fast enough for me. On Sunday afternoon I was on my way to Osceola Mills on my motor scooter.

I found Sharon's street and arrived on time for our first date. After greeting one another, we went for a scooter ride. How exciting it was to be riding through the countryside with Sharon sitting behind me, holding on securely.

We had a very enjoyable scooter ride until it started to rain. When we arrived back at her house, Sharon's father said to me, "You can't ride your motor scooter home in the rain. Put it in our basement."

As I pushed my scooter into their walk-in basement, he said, "Why don't you eat supper with us and then I'll drive you home." I thought to myself, *Yes! That means I'll have to come back another day to get my scooter!* "All things work together for good" (Romans 8:28), even when it rains. Soon I would get to see Sharon again.

God is so amazing in the ways He works in the lives of His children. His invisible hand had moved a mountain to bring Sharon into my life and shortly after we began to date I found out she was a Christian. This was also a tremendous answer to prayer. I had been praying that God would bring a Christian girl into my life who loved Jesus Christ and wanted His will for her life. I believed this was not just a coincidence, but the hand of God working in two lives to bring us together. Psalm 126:3 states, "The Lord has done great things for us, and we are filled with joy." Sharon and I were both filled with great joy; we wanted to get to know one another more and grow together in our faith.

## Moving Toward Marriage

Sharon and I dated throughout our senior year of high school and for almost three more years while I was a student at Houghton College. This was a period of waiting. Psalm 27:14 says, "Wait for the Lord; be strong and take heart and wait for the Lord."

We believed God led us to each other and we often talked about getting married someday. One of the ways I knew Sharon was the one I wanted to marry was because she was the only girl I ever dated who would let me look into her eyes. When I looked into the eyes of the other girls I dated they would say, "Why are you looking at me like that?" This always troubled me, but not with Sharon. She seemed to enjoy it and so did I.

God's timing is perfect, and we didn't want to miss His timing. Solomon wrote in Ecclesiastes 3:1,5, "There is a time for everything, and a season for every activity under heaven: a time to embrace, and a time to refrain."

We enjoyed our times together, and we were getting to know one another's family. I was getting to know Sharon's dad and mother and her sister Peggy, who was almost four years younger than Sharon. Sharon was getting to know my parents, my older brother Dennis, and younger sister Rosalie.

I soon discovered that not only was Sharon quiet and reserved, but her whole family on her mother's side was as well. They enjoyed being together, but never spoke much to each other. I remember being with Sharon at her grandparents' house at Christmastime. Her mother had four brothers and one sister. A typical conversation with Sharon's uncles was always very brief. If I asked her one uncle, "How are you?" he would reply, "Pretty good." If I extended the conversation and inquired, "Do you still work at Penn State as a carpenter?" his response was usually, "Yep, I'm still there." That was the extent of our conversation. If there had not been grandchildren sitting on the living room floor making noise while they opened their Christmas presents, there could be long periods of total silence. It took time for me to adjust to the quietness of Sharon's family, but it probably took them much longer to adjust to Sharon's "talkative boyfriend."

One Christmas, I couldn't take the silence any longer, so I thought that I would liven things up a bit. I noticed that one of Sharon's aunts was sitting on a chair directly under mistletoe that was hanging from the archway above her head. I jumped up and kissed Sharon's aunt on the cheek. Everyone laughed. The silence was broken and her aunt and I became good friends through the years.

## Two Significant Events

There were two events that happened during our senior year of high school that were especially significant to our relationship. One event happened in Sharon's Christian Missionary Alliance Church in Osceola Mills, and the other event took place in my church, Forest Baptist Church.

I often attended the Sunday evening service with Sharon and her family at her church. One Sunday night, at the close of the service, Sharon and I went to the kneeling rail at the front of the sanctuary and knelt to pray. I don't remember anything specific that we were praying about, but I do remember pouring my heart out to God in fervent and extended prayer. Psalm 62:8 declares, "Trust in Him at all times, O people; pour out your hearts to Him, for God is our refuge." I can't quite explain it, but the Holy Spirit came upon me with mighty power. It was such an awesome experience, and having Sharon kneeling beside me seemed to seal my love for her even more.

The other significant event happened during the winter months of our senior year of high school. I had one of the leading roles in my senior class play. My parents planned a party at our house after the play for members of the cast. When the party had ended, Sharon and I returned several folding chairs to my church. After we unloaded the chairs, I said, "Sharon, let's go to the front of the sanctuary and pray together." We knelt and prayed. What happened next was spontaneous and totally unrehearsed. As we were kneeling, I felt so stirred in my emotions that I said something like, "Sharon, I love you. I know it will probably be several years before we can get married, but will you marry me, someday?" Without any hesitation she answered, "Yes." I think we were both shocked and overjoyed by what had just taken place. I had no idea, plan, or forethought that I would propose to Sharon that night, but I did. Was it the invisible hand of God at work in our lives at that moment? Only God could keep us faithful to the promise that we had just made to each other. I Thessalonians 5:24 gave us confidence that He would help us. "The One who calls you is faithful and He will do it."

Two and a half years later, Sharon and I were ready to formally announce our engagement. In September of 1968, I gave her a diamond engagement ring, and on March 29, 1969, we were married at the altar in her church in Osceola Mills. I proposed to her at the altar in my church and married her at the altar in her church. In my mind, this was another example of the invisible hand of God at work in our lives. "He who finds a wife finds what is good and receives favor from the Lord" (Proverbs 18:22).

## Learning To Trust God As Newlyweds

As a newly married couple, we had a lot of love, but not a lot of money. When Sharon and I got married it was near the end of my junior year at Houghton College. We lived in a mobile home in Fillmore, New York, which was about three or four miles from the Houghton campus. Our rent was $75 a month, and that amount included utilities as well. The only income we had at the time was $33 a week that I received as a youth pastor at Knox United Presbyterian Church in Buffalo. We had to watch our spending very carefully, especially since we had very little to spend.

God was teaching us to depend on Him to meet our needs. He promised to meet all our needs, but would we have the faith to trust Him? Philippians 4:19 was a tremendous promise for us to hold on to and watch what God would do. "And my God will meet all your needs according to His glorious riches in Christ Jesus." We had many needs— food, clothing, shelter, gas for our car, money for insurance, tuition, books, and many other things. If God promised to meet all our needs, then we needed to trust Him to keep His promises. If our needs were not met, the problem was not with God, but with us. God didn't promise to meet all our "wants," but all our needs.

In the Sermon on the Mount, Jesus told His disciples not to worry, but to focus their attention on Him and His kingdom. He knew more about their needs than they did. In Matthew 6:25, 31-33, Jesus told them, "Therefore I tell you, do not worry about your life, what you will eat or drink; or about your body, what you will wear. Is not life more important than food, and the body more important than clothes? So do not worry, saying, 'What shall we eat?' or 'What shall we drink?' or 'What shall we wear?' For the pagans run after all these things, and your heavenly Father knows that you need them. But seek first His kingdom and His righteousness, and all these things will be given to you as well. Therefore, do not worry about tomorrow, for tomorrow will worry about itself. Each day has enough trouble of its own." God was teaching us to trust in Him and not worry about all the things we needed.

## A Time Of Testing

Within the first month or two of our married life, we faced a time of testing regarding our needs. We were learning to trust God, regardless of how small or large our needs may have been. How would God meet a very small need we had?

One Friday night, Sharon and I went to a grocery store across the street from our mobile home. We needed to buy several items for a picnic we were planning to have at Letchworth State Park the next day. Sharon's parents were coming to visit us. They planned to arrive from Pennsylvania in time to have breakfast with us, and then we would go to the park for the picnic lunch. After the picnic, Sharon and I would drive to Buffalo to do our youth ministry, and her parents would return home to Pennsylvania.

When we arrived back at our mobile home after being at the grocery store, we discovered we had forgotten to get an item, so I returned to the store. When I returned home the second time, we discovered there was still yet another item we needed. By now we were almost totally broke. I said, "Sharon, the only money we have is some change in a container on my dresser."

I took the container of change and went back to the grocery store for the third time. (As newlyweds we had problems making complete grocery lists.) When I went to the checkout counter, the clerks all laughed as I poured the change out of the container. I remarked, "You won't see me again tonight, for this is all the money we have. We are totally broke." I paid for the item we needed and returned to our mobile home.

We were now satisfied that we had everything we needed for the picnic. But suddenly I became aware of another problem. In fact, we had two potentially embarrassing problems. What would we eat for breakfast? We discovered we had no bread and no milk. We couldn't have toast without bread. We couldn't have cereal without milk. We were so focused on the picnic we hadn't thought about breakfast. "Oh well, we'll make out somehow!"

Then I thought of another problem. We were now totally broke, but I needed fifty cents to park our car at Letchworth State Park. I didn't have fifty cents for parking. Sharon's parents would follow us in their car into the park and what an embarrassment it would be to not have money for the parking attendant. I thought maybe Sharon's parents would want to take my new bride back to Pennsylvania with them if they discovered how poor we were.

What were we to do? It was now late in the evening. Should I go to a friend and borrow some money? I remember trusting God that somehow He would provide for our needs and spare us from embarrassment.

As we prepared to go to bed, I heard a noise outside. It sounded like the wind had blown something against the side of our mobile home. I opened the door and, to my surprise, I found a Coca Cola can tied to the outside doorknob. I thought, *What in the world is this?* As I untied the Coke can I heard the sound of coins. *Is there money in this Coke can? How could this be? Where did it come from? Did God send an angel from heaven to meet our needs?* I was totally shocked, but no longer totally broke. Then I heard laughter from the side of our mobile home. Out stepped several clerks who worked at the grocery store across the street. They felt so sorry for this newlywed couple who were totally broke, so before they went home they took up a "love offering" for us. It totaled $1.56. It was just enough to meet our needs.

The next morning, before Sharon's parents arrived for breakfast, I returned to the grocery store with the clerks' money to buy milk and bread. It's amazing to think of what $1.56 could buy forty-seven years ago. I also had fifty cents left over to pay the parking attendant at Letchworth State Park.

This was one of the most exciting and memorable miracles of God's provision we have ever experienced. We discovered God was concerned about the little needs in our lives as well as the big needs. We were learning to trust Him to meet all our needs.

## God Supplied Our Needs Through Dictionary Sales

During my freshman year at Houghton College, I met a student who was a junior at Houghton. He handed me a Webster's Dictionary and said, "I want you to use this book and tell me if you like it. If you're sold on the book, I'd like you to join my sales team next summer. You could make good money in this sales job."

I used the dictionary for several months and found it very helpful not only as a dictionary, but as a student handbook that also included several hundred pages of useful information. I was sold on the book and believed it would be helpful to any family. As I prayed and asked the Lord if He wanted me to accept the job offer for the summer, He led me to take the job. I spent four summers selling dictionaries for the Southwestern Company in Nashville, Tennessee. Each summer I spent the first week in Nashville at their sales training school. Hundreds of college students had been recruited to sell for Southwestern.

My first summer, in 1967, I sold dictionaries in Mankato, Minnesota. The second summer I spent in La Crosse, Wisconsin. The next two summers, after Sharon and I were married, I sold dictionaries in Delaware, Ohio and Piqua, Ohio.

The training and experience I gained in selling dictionaries was of great value in preparing me for the ministry. I learned quickly that not everyone liked door-to-door salesmen. Many people had been lied to, tricked, or manipulated into buying something they didn't need or didn't want. As a Christian salesman, I was committed to honesty, integrity, and pure motives in my sales approach. I Corinthians 10:31 was a guiding principle for my sales work. "So whether you eat or drink or whatever you do, do it all for the glory of God." I wanted to glorify God and be a witness for Christ as I talked with people each day. I prayed that God would open doors and hearts, and that I would have many opportunities to share my faith in Jesus Christ.

God heard my prayers and answered them. I realized I was not sent to hundreds of homes just to sell dictionaries, but to be an ambassador for Christ. I tried, by God's grace and wisdom, to "seek first the kingdom of God and His righteousness" (Matthew 6:33), and as I focused on Him He prospered my sales.

I remember sharing the good news of the gospel with a lady who stood on her porch and listened for over two hours. In the back of my mind I was thinking, "I'm not selling any books." On a good afternoon I would sometimes be able to sell five or six dictionaries. God was teaching me to trust Him for the sales and not be concerned about the time I was spending in sharing the gospel. When I left that lady's house, I found people who were interested in buying a dictionary at the next three houses. In fact, each family bought two dictionaries—the children's version and the adult version. God blessed me with six sales in a very short period of time. It didn't always happen that way but I sensed God saying to me, "Trust me, trust me," and as I trusted Him and did His will, He prospered my sales.

The Bible says this about King Uzziah, the king of Judah, "As long as He sought the Lord, God gave him success" (II Chronicles 26:5). The book of Psalms speaks about the person who is blessed by the Lord: "But his delight is in the law of the Lord, and on His law he meditates day and night. He is like a tree planted by the streams of water, which yields its fruit in season and whose leaf does not wither. Whatever he does prospers" (Psalm 1:2-3).

I enjoyed selling dictionaries and had great fun as well. When I knocked on a door most of the time the lady of the house opened the door. I began my approach by saying, "Hi, I'm Larry Burd and I'm a salesman." In that one sentence my prospective customers knew my name and why I was there. I was not trained to say I was a salesman, but that's what I was so why not be honest immediately with people? Some salesmen try to deceive people into thinking they are not a salesman. I didn't want to be caught in that trap.

After telling my prospective customer my name and why I was there, the usual response was, "I'm not interested." I would respond by saying, "Most people aren't interested, but since I'm here anyway let me show you quickly what I'm selling." I would pull a dictionary out of my leather carrying case and hold it up so she could see it. She would say, "Oh, it's a dictionary." I would reply," Yes, but it's more than a dictionary. It also has a section of biological terms, musical terms, a complete outline of musical history, chemistry, physics, how to write a theme, secretarial service, parliamentary law, population and space statistics. Isn't that a lot of helpful information?" Then I would say, "Mrs. Jones (or whatever her name was), do you ever get words mixed up like accept, except, effect, affect, put and place, sit and sat, teach and learn, lend and loan?" If she answered "yes," then I would say something like, "You can see how helpful this book could be to you." By this time she may or may not be interested in hearing anymore. If she wasn't interested, I would politely thank her for her time and then ask if there were any families in her neighborhood that had children.

Families with children were the best prospects for an up-to-date dictionary. She would usually be willing to answer my question and point out the families by name that had children. I learned to quickly remember those names so I could greet my customers by name. Dale Carnegie once said, "Remember that a man's name is to him the sweetest and most important sound in any language."[18] I discovered people light up like a Christmas tree when they are spoken to by name. Remembering names is very important in sales work, in the ministry, or in any profession.

When I sold dictionaries in the evenings, there was a scenario I experienced over and over again. Forty-seven years ago, most families I visited did not have air conditioning. They had screen doors. I would knock on the screen door and Mr. Jones, who was sitting in the living room reading the newspaper while watching the evening news on television, would call to his wife and say, "Agnes, there's somebody at the door." Why Mr. Jones wouldn't come to the door I never knew.

Mrs. Jones was usually washing dishes in the kitchen and as she walked to the front door she would remove her apron. I went into my typical greeting, being very aware that Mr. Jones was listening to every word I said to his wife. Before long he would

---

[18] Carnegie, Dale, *How to Win Friends and Influence People* (New York: Pocket Books, Inc., 1936), 83

say to her, "Get rid of the kid, Agnes." I would then speak through the screen door to Mr. Jones and say, "Mr. Jones, I know you and your wife are not interested in buying a new dictionary, but before I leave I would like to show you how much milk there is in this book." Now his curiosity was aroused and he would come to the door. He had no idea if I had a little hose hooked up to the dictionary that would drip milk, or what crazy thing he was about to experience. When he came to the door, I would turn in the dictionary to page 475 where the word 'milk' was listed. I would point to the word 'milk,' and then as quickly as possible, say from memory all the words that began with the word "milk": Milk, milk and water, milk leg, milk maid, milk man, milk of human kindness, milk of magnesia, milk shake, milk shed, milk snake, milk sop, milk sugar, milk toast, milk tooth, milky and Milky Way. "That's a lot of milk, isn't it?" If I could get Mr. Jones to laugh, I could get him to listen to what I had to say about the dictionary. Quite often, Mr. Jones would say, "Let the kid in, Agnes. You know we need a new dictionary."

There was one line I used at the end of my sales talk that often prompted interesting comments. I would be very serious when I said this line and the challenge to me was to say it without cracking a smile. I would say, "Mr. and Mrs. Jones, there are many features people like about this dictionary, but there is one feature people seem to like the most. It's the fact that all the words are in alphabetical order." Some people would roll their eyes at me and say, "I can't believe you just said that." Other people would say, "Oh, that would be helpful. Let me see that." I had so much fun just hearing and seeing the reactions on my customer's faces.

The Bible says, "Those who honor Me I will honor" (I Samuel 2:30). I sought to humbly honor God in selling dictionaries and He honored me with many sales. My first summer on this job, 1967, I made $1,900. My second summer I recruited eight college students to be on my sales team and I made $3,900. I don't remember how much I made my third and fourth summer, but it was a significant amount of money. This summer job paid far more than most summer jobs when I was in college. I once calculated that over the four summers when I sold dictionaries I had personally talked to over 10,000 people. Many things God taught me on this job have been helpful during the years of my ministry.

God used this summer job to meet our needs as a newly married couple. I also worked a few hours a week during the school year, cutting hair at Ted's Barber Shop in Houghton. My wife, Sharon, had a job as a secretary at Houghton, and God used her income to help meet our needs as well. God's grace abounded toward us as II Corinthians 9:8 declares, "And God is able to make all grace abound to you, so that in all things at all times, having all that you need, you will abound in every good work." God's invisible hand was at work in providing, guiding and preparing us for the ministry He had in store for us. We were learning to trust God to meet our needs and He was always faithful in keeping His promises.

## God Supplied Our Need For Friends

Charles Spurgeon said, "Friendship is one of the sweetest joys of life. Many might have failed beneath the bitterness of their trial had they not found a friend."[19]

During the summer of 1966, not long before I went to Houghton College for my freshman year, Grandpa Burd told me about Scott Weldon. He knew Scott and his family who lived in New Buffalo, Pennsylvania. Scott was also an incoming freshman student at Houghton. My grandpa told Scott about me and that he hoped the two of us could meet each other. When we met, we became friends immediately. Scott was quiet and I was talkative, and we became roommates. We both had experienced God's call to the ministry. God gave us the privilege of being youth pastors together in the same church, Knox United Presbyterian Church in Buffalo, during our junior and senior years at Houghton. Scott ministered to the junior high students and I ministered to the senior high students.

The senior pastor of the church, Frank Kik, and his associate pastor, Alvin Jensen, were both graduates of Gordon-Conwell Theological Seminary in South Hamilton, Massachusetts. While Scott and I ministered with them they influenced both of us to

---

[19] Cory, Lloyd. *Quotable Quotes.* (Victor Books, 1985), 146.

attend the same seminary, which we greatly enjoyed attending from 1970-1973.

The Bible tells us about the friendship of Jonathan and David. "Jonathan became one in spirit with David, and he loved him as himself" (I Samuel 18:1). The invisible hand of God was at work in our friendship and Scott and I became "one in spirit." We became prayer and accountability partners. Prayer has been the bond that has held our friendship together over the past fifty years. We pray for one another daily, and whenever we are together we always try to make time to pray.

During my freshman year at Houghton College, I was discipled by a man, Bill Meyers, who had worked with the ministry of the Navigators while he was in the U.S. Air Force. Bill taught me the value of daily Bible study, meditation, prayer, and Scripture memory. He challenged me to find someone to disciple and pass on what I had been taught. II Timothy 2:2 was Paul's instruction to Timothy: "And the things you have heard me say in the presence of many witnesses entrust to reliable men who will also be qualified to teach others." As I prayed for someone to disciple, I believe God wanted me to disciple Scott. Our friendship was deepened because of the time we spent together in Bible study and prayer. Scott also worked for Southwestern and we were roommates during the summer of 1967 as we sold dictionaries in Mankato, Minnesota.

Scott has always been there for me through the years. He has carried my burdens and shared my joys. The amazing timing of his phone calls when I have been discouraged, needed advice or simply needed a friend, had to have been directed by the invisible hand of God.

When the apostle Paul and his missionary team needed encouragement, God sent Titus to them: "For when we came into Macedonia, this body of ours had no rest, but we were harassed at every turn—conflicts on the outside, fears within. But God, who comforts the downcast, comforted us by the coming of Titus" (II Corinthians 7:5-6). Scott has been like Titus to me and has been a friend who "sticks closer than a brother" (Proverbs 18:24).

When Scott started to date a young lady named Joy, who was also a student at Houghton and would become his wife, he brought her to our mobile home in Fillmore, New York for their first date. We played Monopoly together. My wife Sharon and Joy also bonded together and have had a lifelong friendship. No matter where we lived through the years, we always kept in close contact with Scott and Joy and visited with one another. Scott participated in the weddings of our two daughters, Amy and Lisa, and I participated in the wedding of his daughter, Daphne. Scott has agreed to speak at my funeral someday just as I have agreed to speak at his. Someone is going to lose out on this deal unless Jesus returns and we are both raptured into heaven without facing death (I Thessalonians 4:13-18).

Proverbs 27:17 says, "Iron sharpens iron, so one man sharpens another." Scott Weldon has done this for me for the past fifty years, and I will always be grateful to God for his friendship. Henry Ford once wisely stated, "My best friend is the one who brings out the best in me."[20] The Bible says in Ecclesiastes 4:9-10: "Two are better than one, because they have a good return for their work: if one falls down, his friend can help him up. But pity the man who falls and has no one to help him up!" Someone said, "A friend is someone who walks in when the rest of the world walks out." Scott has always been there for me. His friendship is one of the greatest joys I have ever experienced. Our friendship has been the kind of friendship Jesus described in John 15:13, "Greater love has no one than this, that he lay down his life for his friends."

As a newlywed couple, the invisible hand of God provided for all our needs, including the need for lifelong friendships.

## Think About It

- If you are married, did you experience the invisible hand of God at work in bringing the two of you together?
- If you are not married (and it certainly is not God's will for everyone to be married), are you seeking God's will in this area of your life?

---

[20] Quotationsbook.com/quote/16072

- Do you have stories to tell about how God has provided for you? Share some of those stories with someone this coming week.
- Are you developing lifelong friendships with those with whom you have become "one in spirit"?

CHAPTER 6

# *THE INVISIBLE HAND OF GOD AT WORK IN MY FAMILY*

*"He did this so that all the people of the earth might know that the hand of the Lord is powerful, and so that you might always fear the Lord your God" (Joshua 4:24).*

## God's Miracles For His People

God does miracles in the lives of His people. The Bible is a book full of miracles. From the book of Genesis through the book of Revelation, we read about the God who performs miracles. The Bible says, "You are the God who performs miracles; You display Your power among the peoples" (Psalm 77:14). God displays His power, mercy, grace, love, righteousness, holiness, discipline, and wrath through miracles. All of the attributes that describe God are displayed in His miracles in one way or another.

Moses needed a miracle to cross the Red Sea. God had just performed ten miracles in the form of the plagues He brought upon Pharaoh and the Egyptians. Finally, Pharaoh had had enough of God's judgment upon him and his people, and he released Moses and the children of Israel from their bondage.

After four hundred years of slavery, the Israelites left Egypt. God guided His children upon their departure. In Exodus 13:18 we read, "So God led the people around by the desert road toward the Red Sea. The Israelites went up out of Egypt armed for battle."

How did God lead the Israelites? They couldn't see His invisible hand at work in leading them, but He led them by a pillar of cloud and a pillar of fire: "By day, the Lord went ahead of them in a pillar of cloud to guide them on their way, and by night in a pillar of fire to give them light, so that they could travel by day or night" (Exodus 13:21). As the Israelites followed God's guidance, He led them to the edge of the Red Sea.

How would they ever be able to cross the Red Sea and escape from the Egyptians who were in hot pursuit of them?

God performed a miracle for His children in a time of great need. The Israelites were terrified as they saw the Egyptians approaching. As they complained to Moses and questioned his leadership in bringing them out of Egypt, Moses said, "Do not be afraid. Stand firm and you will see the deliverance that the Lord will bring you today. The Egyptians you see today, you will never see again. The Lord will fight for you; you need only to be still" (Exodus 14:13-14). Sometimes God's command to His people in a time of great need is to simply remain "still" and at other times He uses His people to be part of the solution to the need.

Then the Lord said to Moses, "Raise your staff and stretch out your hand over the sea to divide the water so that the Israelites can go through the sea on dry ground. I will harden the hearts of the Egyptians so that they will go in after them. And I will gain glory through Pharaoh and all his army, through his chariots and his horsemen. The Egyptians will know that I am the Lord when I gain glory through Pharaoh, his chariots, and his horsemen" (Exodus 14:16-18). God's ultimate purpose in performing this incredible miracle was to gain glory in the sight of the Egyptians and that they would know who He was.

Moses saw the miracle-working power of God as he stretched out his hand over the Red Sea. "And all that night, the Lord drove the sea back with a strong east wind, and turned it into dry land. The waters were divided, and the Israelites went through the sea on dry ground, with a wall of water on their right and on their left" (Exodus 14:21-22).

Moses and the Israelites saw another miracle as the Lord destroyed the Egyptian army. When the Egyptians followed the Israelites into the Red Sea, the Lord fought against them. "He made the wheels of the chariots come off so that they had difficulty driving. And the Egyptians said, 'Let's get away from the Israelites! The Lord is fighting for them against Egypt'" (Exodus 14:25). Then the Lord told Moses to stretch out his hand again over the Red Sea and the water swept the Egyptians into the sea and they were drowned. "Not one of them survived" (Exodus 14:28). God's victory over the Egyptians was complete.

Through this great miracle God displayed His power against the Egyptians. "That day the Lord saved Israel from the hands of the Egyptians, and Israel saw the Egyptians lying dead on the shore. And when the Israelites saw the great power that the Lord displayed against the Egyptians, the people feared the Lord and put their trust in Him and in Moses, His servant" (Exodus 14:30-31). Not only did the Israelites see the mighty power of God at work increasing their faith, but they trusted in Moses, God's appointed leader who obeyed God.

God's invisible hand at work had performed great miracles for Moses and the children of Israel. Although God's hand could not be seen, it was at work on behalf of God's people. The Bible says, "For the Lord brought you out of Egypt with His mighty hand" (Exodus 13:9). The invisible hand of God at work in performing miracles is far mightier than anyone could ever comprehend. Why don't we trust God to perform more miracles in our lives? If we could only learn to take God at His word and believe what He says we would see far more miracles in our lives today.

## God's Miracles Continue For His People

Joshua needed a miracle to cross the Jordan River. In Joshua chapters three and four, we find the Israelites at a time of crisis again. How would they ever be able to cross the Jordan River, especially "at flood stage" (Joshua 3:15)? Perhaps some of the Israelites had already forgotten the great miracles God performed to enable His people to cross the Red Sea on dry ground. How quickly God's people can forget what God did for them in the past.

Would God perform another miracle like He did when they crossed the Red Sea? Yes, God delights in doing miracles for His people, those who are part of the family of God.

"Joshua told the people, 'Consecrate yourselves, for tomorrow the Lord will do amazing things among you'" (Joshua 3:5). God confirmed the leadership role of Joshua, much like He did for Moses. "And the Lord said to Joshua, 'Today I will begin to exalt you in the eyes of all Israel, so they may know that I am with you as I was with Moses'" (Joshua 3:7).

God doesn't always do His miracles the same way each time He displays His mighty power. With Moses, God told him to stretch out His hand over the Red Sea and the waters parted. With Joshua, God worked in a different way: "See, the ark of the covenant of the Lord of all the earth will go into the Jordan ahead of you. Now then, choose twelve men from the tribes of Israel, one from each tribe. And as soon as the priests who carry the ark of the Lord—the Lord of all the earth—set foot in the Jordan, its waters flowing downstream will be cut off and stand up in a heap" (Joshua 3:11-13). This is exactly what happened. The Israelites were able to cross the flooded Jordan River on dry ground.

## God's Miracles Were To Be Remembered

When God did miracles for His people, they were to remember what He did for them. The Lord told Joshua to have twelve men, one from each of the twelve tribes, carry a stone from the Jordan River. These stones were piled up together to be a sign and memorial to the people of Israel. They were to always remember what the Lord had done for them and how He had performed miracles for them.

When God does miracles for His people, they are to share them with their descendants. Their children, grandchildren, and great-grandchildren are to hear about the wonderful works of God.

The Lord said to His people, "In the future, when your descendants ask their fathers, 'What do these stones mean?' Tell them, 'Israel crossed the Jordan on dry ground. For the Lord your God dried up the Jordan before you, until you had crossed over. The Lord your God did to the Jordan just what He had done to the Red Sea when He dried it up before us until we had crossed over'" (Joshua 4:21-23).

Why did God perform these miracles for His people? Was it just for their benefit at that time? No, God had a far greater purpose in performing His miracles. They were not only for the people who experienced them then, but also for their descendants and even for the whole world.

How do we know this? In Joshua 4:24, God tells us exactly why He performed His miracles: "He did this so that all the peoples of the earth might know that the hand of the Lord is powerful and so that you might always fear the Lord your God." God is concerned about the whole world hearing about His miracles and experiencing them in their own lives.

In the preface of this book, I wrote these words: "I feel compelled to write this book." Psalm 145:4 is God's word to His people through David, "One generation will commend Your works to another; and they will tell of Your mighty acts." As Christians, we are to pass on to the next generation what we have experienced of the invisible hand of God at work in our lives. God delights in us when we tell others about the many ways He's been at work in our lives. He wants us to do this and we honor Him when we declare His mighty acts to the next generation.

I want my children, grandchildren, and even my great-grandchildren to have a written account of some of the many mighty acts of God I have experienced in my lifetime. I want to pass on to them what I have seen in the lives of my parents and grandparents about the invisible hand of God at work in their lives. I have no idea how God may use this book in the lives of people who read it. I pray God will use it for His glory, regardless of how few or many that may read it. If only my children, grandchildren and great-grandchildren read it, I will be satisfied. I believe God led me to write this book, and I am seeking to obey Him. If other people read this book and are blessed and encouraged by God is some way, then I will give Him all the glory for using it in their lives.

The words of Mark Batterson in his book, *The Circle Maker*, have challenged me greatly: "Too many authors worry about whether or not their book will get published. That isn't the question. The question is this: Are you called to write? That's the only question that you need to answer. And, if the answer is yes, then you need to write the book as an act of obedience. It doesn't matter if anyone reads it or not."[21]

---

[21] Batterson, Mark, *The Circle Maker* (Grand Rapids: Zondervan, 2011), 77.

## The Miracle Of Birth

Every child born into the world is a miracle. That child may only live a few seconds, or more than one hundred years, but it is still a miracle. Birth is a miracle of God. God is the Creator of all miracles, including the birth of a child.

In Psalm 139:13-18, David prayed:

> "For You created my inmost being; You knit me together in my mother's womb. I praise You because I am fearfully and wonderfully made; Your works are wonderful, I know that full well. My frame was not hidden from You when I was made in the secret place. When I was woven together in the depths of the earth, Your eyes saw my unformed body. All the days ordained for me were written in Your book before one of them came to be. How precious to me are Your thoughts, O God! How vast is the sum of them! Were I to count them, they would outnumber the grains of sand. When I wake, I am still with You."

This passage of scripture makes it very clear that God created human life, even though He uses a man and a woman in His creative process. Such phrases as "You created my inmost being, You knit me together in my mother's womb" and "I was woven together in the depths of the earth, Your eyes saw my unformed body," are such personal words. God takes a personal interest in every life He creates, and He has a purpose for every life.

When my wife Sharon and I were praying about starting a family, I was in my second year at Gordon-Conwell Theological Seminary in South Hamilton, Massachusetts. I was working on my Master of Divinity degree. I had several part-time jobs; I was a youth pastor, worked in a department store as a salesman, and I also cut hair for students at the seminary. My wife was employed as a secretary at a community college. We paid all my seminary expenses so that I could graduate debt-free. We even had money to go out to eat. And we did, quite often.

We purchased expensive medical insurance to cover the birth of a child, and before long, we were expecting. We were higher than a kite on a perfectly windy day.

When Sharon was two-and-a-half months pregnant, she began having complications with the pregnancy. We prayed that God would protect the tiny baby that was being formed.

I remember the morning I was crying out to God to spare the life of our unborn baby. I wanted to be a father with all my heart. I wanted my will to be God's will. I struggled and feared that, if I surrendered to His will, it may be His will that we were not to have this child.

I didn't think I could surrender to His will, although I knew in my heart His will is always best. Finally, I surrendered and prayed, "Lord, Your will be done." The words of the hymn, *I Surrender All*, describe what I experienced that day: "All to Jesus I surrender, all to Him I freely give; I will ever love and trust Him, In His presence daily live. I surrender all, I surrender all. All to Thee, my blessed Savior, I surrender all."[22] After I surrendered to the Lord's will I had peace in my heart, knowing that whatever happened would be His will, even if I didn't understand or like what was happening.

Later that same morning, I was in the seminary library studying when the librarian came to me and said, "Your wife just called and said she needs you." I knew in my heart what that call meant. I was so sad, yet so glad I had put the situation in God's hands and surrendered to His will earlier that morning.

I immediately drove to the community college where Sharon worked and took her to the hospital. After examining Sharon, the doctor in the emergency room tried to console me, but his words were so matter-a-fact and painful. He said, "The baby was not forming properly; you're young, you can try again." Those who have been through a miscarriage know the pain we experienced that day. "The Lord is close to the broken-hearted and saves those who are crushed in spirit" (Psalm 34:18). We were so thankful the Lord was with us, and He comforted us in our loss.

---

[22] Van DeVenter, John W. *The Hymnal for Worship and Celebration.* (Waco: Word Music), 366.

## God Answered Our Prayers For Children

The Bible says, "Unless the Lord builds the house, its builders labor in vain. Unless the Lord watches over the city, the watchmen stand guard in vain. In vain you rise early and stay up late, toiling for food to eat- for He grants sleep to those He loves. Sons (children) are a heritage from the Lord, children a reward from Him. Like arrows in the hands of a warrior are sons born in one's youth. Blessed is the man whose quiver is full of them. They will not be put to shame when they contend with their enemies in the gate" (Psalm 127: 1-5).

Children are a gift from God. They are on loan to us from God. God created them, and they are His. God allows parents to have the joy of loving, nurturing, caring, and providing for His children. We are only stewards of all that God has entrusted to us. What a great privilege and awesome responsibility it is to be a parent!

Dr. James Dobson, founder of Focus on the Family, said, "Children are not casual guests in our home. They have been loaned to us temporarily for the purpose of loving them and instilling a foundation of values on which their future lives will be built."[23] As parents we have a strong tendency to claim God's children as "our children." When parents dedicate their children to the Lord they are recognizing that they are giving their children back to God in an act of consecration. We need to continually remind ourselves that these children are "His children."

Chuck Colson, founder of Prison Fellowship, made this observation of the family unit: "The family is the most basic unit of government. As the first community to which a person is attached, and the first authority under which a person learns to live, the family establishes society's most basic values."[24] If we are ever to have a strong government we must first have strong families. Families are like building blocks in the foundation of a building. If the foundation is strong and well established, then the building will be able to withstand the storms it will encounter. The same is true for a family that is founded on the solid

---

[23] Sweeting, George, *Who Said That?* (Chicago: Moody Press, 1994), 86.
[24] Ibid., 192.

foundation of Jesus Christ and His Word; it will withstand the storms of life.

About a year after our miscarriage, God heard and answered our prayers for a child. God entrusted to us a son, our firstborn. We named him Nathan. His name means "gift of God" and he truly was God's gift to us as parents.

Nathan was born in 1973 in Beverly, Massachusetts, just a few weeks before I graduated from Gordon-Conwell Theological Seminary. How excited we were as new parents! No one could miss seeing Nathan through the hospital nursery window. He was the only baby in the nursery with golden-blond hair.

Two songs that Sharon and I learned in Sunday school when we were children took on new meaning for us as parents. "Jesus loves the little children, all the children of the world. Red and yellow, black and white, all are precious in His sight. Jesus loves the little children of the world."[25]

Jesus loved our little newborn son more than we could imagine. Now that we were parents, the words of Mark 10:16 became very special to us. "And He (Jesus) took the children in His arms, put His hands on them and blessed them." Even though we could not see the loving hands and arms of Jesus holding our little baby boy, we believed that just as Jesus blessed children in the past, He continued blessing them in the present. Hebrews 13:8 assures us that the same Jesus that walked on the earth and cared for children over 2,000 years ago is with us today: "Jesus Christ, the same yesterday, today, and forever."

The other song that meant so much to us as parents of a newborn baby was the most familiar of the children's songs, "Jesus Loves Me." "Jesus loves me, this I know, for the Bible tells me so; little ones to Him belong, they are weak, but He is strong! Yes, Jesus loves me! Yes, Jesus loves me! Yes, Jesus loves me, the Bible tells me so!"[26] In becoming parents we humbly experienced a new depth in recognizing how much God loved us and the precious child He entrusted to our care.

---

[25]www.metrolyrics.com/jesus-loves-the-little-children-lyricsveggie
[26] Warner, Anna B., The Hymnal For Worship and Celebration (Waco: Word Music), 579

God continued to hear and answer our prayers for children. In 1976, we moved from Melrose, Massachusetts — where I was the pastor of Green Street Baptist Church — to the area of Buffalo, New York — where I became the pastor of Bethel Baptist Church in Getzville, a suburb of Buffalo. I've often chucked about how God kept the Burds and the "Bs" together; I've pastored churches near Boston, Buffalo, and now Bethlehem. It was in Buffalo where our three other children were born.

Amy was born in 1976, Evan in 1981, and Lisa in 1982. God gave us four children in the order of boy, girl, boy, girl. While Sharon was pregnant and carrying our third child Evan, I prayed that God would give us twins. He didn't give us twins, but almost. Evan and Lisa were born eleven months apart. They were like twins as they played and grew together. We even had a double stroller, and when they were together in the stroller many people thought Evan and Lisa were twins.

We experienced the invisible hand of God guiding us through several quick deliveries. Some women spend many, many hours in labor — but not my wife. After the birth of our first child, we didn't count the hours of labor, but the minutes after we arrived at the hospital until each of our other three babies were born.

With Nathan, Sharon's labor was about six hours. Ironically, when my mother went into labor before giving birth to me, my grandfather said it was because she had eaten too many potato pancakes the night before. When Sharon went into labor before Nathan was born, I said that it was because Sharon had eaten too much cranberry pie. I admit that cranberry pie is delicious, but really? *Three pieces?*

The night before Nathan was born, Sharon and I had been visiting with a couple we met when I was in seminary. We were invited to their house for dinner. We had a piece of cranberry pie after dinner, another piece around ten o'clock, and then a third piece around one a.m. before we went home. It didn't surprise me when Sharon awakened me at six a.m. and said, "The baby is coming." "Yep," I thought, "The cranberry pie did it."

When Amy was born in 1976, it was only thirty-one minutes after we arrived at Children's Hospital in Buffalo. That was a quick delivery, but surely we could beat that record on our next child, and we did.

In 1981 we were expecting our third child, Evan. Sharon's doctor, being aware of her exceptionally quick deliveries, advised us to take an ambulance to the hospital when it was time for the baby to be born.

Sharon didn't think that it was necessary, but I did. When the time arrived to take her to the hospital, I called our local police department to request an ambulance. We were totally unprepared for what happened next. I thought an ambulance would arrive and perhaps a police escort to get us safely to the hospital.

Suddenly, we saw red lights flashing in the darkness. When I looked out the window, I saw a huge fire truck, two ambulances, and fourteen volunteer firemen who came to assist my wife. I had no idea that's what you get when you call for an ambulance in Getzville, New York at one o'clock in the morning.

The fourteen eager volunteer firemen, who had left the comfort of their beds that early in the morning, were almost tripping over one another as they all tried to assist my wife. It was rather comical to watch them carrying her on a stretcher down the steps of our two-story house.

The only thing that could have added more drama to the situation would have been the sound of the sirens of the fire truck and ambulances. Thank the Lord, they didn't turn on the sirens. We had enough excitement with red lights flashing all over the neighborhood.

After the fourteen firemen had safely loaded Sharon into one of the ambulances, the driver said to me, "What hospital are we going to?" I quickly responded, "Children's Hospital in downtown Buffalo," which was about a half-hour drive. The ambulance driver then said, "We better take the other ambulance." I didn't question, "Why?" I simply watched as the firemen carried my wife from one ambulance to the other. Finally, we were on our way to Children's Hospital.

After a few minutes in the ambulance, Sharon felt like the baby was going to be born very soon. The ambulance driver said, "We can take her to Millard Fillmore Hospital, which is much closer." I firmly replied, "Her doctor is waiting for us at Children's

Hospital, and that's where we want to go." The driver reluctantly said, "Okay," and I responded, "You drive, I'll pray."

When we arrived safely at the hospital, I looked at my watch and noted the time. Sixteen minutes later, Evan was born. Wow, we cut Amy's thirty-one minute delivery time, after arriving at the hospital, down to a mere sixteen minutes for Evan's arrival. God answered our prayers that we arrived at the hospital before Evan was born in the ambulance. Had he been born in the ambulance, I would have been his untrained obstetrician. Praise the Lord that did not happen.

Eleven months later, we were on our way back to Children's Hospital in Buffalo for the arrival of Lisa, our fourth child. Sharon absolutely refused to let me call for an ambulance this time. One unforgettable ambulance experience was enough for her. Sharon wanted me to take her to the hospital. But I was extremely concerned because of her track record of quick deliveries, and this time I was the driver. I was convinced that it was virtually impossible to drive a car and deliver a baby at the same time. I was very nervous, but complied with my wife's request that I drive her to the hospital.

It was around three o'clock in the morning when I helped Sharon into our car, put on the four-way flasher lights, and drove as fast as I could to downtown Buffalo. I actually hoped a police officer would see me speeding and offer to escort us to the hospital, instead of giving me a ticket for speeding. That didn't happen.

As we drove to the hospital, Sharon kept repeating, "The baby's coming, the baby's coming." I thought surely she would push her feet through the floor in our car. I told her to hold on, and that I would get her to the hospital.

God answered our prayers again and we arrived safely at the hospital. I looked at my watch as we entered the hospital and thought, "Will we break the sixteen minute record?"

No, the invisible hand of God must have been at work in turning Lisa's little body in a posterior position. We had to wait forty-five long minutes for her arrival. The doctor, who delivered Lisa, said to us, "If the baby had not been in the posterior position, you would have had the baby in the car." We chose to believe the invisible hand of God was at work in Lisa's delivery.

Psalm 60:5 was a reality for us when Lisa was born. "Save us and help us with Your right hand, that those You love may be delivered." Lisa, our fourth and final child, was delivered safely and we were filled with praise to our God.

## God Intervened In Times Of Crisis

It is comforting to know God is always with us and available to help us in times of need. Psalm 50:15 has become one of my favorite verses of scripture. "And call upon Me in the day of trouble; I will deliver you, and you will honor Me." The Bible also says, "Let us then approach the throne of grace with confidence, so that we may receive mercy and find grace to help us in our time of need" (Hebrews 4:16). We never know when "a time of need" may arise, but God is always there for us when we call upon Him by faith.

Like many other parents, emergency rooms and hospitals are not strangers to us, nor to our children. Rare is the family that hasn't rushed off to the hospital with one of their children in their arms or at their side.

When Nathan was eight months old, he had a stomach virus. We hesitated to call the doctor and disturb him, because it was New Year's Day, but we did. We explained to the doctor that Nathan wasn't eating anything, and we were concerned. The doctor told us to give him fluids and keep checking his diaper to be sure he was urinating. Over the next couple of hours we checked his diaper and it was dry, so we called the doctor again. He told us to take Nathan to the emergency room at the hospital.

When the emergency room staff saw how weak and lethargic Nathan looked, they hurriedly put an intravenous tube into the top of his head. He was in the hospital for several days, but then recovered from the virus. *Was it the unseen hand of God that led us to call the doctor when we were hesitant to do so? Was the invisible hand of God at work in guiding us to the emergency room at the hospital?* We can only imagine what may have happened to our eight-month old baby if we had not called the doctor and followed his advice.

The Word of God says, "Help me, O Lord my God; save me in accordance with Your love. Let them know that it is Your hand, that You, O Lord, have done it" (Psalm 109:26-27). God's invisible hand is at work in far more ways that our human minds can comprehend. It is so wonderful to know we can always trust this invisible God who cares so deeply for His children.

### An Immediate Answer To Prayer

The story that I am about to share was perhaps the most immediate answer to prayer my wife and I ever experienced. It was truly a miracle in a time of crisis.

It was a beautiful fall day. The leaves were brilliant with color. Sharon and I decided to spend the day with our two children, Nathan and Amy, at Letchworth State Park in upstate New York. What a wonderful day to be together as a family. Nathan was five years old at the time and Amy was two and a half.

As we walked through the park, we came to an area where there were several swings and a very high sliding board. Amy climbed the sliding board and slid down rapidly as her mother caught her at the bottom of the slide. I was amazed that Amy was not afraid to climb to the top of the sliding board alone.

We were having so much fun as a family. We had no idea of the crisis we would be facing in the next few minutes. Life is so fragile and unpredictable.

Once again, Amy climbed to the top of the sliding board. But this time, instead of sitting down, she stood at the top. Her brother Nathan was standing at the bottom of the slide. He wanted to catch her, but Amy did not want her brother to catch her. She waved her arms for him to move. Suddenly, Amy lost her balance, and fell head first to the hard-packed ground below. I thought surely she had broken her neck or back. I ran to her limp body lying on the ground. I knelt beside her, and did the only thing I knew to do in a crisis. I prayed, "Oh Jesus, help us. Please help us." As I picked her up her limp body in my arms, her eyes were rolling, and she was gasping for air.

There were several people sitting at a picnic table about a hundred yards from us. I said to Sharon, "Run quickly; see if you can find a nurse." As she ran toward them, I held Amy tightly in my arms and continued to pray, "Oh Jesus, help us, please help us."

I glanced behind me and saw a lady and a little girl walking together toward me. In utter desperation, I blurted out, "Are you a nurse?"

"No," she responded, "I'm a doctor." *A doctor?!* God had heard and answered my prayer for help, just as He promised in Psalm 50:15.

When my wife came running back I said, "Sharon, God sent us a doctor!" The doctor was thousands of miles from her home country of Egypt. She was working in a hospital in Rochester, New York, and had come to Letchworth State Park that day to spend time with her daughter.

Dr. Zacky carefully examined Amy to see if she had any broken bones or signs of a concussion. She stayed with us for about thirty minutes to assure us that Amy had not been injured when she fell from the sliding board.

Amy was wearing a little hooded jacket, but the hood was down when she fell from the sliding board. We concluded that the hood around the back of her neck was like a football player's shoulder pad and protected her neck and back when she fell.

Amy had the air knocked out of her, and certainly was afraid, but she was not injured. God heard and mightily answered our prayers. Sharon and I were filled with praise for the miracle of God's divine protection in a time of crisis.

As we expressed our gratitude to Dr. Zacky for her compassionate concern for Amy in a time of crisis, I noticed she was wearing a gold necklace that had a very small cross on it. I asked her, "Are you a Christian?"

"Yes," she responded, "I'm a born-again Christian." Then she asked us, "Are you Christians too?" We assured her that we knew the same Jesus as our Savior and Lord as she did. We rejoiced together in our common faith and marveled at how God brought us together that day. We prayed together and thanked God for the miracle we experienced and the answer to prayer that God had given to us.

The fact that the doctor was already walking in the direction toward us, even before Amy fell, is an evidence of the truth of what Isaiah 65:24 teaches: "And it shall come to pass that, before they call, I will answer; and while they are yet speaking, I will hear." Before we departed from one another, Dr. Zacky made a statement I will never forget. She said, "Sometimes God allows things to happen to us just to show us His mercy." God had truly been merciful to us that day.

## Emergency Room Visits

Oh yes, we had our times of crisis when we rushed off to the emergency room with Evan and Lisa as well.

One Saturday morning, when Evan was nine years old, he was playing with his friends at their house. His friends had an ATV (all-terrain vehicle) and were riding it around their property. Within a few hours, we received a phone call that Evan had been in an accident on the ATV, and his friends' parents were taking him to the emergency room at the hospital. He needed stitches in his eyebrow and at the top of his nose.

Sharon and I rushed to the emergency room with Amy and Lisa at our side. When Amy saw blood on Evan's face, she nearly fainted and had to leave the emergency room. This experience convinced Amy that God would never call her to be a nurse. However, Lisa, her younger sister stayed in the emergency room with us and watched every move as the doctor stitched Evan's lacerations. Today, Lisa is a nurse.

The emergency room doctor instructed us to take Evan to our family doctor on Monday to be checked for any signs of infection around his stitches.

Sharon was concerned about Evan the whole weekend. She said to me, "Should I take off work on Monday and take Evan to the doctor?" I assured her that I was off on Monday and could take him, and she should go to work.

What neither of us realized was that I would be taking Evan to one doctor on Monday, and Lisa to another doctor the same day. It was now Lisa's turn to be rushed off to see a doctor in the emergency room at the hospital.

Monday morning arrived, and the children had off school that beautiful October day. Sharon went to work reluctantly, and I started to do some work in front of our house.

Lisa decided to go roller skating on our quiet street, also in front of our house. A few minutes later I heard Lisa scream. It was the kind of scream every parent recognizes: "I'm hurt! Come help me!"

Lisa was crying and holding out to me her broken wrist. I quickly wrapped it in a towel and drove to the emergency room at Muhlenberg Hospital in Bethlehem. On the way to the hospital, Lisa continued to cry. She was not only in great pain, but was afraid.

I said, "Lisa, what are you supposed to do when you are afraid?" We had taught our children to turn to the Lord in their time of need. Through her tears, Lisa whimpered, "When I am afraid, I will trust in Thee" (Psalm 56:3). This was a verse we had our children memorize to help them in times when they would face a crisis or be afraid.

After the hospital staff took x-rays of Lisa's wrist, I was told to take her to see an orthopedic doctor in his office. I called the doctor's office and made an appointment.

I decided to call Sharon at work and let her know how my day was going. When she answered the phone at work, she anxiously asked about Evan. I assured her that Evan was fine, and that his doctor's appointment went well and that there was no sign of infection.

Then I told Sharon what had happened with Lisa and how she had broken her wrist while roller skating. If it's possible to see a mother's heart sink in her chest while you're talking to her on the phone, then I think that's what happened. I am sure Sharon had wished she had stayed home from work that day.

When Sharon arrived home later in the afternoon, we took Lisa to the orthopedic doctor's office. He told us we had three options regarding Lisa's broken wrist and that we needed to make a decision as to what we wanted to do.

The doctor said, "You can do nothing with Lisa's wrist, which is not a good option. You can put her in the hospital and I will set her wrist while she is asleep in the operating room, but that's traumatic for a young child. Or, I can set her wrist back into place right now. It will be painful, but it will only take a second or two."

We decided to have the doctor set her wrist in place right then. As we held our eight-year-old daughter on a table in the doctor's office, he quickly set her wrist in place again.

This was a very painful experience for a little girl, but before Lisa could let out a loud scream, the doctor said, "Don't cry, honey, we're all finished." The doctor put a cast on Lisa's wrist and we were soon on our way home.

Parents never know when they will be faced with a crisis in their family. Christian parents who have a close relationship with God through faith in Jesus Christ have the assurance that God's invisible hand is available to help them at any time. "For I am the Lord, your God, who takes hold of your right hand and says to you, 'Do not fear; I will help you'" (Isaiah 41:13). We experienced God's invisible hand at work numerous times when we faced family crises.

## Think About It

- Do you believe God performs miracles today for His people?
- How have you experienced the invisible hand of God at work in your family?
- What specific answers to prayer can you recall regarding your family?
- Share with a family member or friend about a time of crisis when God intervened in your life or in the life of another member of your family.
- Take a moment to thank God for His divine intervention in your life and family.

CHAPTER 7

# *THE INVISIBLE HAND OF GOD AT WORK IN RAISING CHILDREN*

*"He did this so that all the peoples of the earth might know that the hand of the Lord is powerful and so that you might always fear the Lord your God." (Joshua 4:24)*

## Raising Children God's Way

Abraham was a man of great faith. When God called him to leave his own country and go somewhere else to live, he obeyed Him. God didn't tell him where his new place of residence would be, so he had to walk with God "by faith." Hebrews 11:8 says, "By faith Abraham, when called to go to a place he would later receive as his inheritance, obeyed and went, even though he did not know where he was going." God is delighted when His people walk with Him by faith. "And without faith it is impossible to please God, because anyone who comes to Him must believe that He exists and that He rewards those who earnestly seek Him" (Hebrews 11:6).

Abraham was a man God promised to bless. The Lord had said to Abram (his name was later changed to Abraham), "Leave your country, your people and your father's household and go to the land I will show you. I will make you into a great nation and I will bless you; I will make your name great, and you will be a blessing. I will bless those who bless you, and whoever curses you I will curse; and all peoples on earth will be blessed through you" (Genesis 12:1-3).

Abraham was a man God trusted to raise his children God's way. God said, "For I have chosen him, so that he will direct his children and his household after him to keep the way of the Lord by doing what is right and just, so that the Lord will bring about for Abraham what He has promised him" (Genesis 18:19). God had confidence in Abraham that he would be a faithful father and raise his children to honor and serve the Lord.

Jonathan Edwards (1703-1758) was a man used mightily by God during the First Great Awakening in America. He was a godly man and left a godly legacy for his family when he died. Max Jukes was an ungodly man and left an ungodly legacy for his family when he died. What is so interesting about the comparison study on these two men is that "like begets like."

"Max Jukes was an unbelieving man and he married a woman of like character who lacked principle. And among the known descendants, over 1,200 were studied. There were 310 who became professional vagrants; 440 physically wrecked their lives by a debauched lifestyle; 130 were sent to prison for an average of thirteen years each, seven of them for murder. There were over 100 who became alcoholics; sixty became habitual thieves; 190 public prostitutes. Of the twenty who learned a trade, they learned the trade in a state prison. This family cost the state about $1,500,000 and they made no contribution whatever to society.

In about the same era, the family of Jonathan Edwards came on the scene. And Jonathan Edwards, a man of God, married a woman of like character. And their family became a part of this study that was made. Three hundred became clergymen, missionaries, and theological professors; over 100 became college profs; over 100 became attorneys, thirty of them judges; sixty of them became physicians; over sixty became authors of good classics, good books; fourteen became presidents of universities. There were numerous giants in American industry that emerged from this family. Three became United States congressmen and one became the vice president of the United States."[27] If Christian parents are to pass on a godly legacy to their children, what must they do to impact their children for Jesus Christ while the parents are still living? How can a godly legacy be passed on from one generation to the next?

---

[27] www.unlockingthebible.org/jonathan-edwards-leaving a godly legacy

## Teach Children The Word Of God

What a wonderful privilege it is for parents to teach their children the Word of God. Moses passed on to the children of Israel this command from God: "These commandments that I give you today are to be upon your hearts. Impress them upon your children. Talk about them when you sit at home and when you walk along the road, when you lie down and when you get up" (Deuteronomy 6:6-7).

Timothy had a godly mother and godly grandmother. They had a great impact upon Timothy's faith and character development. The apostle Paul said to Timothy, "But as for you, continue in what you have learned and have become convinced of, because you know those from whom you learned it, and how from infancy you have known the holy Scriptures, which are able to make you wise for salvation through faith in Christ Jesus" (II Timothy 3:14-15).

Jesus was the master teacher. He taught by using stories, parables, and illustrations of everyday life. People could easily relate with Him and what He taught them. He often used children in His teaching ministry. When Jesus wanted to teach His disciples about humility and true greatness, "He took a little child and had him stand among them. Taking him in His arms, he said to them, 'Whoever welcomes one of these little children in My name welcomes Me; and whoever welcomes Me does not welcome Me but the One who sent Me'" (Mark 9:36-37).

In our home, the main teaching time was right after our evening meal. It was always a challenge to teach our children the Word of God as a group, because we had two older children and two younger children. I had to continually gear our family devotional time either up, so I could relate to our two older children, or down, so I could relate to our two younger children.

Parents are commissioned by God with the main responsibility for teaching their children the Word of God. Some parents relegate this responsibility to their children's Sunday school teachers, Christian school teachers, children's pastor, or youth pastor. But the Scriptures indicate that the parents are to have this primary responsibility. The father is to be the spiritual leader of his home. "Fathers, do not exasperate your children; instead, bring them up in the training and instruction of the Lord" (Ephesians 6:4).

Joshua said, "As for me and my household, we will serve the Lord" (Joshua 24:15). Joshua was the spiritual leader in his home, and Christian fathers today should take seriously the spiritual leadership of their homes. In many homes the spiritual leadership of the father is either neglected or passed on to his wife. Thank God for spiritual mothers who are willing to fulfill the role of the spiritual leader in their home, if the father is unwilling to do so.

What a joy it is for parents to teach their children about Jesus and His love, forgiveness, and plan of salvation. Jesus said, "Let the little children come to me, and do not hinder them, for the kingdom of God belongs to such as these" (Mark 10:14). Jesus wants our children to come to Him and receive Him into their lives as their Savior and Lord. All four of our children opened their hearts and received Jesus as their Savior and Lord at an early age. R. A. Torrey said, "It is easiest to lead a child from five to ten years to a definite acceptance of Christ. The younger we get a child to accept Christ and begin Christian training, the more beautiful the product."[28]

## Teach Children To Pray

One day, Jesus was praying in a certain place. When He finished, one of His disciples said to Him, 'Lord, teach us to pray, just as John taught His disciples'" (Luke 11:1). The disciples wanted to learn how to communicate with God in prayer. God speaks to us through the Scriptures and we speak to Him in prayer. In this way, we have a two-way conversation with Him.

Sometimes children will pray and say things in their prayers that are both humorous and embarrassing. A family was having a picnic with relatives and friends from their church. The father asked his little son to say the prayer before they began to eat. The boy was hesitant and said that he didn't know what to say in his prayer. The father said, "Just say what you hear your mother

---

[28] Sweeting, George, *Who Said That?* (Chicago: Moody Press, 1994), 87.

saying." The boy bowed his head and prayed: "Lord, why did we invite all these people on such a hot day?"

When we teach children how to pray we are putting them in touch with God. God is the One they need to rely upon for comfort, strength, courage, and help in times of need. We must teach them to trust God to meet all of their needs. As children are taught how to pray, they can have fellowship with God. In 1 John 1:3 God's Word declares, "We proclaim to you what we have seen and heard, so that you also may have fellowship with us. And our fellowship is with the Father and also with His Son, Jesus Christ." Children will be excited and will grow spiritually when they experience answers to their prayers.

When our daughter Amy was about four years old, she taught me a valuable lesson about prayer. Prayer should always be our first response, not our last resort.

We arrived home from a vacation, and everyone was tired. I went downstairs to our basement to put something in the freezer. We apparently had a lot of rain while we were away, and our sump pump stopped working. We had four or five inches of water all over the basement floor. I was so frustrated and angry that I started hollering upstairs to my wife. "Sharon, you won't believe this, but our Christmas decorations are floating in water and lots of things are ruined!"

I continued to mumble and grumble. Amy walked down the basement stairs and said, "Daddy, why don't we sit down and just pray about it?" I felt so ashamed of my reaction. We had taught our children to turn to God in prayer when they had a problem, and that's exactly what Amy did. I sat down on the steps with her and we prayed together. I still had a mess to clean up, but my attitude changed and the peace of God was in my heart.

Sometimes, the roles are reversed and God uses our children to teach some very valuable lessons to us, as parents.

## Teach Children To Obey

Children need to be taught to obey their parents as well as to obey God. "Children, obey your parents in the Lord, for this is right. Honor your father and mother- which is the first commandment with a promise- that it may go well with you and that you may enjoy long life on the earth" (Ephesians 6:1-2).

A child that has a difficult time obeying his or her parents will also have a difficult time obeying teachers, police officers, God, or anyone in a position of authority.

Obedience must be taught in the home if it is ever to be practiced in society.

Jesus said, "Why do you call Me, 'Lord, Lord,' and do not do what I say?" (Luke 6:46). If Jesus is our Lord, then we will want to obey Him. Teaching children to obey God and their parents can be very frustrating but also very rewarding. When someone comments to a parent about the obedience that they observed in their child, the parent is thrilled. III John 4 says, "I have no greater joy than to hear that my children are walking in truth."

When children are taught to love the Lord and obey Him, they discover how real Jesus can become to them. My favorite verse of Scripture is John 14:21. This verse assures us that Jesus will "show" or "manifest" Himself to those who love Him and obey Him: "Whoever has My commands and obeys them, he is the one who loves Me. He who loves Me will be loved by My Father, and I too will him and show Myself to him." Obedience is the very best way to show that we believe.

## Teach Children By Example

The most powerful way to teach children is by modeling a good example before them. Children will learn far more from what they see than from what they hear. The old adage, "Actions speak louder than words" is true because people remember far more what we do than what we say. Proverbs 20:11 declares, "Even a child is known by his actions, by whether his conduct is pure and right."

As parents we are concerned about the actions of our children, but we must be even more concerned about what is happening in our children's heart. What happens in the child's heart will be manifested in their behavior. Proverbs 4:23 says, "Above all else guard your heart, for it is the wellspring of life."

The heart commonly refers to the mind, emotions, and the will. A child's speech and behavior is controlled by their heart. We must seek to shepherd our children's hearts in the ways of the Lord by teaching them the Word of God and by doing all we can as parents to put into practice in our lives what God's Word says.

In my office at the church I have a sign that says, "The best sermon is a good example." This is a reminder to me as a pastor, father, and grandfather of how important it is to set a good example. We must practice what we preach, and when we fail, which we do, we must humble ourselves and ask for forgiveness not only from God but from those who have observed our words and actions. Sometimes parents must ask their children for forgiveness for something they said or did. This kind of honesty and humility on the part of a parent can have a great impact in the lives of their children.

The apostle Paul said, "Follow my example, as I follow the example of Christ" (I Corinthians 11:1). If we are not following Christ as parents, we will have a very difficult time teaching our children to follow Him. Our bad example can lead our children astray. Parents can become stumbling blocks to their children and hinder their spiritual growth if they do not live a godly example before them. How sad if that is true of us as parents.

Timothy was a young pastor. Paul instructed him, "Don't let anyone look down on you because you are young, but set an example for the believers in speech, in life, in love, in faith, and in purity" (I Timothy 4:12).

A father felt convicted and realized he needed to stop making unkind statements about other drivers when he was driving his car. One day, someone cut him off and he remained silent, but his three-year-old son in the backseat shouted, "Get out of the way, you jerk." The father didn't have to wonder about where his son heard those words.

When parents discover that a clerk in a store didn't charge enough for an item, what do they do? If they go back to the store and pay the proper amount, and their children observe this, they are teaching their children the importance of honesty. If they don't go back and make things right, they are teaching their children dishonesty.

In a situation like this, it is important to explain to our children why we are returning to the store to pay the proper amount of money that we owed for the item we purchased. God knows that we were not charged the proper amount and He calls us to respond out of love and obedience to Him—even if no one else knows what happened. It is out of our love for the Lord and what He has done for us that we obey Him by doing what is right.

As parents, we must never underestimate the power of a godly example in teaching our children the Word of God and what is right and wrong. Godly Christian parents will know the way, go the way, and show the way for their children to follow.

## Teach Children By Disciplining Them

Children need to be disciplined in one way or another at one time or another. Children need to learn that their parents are in charge and they are not. Parents who do not discipline their children when they are young will find it increasingly difficult as their children grow older.

God loves us so much that He disciplines us when we need to be disciplined:

> "My son, do not make light of the Lord's discipline, and do not lose heart when He rebukes you, because the Lord disciplines those He loves, and He punishes everyone He accepts as a son (or daughter). Endure hardship as discipline; God is treating you as a son. For what son is not disciplined by his father? If you are not disciplined (and everyone undergoes discipline), then you are illegitimate children and not true sons. Moreover, we have all had human fathers who disciplined us and we respected them for it. How much more should we submit to the Father of our spirits and live! Our fathers disciplined us for a little while as they thought best; but God disciplines us for our own good, that we may share in His holiness. No discipline seems pleasant at the time, but painful. Later on, however, it

produces a harvest of righteousness and peace for those who have been trained by it" (Hebrews 12:5-11).

I was disciplined by my father and mother when I needed it, which was quite often. Sometimes I was disciplined, usually by my dad, by getting a painful spanking on my backside. Proverbs 13:24 says, "He who spares the rod hates his son, but he who loves him is careful to discipline him." No parent likes to spank or discipline a child, but there are times when it is needed.

Too many parents are not on spanking terms with their children. "Folly (or foolishness) is bound up in the heart of a child, but the rod of discipline will drive it far from him" (Proverbs 22:15). Just as my father spanked me, I spanked all four of our children when it was needed. Sometimes discipline was in the form of a stern look; that worked best with our two daughters, but not with our two sons. There were also times when time out worked best. Sometimes depriving a child of something they want or somewhere they want to go is an effective form of discipline.

As followers of Christ, we should also never practice or tolerate abuse, especially in our home. This includes all forms of abuse: physical, emotional, sexual, and verbal. There is a fine line between firm discipline and child abuse. Only God can give a parent the wisdom and strength to not cross that line.

Parents are to discipline their children in love, not in anger. If our children used abusive or disrespectful language towards their mother or me, they would be disciplined. It was my duty as a husband to protect my wife from verbal abuse from our children.

Children need to see their parents as united. God calls the husband and wife to be one flesh, and the children should see them as fully supporting one another in terms of mutual respect and united in their discipline of the children. Otherwise, the children will play one parent against the other. This is manipulation, which is the opposite of biblical love. Jesus defines love as honoring one another, and putting another's needs above his/her own.

Ephesians 6:4 contains a warning to parents and especially to fathers:

"Fathers, do not exasperate your children; instead, bring them up in the training and instruction of the Lord." If parents exasperate their children they may provoke them to anger and frustration, which may lead to rebellion and even greater forms of misbehavior. Parents must avoid disciplining their children out of anger. They must discipline out of love and not in a rigid and domineering manner like a drill sergeant in the military. There must be a healthy balance between love and discipline.

Some parents express great love to their children, but neglect to discipline them. The same parents may take their dog to obedience school and let their children run wild. Other parents discipline their children continually, but do not express their love to them. Again we must be reminded of Hebrews 12:6, "The Lord disciplines those He loves." Parents must ask the Lord to help them be patient in bringing up their children in the training and instruction of the Lord.

Billy Graham once said, "The Bible calls for discipline and a recognition of authority. If children do not learn this at home, they will go out into society without the proper attitude towards authority and law. There is always the exceptional child, but the average tells us that the child is largely what the home has made him. The only way to provide the right home for your children is to put the Lord above them, and fully instruct them in the ways of the Lord. You are responsible before God for the home you provide for them."[29]

## Teach Children By Spending Time With Them

Jesus spent time with His apostles. "He appointed twelve—designating them apostles—that they might be with Him and that He might send them out to preach" (Mark 3:14). Jesus wanted His apostles to be "with Him" so that He could teach them and model for them the kind of ministry that He wanted them to perform when He went back to heaven.

Parents need to spend quality time with their children, but they also need quality time with one another as a husband and wife. The marital relationship is the primary relationship in a home.

---

[29] Sweeting, George, *Who Said That?* (Chicago: Moody Press, 1994), 193

When a husband and wife have a strong marriage, it brings stability to the children. In a Christian home, the priorities should be God first, the marriage relationship second, and the children third.

There has only been one perfect marriage in history and it didn't last long. Before Adam and Eve sinned in the Garden of Eden, their marriage was perfect in every way. After they sinned, their marriage was no longer perfect, but dysfunctional. Still, at least Adam didn't have to listen to Eve talk about all the other men she could have married, and Eve didn't have to listen to Adam talk about what a good cook his mother was.

Parents must plan time in their schedule for their children. Our children loved to wrestle on the floor or lawn with me. My wife would holler at me, "Larry, you're going to hurt the kids!" I don't remember anyone getting hurt, but I do remember the laughter, the giggling, the tickling, and the bonding that took place.

One night, I was wrestling with Evan and Lisa before a TV program came on that they wanted to watch. We lost track of time and I was tired enough to stop. I said, "Hey kids, your program is on TV." They said, "We don't want to watch it. This is more fun."

Some of my fondest memories are times when we did things together as a family and went places with our children. We spent time together at parks, picnics, parties, and school or church programs. I had many great times hunting and fishing with my two sons. I remember lots of bike rides with my daughters and times that we spent at the mall or just playing games together.

Vacations were always a great experience for us as a family. We went to many North American Baptist conferences in various states and in Canada. One summer, we spent three weeks traveling across Canada and the United States, stopping at state parks, Yellowstone National Park and the Grand Canyon. That was one of the best vacations we had as a family.

Pastors and missionaries, like everyone else, need time off from their ministry to relax, refresh, restore, and be revived. When a lady heard her pastor say that he was going on vacation, she was very upset. She confronted him at the door of the church after the morning service. "Pastor, did I hear you say that you were going to take a vacation?" "Yes," the pastor responded, "I need to get away and spend some time with my family." The lady growled, "Don't you know that the devil never takes a vacation?" The pastor replied, "I know that, and if I didn't take one I'd be just like him."

Jesus said to his disciples, "Come apart into a desert place, and rest a while" (Mark 6:31). Someone commented on this verse by saying: "If you don't come apart and rest a while, you will just come apart."

As I look back over the past forty-three years of ministry, I know that I have made many mistakes. One of my greatest regrets is that I didn't spend more time with my wife and children, especially when my children were young. I often put the people of the church and my ministry ahead of my family. I have asked the Lord to forgive me for this and I pray that He will give me much quality time in my later years with my wife, our four children, their spouses, and our nine grandchildren. Time is one of the greatest gifts that we could ever give our family. Another way to spell love is T-I-M-E.

When our daughter Lisa was about six or seven years old, she came to me while I was working in our garden. She said, "Daddy, can you take me for a bike ride?" I was willing to go for a bike ride with her, but I thought that I would have fun kidding with her. I said, "Lisa, today is my day off and I have to work in the garden." She put her hands on her little hips, looked right into my eyes, and said, "Daddy, don't you know that the Bible says that you are supposed to spend time with your children?" I wanted to play along with her, so I said, "Lisa, where in the Bible does it say that a father is supposed to spend time with his children?" By now, Lisa was thoroughly frustrated and said, "I don't know where it says it, but I know it's in the Bible." As parents, our time with our children passes quickly and we must take advantage of every opportunity we have to spend quality time with them. When we are raising our children, the days seem long, but the years are short.

Fridays have always been my busiest days in studying and preparing for Sunday's message to the congregation that I serve. One Friday I had a funeral and funeral luncheon to attend. As I was driving back to the church, I decided to reschedule an appointment I had later in the afternoon. I called my son Evan on my cell phone and said, "Evan, would you like to go fishing?"

He said, "Dad, don't you have to go back to the church?"

I replied, "I cancelled my appointment and thought I would like to take you fishing."

There was dead silence and then Evan said, "Dad, I've waited sixteen years for this day."

That phone call taught me how much more important my family must be to me than my ministry. I made many changes after that day. One of the changes was that when a member of my family called me, regardless of whether I was counseling someone or in a church meeting, or whatever, I would take that call. My family became my second priority after God.

## God's Hand Upon Our Children

I have experienced the invisible hand of God at work in my family through the years. I am so thankful for my family and that God holds us in His hand. "Surely it is You who love the people; all the holy ones are in Your hand. At Your feet they all bow down and receive instruction" (Deuteronomy 33:3). Not only does God hold us with His hand but He also instructs us in the way we should go in life (Psalm 32:8).

"If I rise on the wings of the dawn, if I settle on the far side of the sea, even there Your hand will guide me, and Your right hand will hold me fast" (Psalm 139:9-10). God is always with His people no matter where they may travel. How encouraging it is to know that God holds His children with His hand and no one can pluck them out of His hand as John 10:29 reminds us.

God promises to guide His children. David experienced the invisible hand of God guiding him. No matter where he went he could say, "Even there Your hand will guide me, and Your right hand will hold me fast" (Psalm 139:10).

God's will is perfect. Psalm 18:30 declares, "As for God, His way is perfect; the Word of the Lord is flawless. He is a shield for all who take refuge in Him." When we surrender to God's will for our lives, He guides us on the paths that He wants us to travel. "Show me Your ways, O Lord, teach me Your paths; guide me in

Your truths and teach me, for You are God, my Savior, and my hope is in You all day long" (Psalm 25:4-5).

Isaiah the prophet wrote about God's guidance. "The Lord will guide you always; He will satisfy your needs in a sun-scorched land, and will strengthen your frame. You will be like a well-watered garden, like a spring whose waters never fail" (Isaiah 58:11). God's guidance and strength is available at all times for those who trust in Him and look to Him to meet their needs.

The hymn writer William Williams wrote the words to the hymn, "Guide Me O Thou Great Jehovah. " "Guide me, O Thou great Jehovah, pilgrim through this barren land; I am weak but Thou art mighty; Hold me with Thy powerful hand; Bread of heaven, Bread of heaven, Feed me till I want no more, Feed me till I want no more."[30]

God's hand was upon our children as they attended school. We planned to have Nathan, our oldest child, attend a public elementary school in our neighborhood, but God had a different plan for his education. When we took Nathan to the school for an orientation session, we had a bad experience with the teacher that he would have had in kindergarten.

There were about twelve prospective kindergarten students and their parents who attended the orientation session. The teacher had the children sit on the floor while she spoke to them as a group. Each child had a name tag. Several times, the teacher said, "Every day when you come to school, you will see Sarah, Jennifer, Billy, and Caleb." She repeated different names of the students, but continually said, "Every day you will see..." Nathan said to the teacher, "Maybe not, maybe someday someone will be sick."

I thought of the same thing as my wife and I stood in the back of the classroom. The teacher scolded Nathan in a manner that we did not appreciate as parents. She scolded him a second time when he tried to get a drink at the water fountain. We left the school that day saying, "We don't want that teacher teaching our son." The same day, we received a letter from a Christian school in our area that offered scholarship assistance if we wanted to

---

[30] Williams, William, The Hynmal for Worship and Celebration (Waco: Word Music, 1986), 51

send our children to their school. We visited the school and believed that God guided us to have our children attend there instead of the public school.

Several years later, we moved from Buffalo, New York, to Bethlehem, Pennsylvania when I became the senior pastor at Calvary Baptist Church. We were delighted to discover the Bethlehem Christian School was renting the church classrooms and space was available for our children. All four of our children attended this school through eighth grade and received a Christ-centered education. God provided the funds for tuition and His hand was upon our children. We were so grateful for the staff and teachers at the Bethlehem Christian School.

After eighth grade, God led us to the Lehigh Valley Christian High School in Allentown, Pennsylvania and Nathan graduated from there in 1991. Our other three children graduated from Freedom High School, a public high school in Bethlehem. Not only does God guide, He also provides. "And my God will meet all your needs according to His glorious riches in Christ Jesus" (Philippians 4:19). God promised to meet all our needs and we trusted Him to provide thousands of dollars for tuition for our children.

Nathan graduated in 1995 from Liberty University in Lynchburg, Virginia. He received a $2,000 scholarship from Liberty for each of his first two years. God graciously supplied all the funds that we needed. Liberty University offered a 10% discount if all tuition costs were paid in full by June 10th. Each year, we saved in advance to get the discount, which was significant. After two years, his scholarship ended.

In the spring of 1993, our faith was tested. Not only would Nathan's two-year scholarship be finished, but we found out that our tax accountant had not done our state income taxes properly for several years, and we owed the state of Pennsylvania $1,600. What could we do? We prayed and asked God to guide us.

We had to pay the taxes, so we took the tuition money that we had been saving to pay the state what we owed. How could we replace $1,600 by June 10th and have the money for Nathan's tuition?

I called Liberty University to find out if they knew of any other sources of scholarships that might be available to us. The secretary in the accounting office put me on hold while she did some research. A few minutes later she said, "Mr. Burd, your son has had good grades, so we will extend his scholarship for the next two years." *Wow!* We just paid $1,600 in back taxes and God gave us $4,000 in scholarship funds. We experienced the invisible hand of God at work again. God also provided a significant amount of Amy's college expenses through scholarships and gifts.

God's hand was upon our children as He led them to their spouses. We had prayed for many years that God would lead each of our children to a godly, Christian spouse someday. God heard and answered our prayers. Having all four of our children married to godly, Christian spouses is certainly one of the greatest joys we have experienced as parents.

Nathan met Mary Smith while he was a student at Liberty University. Nathan and Mary worked in the same restaurant, fell in love, and were married in Virginia in 1995. Mary is a southern girl with much charm. She is also a tremendous cook, which pleases Nathan greatly, as well as many others who sit at her table and enjoy her warm hospitality. Mary is a wonderful addition to our family and she fits in well with everyone.

Amy met Darryl Robbins, a native of Canada, while she was a student at Houghton College in Houghton, New York. Darryl and Amy were chosen to be the homecoming king and queen. They fell in love and were married in 1999. When my dad first met Darryl, he called him "Luther" and sometimes to be silly, I call him Luther as well. Darryl has a great personality and is a lot of fun to be around.

Lisa met her husband-to-be through a Christian internet site. She asked me to have breakfast with Gregg Rader and "check him out" before she went out with him. I met with Gregg and liked him very much. He shared his testimony with me about how he became a Christian. He also shared his views on tithing, saving, and getting out of debt. I was skeptical when Lisa said she met Gregg "online," but after getting to know him, my wife and I gave Lisa our approval to date him. They were married in 2001.

Evan was the last of our four children to be married. One Sunday, when he had a weekend off from the Air Force, he attended our church and saw a young lady named Sarah Lyman. It had been eleven years since they last saw each other at Bethlehem Christian School where they had both been students.

Sarah lived in Florida and only attended one worship service at our church in 2003, but by God's divine guidance and invisible hand at work in their lives that was the day she and Evan reconnected and began to show an interest in one another.

Sarah came to worship services at our church a number of times during her college years and I always liked her and enjoyed interacting with her. She loved the Lord and enjoyed talking about spiritual things. She had been on a couple mission trips and had a passion for reaching people for Christ. I was so excited when Sarah and Evan began to date. Sarah is a very compassionate and caring person.

Ironically, I took Sharon for a scooter ride on our first date and Evan took Sarah for a motorcycle ride on their first date. They were married in 2004.

As a father and pastor, I had the overwhelming joy of not only baptizing all four of our children after they received Jesus Christ as their Savior and Lord, but I also performed the wedding ceremony for each of our children. In Psalm 23:5, David wrote, "my cup overflows." The overflowing joy of the Lord is what Sharon and I have experienced in seeing our four children be married to godly, Christian spouses.

## The Blessing Of Having Grandchildren

A lady was asked, "What do you want your next child to be?" She answered, "A grandchild."

Eleven years ago we didn't have any grandchildren and I asked the people in our church if they would pray for us and ask the Lord to bless us with grandchildren. The people began to pray and within less than four years we had eight grandchildren. God blessed us with three granddaughters: Madelyn, Chloe, and Liza, and five grandsons: Benjamin, Elliot, Everett, Jack, and Owen. In December 2012, our ninth grandchild, Timothy, was added to our family. We would be delighted to have even more grandchildren if the Lord has more in His divine plan for us.

Sharon and I treasure our role as grandparents. Psalm 115:14-15 has become very special to me since we became grandparents. "May the Lord make you increase, both you and your children. May you be blessed by the Lord, the Maker of heaven and earth." God has truly blessed us as a family and He has increased us.

God is a God of miracles. Every child and grandchild is a miracle from God. Both of our sons and their wives had difficulties in having a family. After going to fertility clinics and having various procedures done, it didn't seem like they were going to have children. Many people were praying for them. I had resigned myself to the thought that it must not be God's will for them to have children. If God didn't want them to have children, then may His will be done. Sharon, however, did not think that way. She never stopped praying or believing that God would bless our sons with children.

Nathan and Mary had been married for thirteen years. They were trying to adopt a child through the country of Ukraine. They had spent thousands of dollars on home studies and other adoption expenses. Emails would come in from the adoption agency telling them that in three weeks they could travel to Ukraine and get their child. Then, before the three weeks had passed, they would get another email saying that all adoptions in Ukraine had been stopped for the next six months.

Their emotions were continually frazzled and they felt like a yo-yo going up and down, up and down. Finally, after two and a half years, they decided to stop the adoption process. They concluded that if God wanted them to have a child, they would have one. If not, God would give them grace to accept His will and recognize that His will is always best, even though they may not be able to understand it at the time.

One year, during their years of struggling to adopt, it was around Christmastime, and Sharon was listening to Christmas music and thinking about the miracle of Christ's birth through Mary, who was a virgin. The thought came into her mind that if God could perform a miracle for Mary, the mother of Jesus, He could perform a miracle for our daughter-in-law, who was also called Mary. Sharon had a deep assurance in her heart that God would hear and answer prayer and enable Nathan and Mary to have a child. When Elliot was born in 2008, Sharon burst into tears of great joy.

Evan and Sarah also wanted a family — but they, too, struggled with infertility for several years. They decided to adopt a child from the Philippines. The day before they were supposed to send an additional $3,000 to the adoption agency, Sarah discovered she was pregnant. When they called to tell us, not only did we hear the amazing news that they were expecting, but that they were expecting twins! A few weeks later Evan and Sarah called again, saying they had just had another ultrasound performed. I asked, "How are the twins?" They said, "The ultrasound technician told us that in twenty-six years of viewing an ultrasound screen, she had never failed to see a fetus until today. She said, 'You're not having twins, you're having triplets!'" In November 2009, Everett, Jack, and Owen safely arrived. Evan and Sarah were very excited to be parents of triplets, but they also felt overwhelmed.

Sharon and I never dreamed of being grandparents of triplets. What an amazing challenge it was to take care of three babies at the same time. As soon as one baby was fed, diapered, and asleep, the next one needed the same loving care, and then the next one. The cycle seemed endless. Our prayers intensified for Evan and Sarah as we realized what an awesome task it was to be the parents of triplets. They needed all the help they could get. Sharon stayed with Evan and Sarah before the triplets were born and for several weeks after they were born. She was gone for nine weeks and I missed her terribly. When I told her how much I missed her, she said, "Just think you're on a mission trip." I responded, "The problem is I am not on a mission trip. I am home all alone." I was so happy when she finally came home.

Sharon and I have experienced the invisible hand of God at work in the lives of our children and grandchildren. The words of Psalm 115:14-15 have become a reality in our family. There are now nineteen in our family who gather at our dining room table when they are all home. If the Lord wants to send us more grandchildren we would welcome them with open arms.

## <u>Think About It</u>

- Will you be leaving a godly or ungodly legacy for your family some day?
- Are you seeking to be consistent in modeling a Christ-like character before your children and grandchildren?
- Are you spending quality time with your family or focusing too much on work?
- Are you disciplining your children appropriately with a godly purpose, method and attitude?
- What biblical truths are you teaching your children and grandchildren?
- In what ways have you experienced the invisible hand of God at work in your family?

CHAPTER 8

# THE INVISIBLE HAND OF GOD AT WORK IN MY MINISTRY AT GREEN STREET BAPTIST CHURCH

*"The Word of the Lord came to Ezekiel the priest, the son of Buzi, by the Kebar River in the land of the Babylonians. There the hand of the Lord was upon him" (Ezekiel 1:3).*

Ezekiel was a prophet and a priest of God. His name means "strengthened by God". Only God could give Ezekiel the strength he needed to fulfill his ministry. He was only twenty-five when he was taken captive in Babylon and thirty when he was called by God to his ministry. His ministry began in 593 B.C. and continued for twenty-two years until 571 B.C. Approximately 10,000 Jews were taken captive into Babylon and Ezekiel and his wife were among them.

Numerous times in the book of Ezekiel "the hand of the Lord" was mentioned. Ezekiel 1:3 tells us "the hand of the Lord was upon him." In Ezekiel 2:9, the Bible says, "Then I looked, and I saw a hand stretched out to me. In it was a scroll, which He unrolled before me. On both sides of it were written words of lament and mourning and woe." Ezekiel 3:14 says, "The Spirit then lifted me up and took me away, and I went in bitterness and in the anger of my spirit, with the strong hand of the Lord upon me." Because the hand of the Lord was upon Ezekiel he had the wisdom, strength, and courage needed to be faithful to the Lord and to accomplish His ministry.

Ezekiel was called to a very difficult ministry. The Israelites were in rebellion toward God. They didn't want to listen to God's Word, but Ezekiel was sent by God with His Words regardless of whether the people listened to him or not. The call of God upon

Ezekiel and the rebellion of the people is recorded in Ezekiel chapter two:

> "He said to me, 'Son of man, stand up on your feet and I will speak to you.' As He spoke, the Spirit came into me and raised me to my feet, and I heard Him speaking to me. He said: 'Son of man, I am sending you to the Israelites, to a rebellious nation that has rebelled against Me; they and their fathers have been in revolt against Me to this very day. The people to whom I am sending you are obstinate and stubborn.' Say to them, 'This is what the Sovereign Lord says.' And whether they listen or fail to listen - for they are a rebellious house - they will know that a prophet has been among them. And you, son of man, do not be afraid of them or their words. Do not be afraid, though briers and thorns are all around you and you live among scorpions. Do not be afraid of what they say or terrified by them, though they are a rebellious house. You must speak My words to them, whether they listen or fail to listen, for they are rebellious. But you, son of man, listen to what I say to you. Do not rebel like that rebellious house; open your mouth and eat what I give you.' Then I looked, and I saw a hand stretched out to me. In it was a scroll, which he unrolled before me. On both sides of it were written words of lament and mourning and woe (Ezekiel 2:1-9)."

Regardless of how rebellious and obstinate the Israelites behaved toward God, Ezekiel was called to be a faithful prophet unto them. He had many reasons to fear the Israelites, but God assured him that he should not be afraid of them. What gave Ezekiel great confidence as he ministered God's Word to people who did not want to hear what God had to say? "The hand of the Lord was upon him" (Ezekiel 1:3). Being assured that the invisible hand of God was upon him enabled Ezekiel to carry out his ministry and be faithful to God's call upon his life.

## God's Call To Preach His Word

Like Ezekiel, I sensed the hand of the Lord upon me when He called me into the ministry. I needed God's wisdom, strength, and courage in my life if I was to be faithful to the Lord and His ministry. I had much to learn about what it meant to preach the Word of God. I was concerned because I didn't know how to preach or what to preach. How would I be able to convince people about the truth of God's Word? I had many fears and doubts about my ability to preach. I was convinced I couldn't do it. If God called me to preach then He would have to preach through me. *How could this happen? How could His Word and His Spirit speak through me?*

God began to give me insights about preaching. At the time of my call to the ministry, He led me to Jeremiah 5:14. God said to Jeremiah the prophet: "I will make My words in your mouth a fire and these people the wood it consumes." The Lord encouraged me greatly through this verse. He said "I will make My words in your mouth a fire." He was the One who put His words in Jeremiah's mouth. Jeremiah was not to speak his own words, but God's words that He had given to him. The Lord's words would be like a fire burning within Jeremiah. Just as a fire burns wood, so God's Word would burn like fire in the lives of people.

## The Power Of God's Word

I discovered I did not have to convince people about God's Word; I simply had to preach God's Word to them. The power was in the Word, not in the messenger. Jeremiah 23:29 says, "'Is not My Word like fire,' declares the Lord, 'and like a hammer that breaks the rock in pieces?'" The Bible is a living, active, and powerful Word from God. Hebrews 4:12 declares, "For the Word of God is living and active. Sharper than any double-edged sword, it penetrates even to dividing soul and spirit, joints and marrow; it judges the thoughts and attitudes of the heart."

God's Word is so powerful that it can pierce a person's heart and reveal everything about that person. After Jesus met the woman at the well in John chapter four she went back to Samaria and said to the people: "Come, see a man who told me everything I ever did" (John 4:29). When Jesus spoke to the woman His words pierced her heart and she concluded that He was the Messiah.

Would God give me the strength and ability to preach His Word? He was teaching me to rely upon Him and not myself. "Not that we are competent in ourselves to claim anything of ourselves, but our competence comes from God" (II Corinthians 3:5). The apostle Paul said to Timothy, a young pastor: "I thank Christ Jesus our Lord, who has given me strength, that He considered me faithful, appointing me to His service" (I Timothy 1:12). If God could give Paul strength to preach and do service for the Lord, then I concluded that He could give me His strength as well. "I can do everything through Him who gives me strength" (Philippians 4:13). I determined to depend upon the Lord and His strength. He would work in me and through me as He promised.

## Disasters In Ministry

I gained valuable experience for the ministry when I was a youth pastor. My first two years of youth ministry were at Knox United Presbyterian Church in Kenmore, New York, a suburb of Buffalo. The senior pastor, Frank Kik, was gracious to me and my friend, Scott Weldon. Pastor Kik gave us the opportunity to preach on several occasions on Sunday nights. I don't remember if my preaching was a disaster—it probably was—but I remember my first public prayer and it was definitely a disaster. The church had a live radio broadcast of its morning worship services. The pastor asked me to offer the morning prayer. He gave me specific directions. "Your prayer should be between five and seven minutes long. There is a clock embedded in the lectern on the pulpit, so keep an eye on the clock and don't go under or over the time limits." I felt so nervous I could have almost passed out. I had never prayed a pastoral prayer before. Knowing the service was broadcast on the radio made me exceptionally nervous.

After the morning services, the pastor didn't say anything about my prayer, he simply asked me to come into his office. He turned on a tape recorder and asked me to listen to my prayer. Every time I said, "Our Father," he made a mark on a piece of paper. When I said "Our Father" for the fifth time he drew a line through the other four marks. When the prayer was finished, he had thirty-four marks on the paper. He didn't need to say another word. I never prayed that way again. I was gaining valuable experience in praying and preaching in public.

During my first two years at Gordon-Cornwell Theological Seminary in South Hamilton, I was a part-time youth pastor at the First Baptist Church in Stoneham, Massachusetts. The senior pastor was out of town when a ninety-two-year-old lady, who attended the church, died. The pastor called and asked if I would preach at her funeral. I had never done a funeral before. I was about to experience another disaster in ministry. The pastor told me a few things I could preach at the funeral service, but the day of the service, I felt very unprepared and more nervous than the day I did my first pastoral prayer.

When I arrived at the funeral home, I met the daughter of the lady who had died. I think she was about seventy years old. She was crying and I tried to comfort her. I said something like, "It was wonderful that your mother lived to be ninety-two. The Bible says our life span is three score and ten, that's seventy." At that point the lady began to wail and I didn't know why. I didn't realize what I had said to her until I was driving home after the funeral service. I guess she concluded her own funeral might not be far off.

What happened next humiliated me. The funeral director told me to turn on the light on the portable lectern where I would be speaking and then turn it off when I was finished. I didn't realize the electrical cord for the light was between my legs while I was preaching. When I finished preaching I turned the light off and began to walk toward the casket to pay my last respects to the deceased. With the electrical cord still between my legs the portable lectern nearly tipped over before I caught it. Someone in the audience gasped in seeing the lectern almost tip over, but the gasp startled me and in my nervousness I thought the lady in the casket must have sat up.

Immediately after standing the lectern upright, I stood at the casket for one second, went into a little room, picked up my top coat and went home. I was so humiliated I didn't want to speak to anyone. If it were not for the grace and invisible hand of God upon my life, I could have quit the ministry that day.

After being a part-time youth pastor for four years, I wanted to gain more experience in preaching, visitation, and other aspects of ministry. I resigned from my youth ministry and prayed that God would open another door where I could gain other experience, especially in preaching. God heard and answered my prayer.

## God's Call To Green Street Baptist Church

Green Street Baptist Church in Melrose, Massachusetts, was without a pastor. Their pastor resigned and went to Europe to study. The church leaders asked if I would be their interim pastor until they called another full-time pastor. I was excited to be preaching every Sunday, but I soon discovered I was not theologically on the same page with many of the people in the church. Our theological differences led to many interesting, and sometimes heated, discussions.

I believed the Bible was the divinely inspired Word of God and that's what I was going to preach. My opinions were no better than those of anyone else so I was not going to preach my opinions, but God's Holy Word. Paul told Timothy, "In the presence of God and of Christ Jesus, who will judge the living and the dead, and in view of His appearing and His kingdom, I give you this charge: Preach the Word; be prepared in season and out of season; correct, rebuke, and encourage–with great patience and careful instruction" (II Timothy 4:1-2).

Not only was I determined to preach the Word of God, but I wanted to lift up Jesus Christ and watch Him draw people to Himself. Jesus said, "But I, when I am lifted up from the earth, will draw all men to myself" (John 12:32).

The death of Christ on the cross for our sins, His burial and victorious resurrection from the dead is the central theme of the gospel. I preached that we must believe the gospel, repent of our sins and by faith receive Jesus Christ into our lives as Savior and Lord.

I continually had opposition to what I preached. One man, who was a Sunday School teacher for many years, told me as I tried to share Christ with him, "I know that's what the Bible teaches, but I don't believe it." Another man said he wasn't sure he believed Jesus Christ rose from the dead.

One day I was visiting in the home of a young couple and I read John 3:1-8 about the necessity of being "born again." The lady said, "Jesus said that? I thought that was your theory." She realized that what I was preaching was God's Word and not my theory. An elderly church member commented one day, "I haven't heard preaching like that in our church for forty years." He was a godly man and part of a remnant of true believers in the church.

Paul wrote to Timothy and warned him about those who would not believe the truth. "For the time will come when men will not put up with sound doctrine. Instead, to suit their own desires, they will gather around them a great number of teachers to say what their itching ears want to hear. They will turn their ears away from the truth and turn aside to myths" (II Timothy 4:3-4). I was committed to preach what the people needed to hear, not just what they wanted to hear. I prayed and sought God's will as to what He wanted me to preach. Sometimes I was afraid to preach what God led me to preach, but I wanted to obey Him and preach His Word with His power and anointing.

I interacted with many people in the church and community that basically believed salvation was by good works. They believed if you were kind and helpful to people and tried to be good you would make it into heaven. If that were true, then we didn't need Jesus. His death on the cross, burial, and resurrection were not necessary.

The Bible says, "For it is by grace you have been saved, through faith–and this is not from yourselves, it is the gift of God–not by works, so that no one can boast" (Ephesians 2:8-9). God's plan of salvation is by grace through faith in Christ alone.

There are not many paths to heaven as some people believe, but only one way, and that is through faith in Jesus Christ alone. "Salvation is found in no one else, for there is no other name under heaven given to men by which we must be saved" (Acts 4:12). Jesus said, "I am the way and the truth and the life. No one comes to the Father except through me" (John 14:6). Anyone who tries to get into heaven except through Jesus Christ will not be accepted. People think that's "narrow-minded thinking," but that's exactly what the Bible teaches. I was committed to preaching the gospel even if people opposed it, and they did.

When the Word of God is preached and Jesus Christ is exalted in all His glory, God draws people to Himself. God will work miracles in the lives of people who believe Him and obey Him. "For nothing is impossible with God" (Luke 1:37).

As the Word of God was preached and Christ was exalted, the church began to grow. After many years of declining attendance, it began to come alive with new people. It was exciting to see the congregation growing. People asked me, "Where are you getting these people?" I didn't have time to be "getting" them. I was a full-time seminary student and had to spend much time studying and preparing to preach on Sundays. Other than preaching, I visited the sick and shut-ins on Wednesday afternoons. But God continued to draw people to Himself and to His church as He was exalted.

### God's Call To Endure Hardship

Near the end of my senior year in seminary the church pulpit committee asked me if I would be willing to be their full-time pastor after I graduated. This was one of the most difficult decisions I ever had to make. On the one hand, I was aware of our theological differences and what problems that could create. There were many things I observed as an interim pastor that I did not agree with and if I attempted to make changes after I became the pastor, I would face great opposition. *Was I willing to endure hardship for the cause of Jesus Christ and His people?* Paul told Timothy, "But you, keep your head in all situations, endure hardship, do the work of an evangelist, discharge all the duties of your ministry" (II Timothy 4:5).

God called me to preach the gospel, the good news of salvation, and I was willing to do the work of an evangelist. There was a great joy in my heart and I wanted to lead people of all ages to a saving knowledge of Jesus Christ and see them become genuine followers of Him. That was one of the greatest desires of my life. With great anticipation I looked forward to many of the duties of the ministry.

I feared that if the church did not call an evangelical, Bible-believing pastor, then many people would not hear the truth but would remain in spiritual darkness. In Colossians 1:13-14 the Bible says, "For He has rescued us from the dominion of darkness and brought us into the kingdom of the Son He loves, in whom we have redemption, the forgiveness of sins."

The question I wrestled with was, "Am I willing to suffer hardship for the cause of Jesus Christ and His church?" I knew I would face hardship and opposition if I accepted the offer to become the full-time pastor.

The apostle Paul and many others faced hardship in their ministry, so why couldn't I, with God's help, face whatever I had to face in accepting the position? Near the end of Paul's life he said, "For I am already being poured out like a drink offering, and the time has come for my departure. I have fought the good fight, I have finished the race, I have kept the faith. Now there is in store for me the crown of righteousness, which the Lord, the righteous Judge, will award to me on that day–and not only to me, but also to all who have longed for His appearing" (II Timothy 4:6-8). If Paul could fight the good fight, finish the race, and keep the faith, then by God's grace and strength I, too, could face whatever I had to face in the ministry.

After much prayer and seeking God's guidance, Sharon and I believed God was calling us to Green Street Baptist Church. We believed that according to the Scriptures, the Holy Spirit is the One who makes pastors and elders overseers in His church. To the elders in the church at Ephesus Paul wrote, "Keep watch over yourselves and all the flock of which the Holy Spirit has made you overseers. Be shepherds of the church of God, which He bought with His own blood" (Acts 20:28). God called us and we accepted His call. I began my full-time ministry at Green Street Baptist about a month after I graduated from seminary in June 1973.

Within the first two weeks of being in this new ministry, I found out there were seventeen—of the eighty members of the church—that did not want me to be their pastor. *How did I know this?* They either told me themselves or someone else told me. Many of them spent the next three years trying to prove to me they didn't want me to be their pastor. My key focus had to be on what God wanted, not on what the people wanted.

One of the first changes I made when I became the pastor was to keep the offering in the sanctuary or chapel until after the service. I didn't like what I observed. Several people would sit in the church kitchen drinking coffee and smoking cigarettes while waiting for the church offering to be taken. They would not attend the church service, but after counting the offering, they would go home. I thought this was not right and it must change. The next Sunday when the ushers came to the front of the sanctuary for the offering prayer, after they had taken the offering, I took hold of the offering plates and placed them on the communion table. From that time forward, the offering was not counted until after the worship service. This made a number of people angry, but I thought it was the right thing to do and stood by my decision despite the opposition.

## Problems With The Parsonage

The next challenge was with the trustees of the church. The church owned a very old parsonage that sat on the hill just up the street from the church. When we accepted the call to the church, we were told the parsonage would be refurbished, any necessary repairs would be done and it would be ready for us to move in. When we moved in we discovered nothing had been done. No painting. No repairs. Nothing. The roof leaked. In one of the bedrooms, we had to have buckets to catch the water when it rained. The plaster on the ceiling was falling off.

The bathroom plumbing did not work properly. When we took a shower, some of the water from the previous day was still in the bathtub. One day when I was running water in the bathroom upstairs, Sharon, who was downstairs, started hollering to me, "Water is pouring out of the chandelier in the breakfast nook!" I raced downstairs to see what was happening. Sure enough, our chandelier had been turned into a water fountain.

It was now August and some mornings were quite cool in New England. With having a four-month-old baby in the house, I thought I'd better check the furnace in case we needed to turn it on to warm the house. Did the invisible hand of God guide me to check the furnace? Did His invisible hand protect us from possible harm? The furnace pipes were so old and rusty that when I touched them, pieces of the pipes fell to the basement floor. The furnace was a fire and health hazard. God showed great mercy to us in protecting us every day we spent in that house.

On a Saturday night around nine o'clock, I heard Sharon crying upstairs. I went to check on her. I recall her saying something like, "I can't live in this house any longer." She was so upset she wanted us to move out.

Nothing had been done to refurbish the house. With a leaky roof, plumbing problems, and now a furnace that couldn't be turned on when we needed heat, I had had enough and Sharon couldn't bear it any longer either.

I didn't make a vow, but I came very close to it. I told Sharon I was going out to try to find one of the trustees of the church. As a twenty-five-year-old pastor, I needed "holy boldness" to confront the trustees about the terrible condition of the parsonage and I trusted God to give it to me.

I went from house to house that Saturday night and couldn't find anyone home. Finally, I found a trustee that had just come home from vacation with his family. Suitcases were all over the living room floor and the man was sitting in a chair sipping on a martini when I arrived. He was surprised to see me so late on a Saturday night. After chatting with him for a few minutes about his vacation, I told him why I was there. I told him about the leaky roof, the plumbing problems, the furnace, and that no painting or any refurbishing had been done on the parsonage. Then I said, "When the pulpit committee was interviewing me about becoming the pastor of the church, they asked me how long I thought I would stay here. I told them maybe six weeks or six years or the rest of my life. I didn't know how long I'd be here. That was up to God to decide."

Then I looked this man in the eyes and said in no uncertain terms, "If the trustees do not immediately begin fixing up the parsonage my wife and I are moving out. Don't worry about the plumbing and furnace problems. I'll contact a plumber and furnace repair man to have the repairs done and I'll give the bills to the church." He replied by saying, "Now, now, Pastor, calm down." I wasn't about to calm down. I had his attention and the trustees needed to take some action and very soon. I looked him in the eyes again and said, "Let me repeat what I just said." I repeated the same words to him, said "goodnight," and walked out the door.

On Monday night, the trustees had a crew of people show up at the parsonage with paint brushes in their hands. Before long the parsonage was refurbished, the necessary repairs were done, and we were willing to live in it. God had given me holy boldness to confront a situation that needed to be confronted. I trusted God for guidance and He guided me: "I will instruct you and teach you in the way you should go; I will counsel you and watch over you." (Psalm 32:8)

## More Challenges

More challenges were to follow. The organist and I did not agree on many things. Our greatest disagreement was in regard to an annual Pops Concert the choir performed three times over a weekend. The church basement was packed for each performance and it was very well done. The problem I had with the Pops Concert was that the music was all secular and not Christian.

My heart ached to have so many people come to our church and not offer them something spiritual. *Were we a church or simply a social organization?*

I took my concerns to the music committee. I asked if I could read something from the Bible or quote a spiritual poem or have some type of Christian witness at the end of the concert? The organist blew up at my suggestion. He angrily moved his right hand back and forth on his left arm and said, "Jesus Christ, Jesus Christ, you want Him in everything."

He understood my point very accurately and stormed out of the room. *Why shouldn't Jesus Christ be part of a concert held in His church?* I believed Jesus Christ should be the focus of everything that took place in His church. In spite of my efforts to have a spiritual component added to the concert program, no changes were made during the three and a half years we were at the church.

## Financial Hardship

We also faced constant financial hardship and found it very difficult to meet the most basic needs of our family. With so many leaders in the church not wanting me to be their pastor, I think some of them may have thought they could starve us out. My salary in 1973 was a mere $6,800. I asked God to provide another source of income for us and He graciously heard my prayer and answered.

I received a call from the dean of North Shore Community College in Beverly, Massachusetts. Sharon had worked as a secretary in his office when I was in seminary. He asked if I could teach a sociology course at the college. I told him I probably could do that since I had taken sociology courses in college, but it would require many hours to prepare to teach. I reluctantly turned down his offer to teach sociology, but I said, "You wouldn't need a speech teacher would you?" I had minored in speech in college and I would enjoy teaching speech. He said, "No, we don't need a speech teacher, but we will keep you in mind if the need ever arises."

About two weeks later the dean called again and said, "Our speech teacher had a heart attack. Can you teach speech on Monday nights?" Monday was my day off, so that opportunity fit my schedule perfectly. I taught speech for three semesters. I loved every minute with my students and was paid $600 a semester. That was just enough to meet our needs. Enough never seems like enough, but enough is always just enough. God kept His promises to meet our needs as we trusted in Him and waited for His perfect timing. In Psalm 37:25 David said, "I was young and now I am old, yet I have never seen the righteous forsaken or their children begging bread."

## God's Call To Prayer

When I accepted the call to Green Street Baptist Church I knew there would be many challenges, hardships, and troubles in the ministry. Paul said to Timothy, "Endure hardship with us like a good soldier of Christ Jesus" (II Timothy 2:3). Jesus faced many trials and He told His disciples they would as well: "But a time is coming, and has come, when you will be scattered, each to his own home. You will leave Me alone. Yet I am not alone, for My Father is with Me. I have told you these things, so that in Me you may have peace. In the world you will have trouble. But take heart! I have overcome the world" (John 16:31-33).

Where would I get the strength, wisdom, and courage to carry on in a very difficult ministry? I had experienced the mighty power of prayer before I was called to my first full-time ministry and I knew God had to be the source of everything I needed to do His will. God releases His power when His people pray and don't give up. I learned the meaning of P.U.S.H: Pray Until Something Happens. Jesus said, "If you remain in Me and My words remain in you, ask whatever you wish, and it will be given you" (John 15:7).

I will never forget my first day of ministry at Green Street Baptist Church. I had an unusual experience that resulted in bringing great strength and stability into my life. My office was on the first floor of the church. The secretary's office, chapel, and fellowship hall were in the basement. I was on my knees in my office praying for direction for the church and for my ministry. God said, "Call to Me and I will answer you and tell you great and unsearchable things you do not know" (Jeremiah 33:3). I asked God what He wanted me to do and a thought came into my mind, "Get the people to pray." *Was that my own thought or was that God speaking to me?* As I continued to pray, a picture of the chapel downstairs came into my mind. I was so moved by this experience that I went downstairs to the chapel and continued praying.

"Is this where you want us to pray, Lord?" It seemed like such a perfect place to pray. I asked, "Lord, when would You want us to pray?" In my mind I heard the words, "Six-thirty Thursday mornings." When I heard those words I laughed and said, "Who will attend a prayer meeting at six-thirty on a Thursday morning?" Then it seemed like I heard words of rebuke, "I'll be here, will you?"

I was so convicted by this experience that I believed I would be disobeying God if I didn't announce to the congregation on Sunday that a prayer meeting would be held on Thursday mornings at six-thirty in the chapel.

When I arrived at the church the following Thursday morning, two godly, elderly ladies were waiting by the door. Before long, several more people joined us. I had announced, "Come when you can. Leave when you must." We had between six and thirteen people come every Thursday morning. Prayer became the most important element in our ministry. Prayer was not the spare tire, but the steering wheel and source of everything good God did in His church during those days. I became the closest to the people who came to pray with me on Thursday mornings. I gained my greatest strength from God through the prayers of His people. When we work, we work, but when we pray, God works.

## If God Can Speak Through A Donkey

I have often felt inadequate in speaking for the Lord. Even though I graduated from college and seminary and have forty-three years of pastoral experience, there are still times when I am afraid I will say the wrong thing and cause more harm than good. There have been times when I remained silent when I knew God wanted me to say something. God taught me a valuable lesson about trusting Him to speak through me even when I felt inadequate and afraid of saying the wrong thing.

Within the first month of my full-time ministry at Green Street Baptist Church, I conducted my second funeral. One afternoon I was in my office at the church when my secretary informed me that she had just received a crisis telephone call. A twenty-one year-old college student whose parents were members of our church had just committed suicide in his bedroom at the family home. Immediately, I left the church and drove to their house.

My mind was racing. This was my first crisis as a young pastor. *What do I say to the parents whose son committed suicide? How can I help them? How can I comfort them? What do I do in a crisis like this?* I felt so inadequate, so unprepared, so afraid I'd say or do the wrong thing. As I drove I prayed, "Please, please help me O Lord. I need You. Help me to know what to say and what to do. I don't want to say or do something stupid. I trust You, Lord, to help me. Speak through me, O Lord."

It was a hot summer afternoon. When I arrived, the family was sitting at a picnic table in the backyard. They were all crying as I sat down beside them. A Bible verse came to mind, "Rejoice with them that do rejoice, and weep with them that weep" (Romans 12:15). I felt their pain in my heart and began to cry with them. I said very little, but somehow believed that just being with them was what they needed most at that moment. We all watched as several police officers came out of the house carrying a body bag. It was a heart-wrenching experience.

I spent a brief time with the family, had a short prayer, and asked if I could come back and visit the next morning. For the time being, I felt the family needed private time together.

As I drove to their house the next morning I prayed again, "Please Lord, don't let me say something stupid. Give me words. Speak through me. I need You. I trust You. Thank You for helping me. In Jesus' name. Amen."

When I talked with the grieving parents in their home, I was nervous and careful about every word I spoke. In the midst of our conversation I asked them, "Were you able to get any sleep last night?" Immediately I regretted what I had said. I thought, *"What a stupid thing to ask parents whose son had just committed suicide the day before."* Of all the words I spoke during our conversation, I wished I could have taken a pair of tweezers and removed that one sentence. I felt so stupid about what I had said. I read a few verses of Scripture, had a prayer with the grieving parents, and walked toward the door to leave.

As I was leaving, the father's eyes filled with tears and he said to me, "Pastor, you will never know how much it meant to us when you asked us if we had gotten any sleep last night." The one sentence I wanted so desperately to remove from our conversation was the very sentence God used to touch the hearts of these grieving parents. The words that I thought were stupid were used by God to communicate His love and concern.

While driving home that morning, I said to the Lord, "If you could speak through Balaam's donkey, (Numbers 22:28), surely you can speak through me anytime, anywhere."

God taught me a valuable lesson that day. Whenever I feel inadequate and afraid that I'll say the wrong thing, I've learned to trust that God will speak through me in spite of my weakness and fear. He only asks that I avail myself to Him. He will do the work. Simply put, God wants each one of us to be a vessel He can speak through to a world that desperately needs to hear from Him.

"Not that we are competent in ourselves to claim anything for ourselves, but our competence comes from God" (II Corinthians 3:5). When God calls us to serve Him He equips us with all we need to do His will.

In II Samuel 23:2 David said, "The Spirit of the Lord spoke through me; His Word was on my tongue." I trusted God to speak through me and I was amazed at what He did. It is truly thrilling to think that Almighty God can and does speak through human beings who are yielded to His Word, His Spirit and His will.

## God's Call To Follow Jesus

The most exciting and rewarding experiences we had at Green Street Baptist Church (1972-1976) were seeing changed lives as people received Jesus Christ as their Savior and Lord. Many people were born again into a new life and became followers of Jesus Christ. Jesus said, "My sheep listen to My voice; I know them, and they follow Me" (John 10:27).

## Leo and Janet

Leo and Janet, a young couple, were among the first to become Christians. Leo's brother, George, had become a Christian and started to attend our church. He invited Leo and Janet to a service. As a married couple they had been going through difficulties in their marriage and were almost ready for a divorce. Struggling financially, but at the same time they were seeking for answers of any sort. They started looking for answers through horoscope books and card readers.

Janet decided to turn to Jesus and ask for His help in their marriage. The very next week they came to our church. I invited them to the parsonage to talk about their situation and to share the gospel with them. After realizing how much God loved them and that Jesus died on the cross for their sins and was raised from the dead so they could have eternal life, they put their faith in Him and their lives began to change. Within months they believed God was calling them into the ministry. They packed their belongings into a U-Haul and along with their two young daughters headed off to Maine to attend a Bible college. We gave them our blessing and knew God had a special ministry planned for them.

## Wing

Wing was a Chinese man who grew up in southern China. He worked with his father in a laundromat. He was brought up to worship his ancestors, so God was foreign to him. The subject of death struck his heart with fear. He refused to read the obituary column in the newspaper. His wife, Marie, and their children attended our church. He was uncomfortable when he saw their Bibles or a cross. God was seeking him even though he did not realize it.

Wing was an engineer at RCA in the Boston area, and he had several friends who were sharing Jesus Christ with him. In no way could he accept the fact that he was a sinner. The Bible says, "For all have sinned and fall short of the glory of God" (Romans 3:23).

He saw himself as a moral, hard working person. His friends continued to share with him how Jesus could change his life.

In his written testimony, Wing wrote: "Wanting to ease their pressure and hoping to keep their friendship, I finally informed them that I would accept Jesus Christ on an 'as needed basis'. Pow! The righteous indignation of my friend's response cut me deeply and on that very day in April 1973 driving home from work I prayed to Jesus Christ to take over control of my life without any constraint." Wing became one of the most dedicated and zealous followers of Christ I have known. He joined his wife and family and became a member of Green Street Baptist Church. Actively involved in prayer meetings, in a men's Bible study, and fellowship group—he was a powerful witness for Christ and served the Lord joyfully. For years he waited impatiently for his family to come out of church so he could drive them home; after he became a Christian, his family waited for him.

### Randy and Philip

Randy and Philip were two young boys about twelve years old who lived near our church. One afternoon, I was waiting for a man to come to my office for counseling. I propped the front door of the church open so he could get into the church. Before he came, I heard noise outside the church. I peeked my head outside the door and saw two boys throwing stones at a large spotlight near the roof of the church. Before I could stop them, the fatal stone struck the light and shattered glass went flying through the air.

The boys were startled when they saw me and knew that I had just observed their behavior. In an official sounding voice I said, "Boys, come with me." I took them into my office and like a police officer I interviewed them. "What is your name and address," I asked each of the boys. By now they were shaking with guilt and felt like they were about to be sentenced to twenty years in the state prison.

I asked them several more questions and wrote down their answers. I then asked, "Boys, what do you think should be done about the broken light?" Randy actually threw the fatal stone, but

Philip spoke up first. "I think we should pay for the light," he said. I replied, "How much do you think a light like that may cost?" Philip spoke again, "It cost eleven dollars the last time we broke it."

I didn't know they had committed the same crime previously. I released the boys without setting bail and in a few minutes they returned to my office with the money. I befriended them and they asked if they could come back another day and have a tour of the church. When they returned for the tour, I gave them each a Bible and invited them to come to a church service.

Randy, his mother Janet, and her boyfriend Ed all began attending our church and all received Jesus Christ into their lives. God used a broken spotlight to bring us together. The Bible says, "And we know that in all things God works for the good of those who love Him, who have been called according to His purpose" (Romans 8:28).

## Jean and Bill

I referred to Jean as "the mystery lady." I saw her sitting in the congregation, but week after week she disappeared after the worship service. I wondered, "Where does she go? How can she escape without leaving through the main church door near the back of the sanctuary?" Finally, I realized she was leaving through a door at the far right corner of the sanctuary that was seldom used. She lived near the church with her husband and two children. They did not attend the church with her at that time.

One day Jean introduced herself to me and asked if I could visit her husband who was not a Christian. I assumed she was a Christian. I visited with them in their apartment and met her husband, Bill. He didn't seem to be interested in spiritual things initially, but I shared my testimony with them and explained what it meant to have a personal relationship with Jesus Christ. When I was leaving, I told them if they ever needed help with anything I would be willing to help them.

A couple weeks later I received a phone call from Bill. "When you visited us you said if we ever needed help we should let you know. Well, I contacted several friends and no one is available to help me carry a couch upstairs to our apartment. Can you help me?"

This gave me an opportunity to help Bill with the couch and we talked more about spiritual things. I challenged Bill to read the Bible, the world's best seller, and to open his heart to the Lord. When I saw Bill and Jean a few weeks later Bill commented that he had been reading the Bible and that it was an interesting book. He also said he had his heart about half way open to the Lord. What an opening to challenge him about making a full commitment to Jesus Christ.

"Bill, if I came to your apartment and you only opened the door half way for me, would I think you really wanted me to come in?" As we talked that day I again challenged Bill to open his heart "completely" to the Lord.

Late one evening, the phone rang at the parsonage. It was Bill and I could hear the excitement in his voice. "Larry, Jean and I just pulled into a parking lot and prayed to accept Jesus Christ into our lives." They had both just made life's most important decision and I celebrated with them. Their whole family began coming to church faithfully; they were growing in their faith.

Bill and Jean decided they wanted to be baptized outdoors and were praying that God would lead them to a special place for their baptism. God heard and answered their prayers and He led them to Redemption Rock in northern Massachusetts. Their baptism was one of the most memorable I have even experienced.

On a summer Sunday afternoon, about twenty-five people from our church drove a considerable distance to Redemption Rock for the baptism of Bill and Jean. It was a cloudy, overcast day. Ed, a cab driver and former alcoholic who had become a Christian, was in our group. He was carrying a video camera and he said to me, "God is going to bless this baptism and the sun is going to shine." I had no doubt about God blessing the baptism, but I had considerable doubt about the sun shining on such a cloudy day.

After walking several hundred yards on a dirt road through a wooded area we came to a little lake. Only God could have led Bill and Jean to this perfect spot for their baptism. I walked a short distance into the lake and began to preach about baptism.

Suddenly the unthinkable happened. Through a small opening in the clouds, the sun shined upon us. I couldn't believe this was actually happening. Bill and Jean walked into the lake while Ed was filming the event from the shore. After sharing a testimony of their faith in Christ, Bill and Jean were baptized. The three of us walked back to the shore and in a few minutes the sun disappeared behind the dark clouds.

The Bible describes what happened when Jesus was baptized in the Jordan River. "As soon as Jesus was baptized, He went up out of the water. At that moment heaven was opened, and He saw the Spirit of God descending like a dove and alighting on Him. And a voice from heaven said, 'This is My Son, whom I love; with Him I am well pleased'" (Matthew 3:16-17). The Son of God certainly blessed the baptism of Bill and Jean and the sun shined upon us as well. A group of us who attended the baptism got together a few weeks later and watched Ed's movie with the sun glistening on the water. Jesus said to His disciples, "O ye of little faith" (Matthew 8:26). Ed had great faith that the sun would shine at the baptism and it did.

We saw many people come to know Jesus Christ as Savior and Lord and become His faithful disciples during the years of our ministry at Green Street Baptist Church. By God's grace and blessing we saw the church grow from about eighty people to about 150-160. Jesus said, "I will build My church, and the gates of Hades [hell] will not overcome it" (Matthew 16:18). Jesus was building His church one person at a time and it was exciting to experience His invisible hand at work in the lives of many people.

God continued to give us His amazing grace, strength and courage to minister the gospel in a church where we faced much opposition and hardship. God's promises sustained us time and time again. "The One who calls you is faithful and He will do it" (I Thessalonians 5:24). God was the One who called us and as we trusted in Him He worked through us in spite of our weakness, limitations, and the challenges we faced.

The Lord was our strength as He promised in Psalm 27:1, "The Lord is my light and my salvation–whom shall I fear? The Lord is the stronghold of my life–of whom shall I be afraid?" He gave us courage to do the ministry He called us to do for His glory. God gave courage to Joshua and He gave us courage as well. "Have not I commanded you? Be strong and courageous. Do not be terrified; do not be discouraged, for the Lord your God will be with you wherever you go" (Joshua 1:9).

## Man's Call For My Resignation

Although we were seeing God do many wonderful things in the lives of people, the opposition increased to the message I preached and the ministry I was doing. Tensions increased, not only against me as the pastor, but against those in the church who wanted a Christ-centered, Bible-based, evangelical ministry. By the end of my third year, the church was divided. There were those who wanted an evangelical ministry and those who didn't. Doing things man's way instead of God's way and following traditions instead of the Word of God were the root causes of many problems we faced in the congregation. I feared for the future of the church if the people refused to follow the Lord and His Holy Word.

Many of the people were like the Israelites when Ezekiel the prophet was sent by God to minister to them. God said to Ezekiel, "Son of man, stand up on your feet and I will speak to you. As He spoke, the Spirit came into me and raised me to my feet, and I heard Him speaking to me. He said, 'Son of man, I am sending you to the Israelites, to a rebellious nation that has rebelled against Me; they and their fathers have been in revolt against Me to this very day. The people to whom I am sending you are obstinate and stubborn'" (Ezekiel 2:1-4).

Ezekiel was called to proclaim God's Word to the people whether they listened to what God said or not. God told Ezekiel not to be afraid of them or of their words saying, "You must speak My words to them, whether they listen or fail to listen, for they are rebellious" (Ezekiel 2:7). With all my heart I wanted to be faithful to the Lord and preach the Word of God as He guided me by the Holy Spirit. David said, "The Spirit of the Lord spoke through me; His Word was on my tongue" (II Samuel 23:2).

We desperately needed a spiritual revival in the church. God was calling the church to repent and return to Him. Jesus said,

"But unless you repent, you too will all perish" (Luke 13:5). God called to His people through Jeremiah the prophet saying, "Return, faithless people; I will cure you of backsliding" (Jeremiah 3:22).

One Sunday morning in January 1976, I was preaching a message at the church and the Holy Spirit came upon me in mighty power. I believe He moved me to say to the congregation, "Unless you repent and turn to the Lord, the day will come when the doors of this church will be closed." It was a piercing statement and I was shocked by it as much as anyone in the congregation.

The following Saturday night I received a telephone call from the man who was the chairman of the pulpit committee when I was called to the church nearly three years prior. He previously told me, at the time of my call to the church, that he was not in favor of me being the pastor, but the pulpit committee wanted me to be voted on by the congregation. In his brief telephone call he said, "I want your resignation tomorrow morning or I will do whatever is necessary to have you removed in the next sixty days."

God gave me grace and calmness and I said, "What's the problem?" He replied, "You know what the problem is. You threw down the gauntlet last Sunday." I said, "I'm sorry you are so upset, but I don't think God wants me to resign. If God wanted me to resign, I would give my resignation to the church, not to you." He responded by saying something like, "Well, you can do whatever you want, but I will be having a meeting with the trustees tomorrow morning after church and we will call for a congregational meeting in two weeks to remove you if you won't resign."

As I prayed for God's guidance and courage to face this challenge, He did not lead me to resign. With every fiber of my human flesh I wanted to resign and be gone from the church, but I had to obey God and do His will. God called me to this church and I wasn't going to resign until God made that clear to me.

The next morning I prayed that God would fill me with His love as I faced this tremendous challenge in my ministry and God heard and answered my prayer. Romans 5:5 says, "God has poured out His love into our hearts by the Holy Spirit, whom He has given us." Even though I would be meeting with the trustees after the worship service and they would be considering calling a congregational meeting to have me removed, I looked into the eyes of the congregation, including the trustees, and felt love in my heart for them.

At the trustees meeting I was again asked to resign, but I refused. I told them I didn't think God wanted me to resign. They decided to call for a congregational meeting two weeks later and let the congregation decide whether I should go or stay as the pastor of the church.

On Sunday afternoon, January 25, 1976, a long congregational meeting was held in the church fellowship hall. Before I walked down the hill from the parsonage to the church, I asked the Lord to give me a verse of scripture. I needed encouragement to face the possibility that I could be voted out of the church and not have anywhere to go with my family. I knew God would provide for our needs regardless of what the congregation decided, but I was still very concerned. God led me to Psalm 21:2. "Thou hast given him his heart's desire, and hast not withheld the request of his lips." My greatest desire was to do God's will regardless of the cost or the consequences.

For over two hours, members of the church spoke either in favor of having me resign or that I should stay and continue my ministry as the pastor of the church. In addition to the theological differences of what many of the people believed and what I was preaching from the Bible, there were two issues I remember being brought up against me.

One member said I wasn't interested in the youth and I wouldn't go to their youth meetings. This wasn't true. I was interested in the youth, but when I tried to attend a youth meeting I was told by the youth leaders that they didn't want me to attend. I was also accused of telling the congregation they shouldn't take communion unless they were born again. That accusation was accurate. Communion was for believers, not for unbelievers. Each person had to decide if they were a believer or not.

When the congregation was finished speaking, the moderator told me I had twenty minutes to speak. I told him I couldn't say what I needed to say in twenty minutes and I would take the time I needed to speak to the congregation. I began by mentioning a few things about the condition of the parsonage when we arrived, but then I decided to keep my comments positive and not negative. The invisible hand of God must have been guiding me because my human flesh wanted to respond to every accusation that was raised against me. Instead of defending myself, I trusted the Lord to defend me. Psalm 35:23 declares, "Awake, and rise to my defense! Contend for me, my God and Lord."

I had made three large posters to show to the congregation. Written in large letters across the top of the first poster, I had printed the words: "WHAT IS AN EVANGELICAL CHURCH?" I opened a church hymnbook to the back of the front cover where our Church Covenant was pasted and read the line that said, "We will strive to support an evangelical ministry among us." The covenant had been in the hymnbook for many years, probably from the days when the church was evangelical.

I explained to the congregation that this was exactly what I was striving to do, to "support an evangelical ministry." I read to them the definition of the word "evangelical" I had written out on the poster: "Of or according to the four gospels or the New Testament; of or having to do with the Protestant Churches that emphasize Christ's atonement and man's salvation by faith as the most important parts of Christianity; evangelistic."

On the second poster, I had a chart of the church attendance over the past three years. They could easily see how the attendance had increased each year.

The third poster was a chart of the giving over the past three years. Giving had approximately doubled.

I then summarized my thoughts by saying something like, "I have tried to be evangelical in my ministry. That's what you say you want when you read the church covenant each month at our communion services. You can see from the charts how the church has grown in attendance and giving, so what is the problem?"

Someone quickly called for the vote. One lady had been tearing her ballot into many small pieces which she threw up into the air. As the pieces fell like snowflakes she blurted out, "I don't know how to vote." When the vote was taken I received a few more votes than the fifty percent majority needed for me to stay as the pastor. The church was deeply divided. One man said, "By September we'll have enough votes to remove you."

Man's call for my resignation was thwarted. God had a different plan for our lives and in a few weeks He would make His plan known to us. God's invisible hand was upon us and the ministry He called us to perform for His glory. The lessons He taught us — about being faithful to His Word, trusting Him to meet our needs, enduring hardship in the face of opposition, the power of prayer, and the need to surrender to His will — have been of great value to us in the ministry over the past forty years since we left that church in 1976.

"The hand of the Lord was upon me…" (Ezekiel 3:22)

## Think About It

- What has God called you to do and are you faithfully doing it?
- Can you recall some examples of times when you've had to endure hardship for the cause of Christ?
- What have you discovered about the amazing power of prayer?
- If God can speak through a donkey, what do you need to do to allow Him to speak through you?
- What are some areas of your life in which you need to ask God to help you begin trusting Him more?
- In what areas of your life are you fully surrendered to God's will regardless of the cost or the consequences?
- In what areas of your life do you need more help from the Holy Spirit to bring about lasting changes?

CHAPTER 9

# THE INVISIBLE HAND OF GOD AT WORK IN MY MINISTRY AT BETHEL BAPTIST CHURCH

*"If I rise on the wings of the dawn, if I settle on the far side of the sea, even there Your hand will guide me, Your right hand will hold me fast" (Psalm 139:9-10).*

God promises to guide His people. In Psalm 139, David could not see God's hand, but he knew he was being guided by it. It is comforting to picture God taking us by the hand and leading us to where He wants us to go. Many Christians have chosen Proverbs 3:5-6 as their life verse: "Trust in the Lord with all your heart and lean not on your own understanding; in all your ways acknowledge Him, and He will make your paths straight."

Isaiah, the prophet, spoke of God's guidance in Isaiah 58:11: "The Lord will guide you always; He will satisfy your needs in a sun-scorched land and will strengthen your frame. You will be like a well-watered garden, like a spring whose waters never fail." In the New Testament we read in Romans 8:14, "Those who are led by the Spirit of God are sons of God." I believe it is truly exciting to be led by the Spirit of God on a daily basis. Life is a great adventure when I ask God to guide me in His way to do His will for His glory.

When a person becomes a Christian, the Holy Spirit comes to dwell within that person's life. The Holy Spirit cannot be seen, but His presence can be experienced. Jesus promised His followers the presence and power of the Holy Spirit. Jesus said, "And I will ask the Father, and He will give you another Counselor to be with you forever – the Spirit of truth. The world cannot accept Him, because it neither sees Him nor knows Him. But you know Him, for He lives with you and will be in you" (John 14:16-18).

161

The unseen presence of God in the person of the Holy Spirit dwells within ever believer. It was the power of the Holy Spirit working in the lives of Christ's disciples that made them fearless witnesses for Him. Jesus promised, "But you will receive power when the Holy Spirit comes on you; and you will be My witnesses in Jerusalem, and in all Judea and Samaria, and to the ends of the earth" (Acts 1:8).

In the book of Acts, the disciples of Christ were continually filled with the Holy Spirit. It was through prayer and the filling with the Holy Spirit that the disciples had boldness to preach, teach, witness, and minister for Christ. In Acts 4:31 Luke wrote: "After they prayed, the place where they were meeting was shaken. And they were all filled with the Holy Spirit and spoke the Word of God boldly." Prayer released the power of the Holy Spirit in their lives. Their boldness was simply unembarrassed freedom of speech to preach and teach about Jesus Christ.

This same unseen Spirit of God fills Christians today with God's presence, power, and boldness to minister for Him. This is the Spirit who promises to guide God's children in their daily lives and ministries. As Christians, we must submit ourselves to God and ask the Holy Spirit to fill us and guide us as to where He wants us to go and what He wants us to do.

### Tensions Increased

After the congregational meeting at Green Street Baptist Church in Melrose, Massachusetts, on January 25, 1976, tensions continued to increase in the church as well as in our lives. People were wondering what would happen next. Would I resign, or would I remain as the pastor of the church? If I stayed, how would I be able to minister in a congregation that was so divided by theological differences? Would those who opposed me call for another congregational meeting in September or even sooner? Would they be able to rally enough votes to remove me if they held another meeting?

This was an especially intense time for my wife. There were times when she would get very anxious when the telephone rang.

She dreaded answering it for fear that it would be someone calling to be critical about something we had said or done.

Our son Nathan was only three years old at the time, so the tension in the church didn't affect him like it affected us as his parents. What would it be like for him if we stayed in a church where nearly half of the people did not want his father to be the pastor? How would he be treated in the church nursery, Sunday school classes, or at church activities? These were genuine concerns for us as parents, especially if we stayed longer term.

## God Sent Encouragement

How did God sustain us during these difficult times? Sharon and I often turned to God and prayed together and asked for the Lord's help and comfort. His Word became so vital to our survival and we read it constantly. God also surrounded us with wonderful Christian friends in the church who helped carry our heavy burdens and prayed with us and for us. Galatians 6:2 exhorts us to "bear one another's burdens" and that is what many Christians did for us.

Our Thursday morning prayer group and Saturday morning men's Bible study and fellowship time were especially helpful to me. Some of our closest friends took us out to eat and encouraged us to be faithful to the Lord. Sometimes I called my prayer partner and closest friend, Scott Weldon, and he was always there for me and listened to my breaking heart and prayed with me and shared valuable insights with me. Scott would also call me, and it seemed like he always knew when to call, especially when I was having an exceptionally depressing day. There were also several women in the church who reached out to Sharon and encouraged her.

God sent a seminary friend and his wife, Paul and Nancy, to our parsonage one day when I was perhaps at my lowest point in my ministry at Green Street Baptist Church. They had no idea of the struggles we were going through, but God knew and He cared enough to send them to me that day. Sharon was not home when Paul and Nancy stopped by. Their visit reminded me of II Corinthians 7:6, where the apostle Paul wrote about a man named Titus: "But God, who comforts the downcast, comforted us by the coming of Titus..." When the apostle Paul and his companions were "harassed at every turn-conflicts on the outside, fears within" (II Corinthians 7:5), God sent Titus to comfort them.

God has amazing ways of comforting, encouraging, and sustaining His servants as they seek to serve Him. Without God's Word, God's Spirit and God's people at work in our lives we could never have survived the ministry He called us to do for His glory. His invisible hand was upon us even though we could not see it. Psalm 55:22 instructs us to "cast your cares on the Lord and He will sustain you," and that is exactly what we did. We needed God's guidance, wisdom, and courage. *What should we do? Should I resign? If I resigned, where would we go?* It's certainly risky to not have a roof over your head and not have a source of income, especially when you have a family who are depending on you to provide for them. If I stayed, could I trust God to give me the grace and strength to minister to people who did not want me to be their pastor?

This was a time when Sharon and I needed to seek God with all our hearts and to trust Him completely. His Word sustained us and His promises became very real to us in this time of trouble. "Call upon Me in the day of trouble; I will deliver you, and you will honor Me" (Psalm 50:15). "Trust in Him at all times, O people; pour out your hearts to Him, for God is our refuge" (Psalm 62:8). God became a refuge or hiding place for us during difficult times. "I can do everything through Him who gives me strength" (Philippians 4:13). What amazing promises God gives to His children. If we would only believe them and live them out each day we would be able to experience the victory He promises.

## Our Faith Was Tested

Our faith was being tested. Would we continue to hold on to God and His Word even if our circumstances became worse? It was difficult to be joyful in a divided church with continual opposition, but the Lord tells us to be joyful in trials. "Consider it pure joy, my brothers, whenever you face trials of many kinds, because you know that the testing of your faith develops perseverance. Perseverance must finish its work so that you may be mature and complete, not lacking anything. If any of you lacks wisdom, he should ask God, who gives generously to all without finding fault, and it will be given to him" (James 1:2-5). Only God could give us the perseverance and wisdom we needed to continue in this ministry.

I knew Sharon and I were young and had much to learn about the ministry. God allowed us to face many trials in our first pastorate. I didn't want to be bitter; I wanted to be better. I was discovering that when I faced trials, tribulations, and temptations, I had a choice as to how I would respond. Would I be bitter or better?

I didn't want to quit until I was certain God wanted me to quit. Pan Fraser wrote the poem "Don't Quit."

### "Don't Quit"

When things go wrong as they sometimes will,
When the road you're trudging seems all up hill,
When the funds are low and the debts are high
And you want to smile, but you have to sigh,
When care is pressing you down a bit,
Rest, if you must, but don't you quit.

Life is strange with its twists and turns,
As every one of us sometimes learns,
And many a failure turns about
When he might have won had he stuck it out;
Don't give up though the pace seems slow-
You may succeed with another blow.

Success is failure turned inside out-
The silver tint of the clouds of doubt,
And you never can tell how close you are,
It may be near when it seems so far;
So stick to the fight when you're hardest hit-
It's when things seem worst that you must not quit.[31]

---

[31]www. Poemhunter.com

We determined, by God's grace and strength, that we would stand firm and continue to serve the Lord regardless of what was happening in our lives or in the church. The apostle Paul, under divine inspiration, wrote these words to the Christians at the church in Corinth: "Therefore, my dear brothers, stand firm. Let nothing move you. Always give yourselves fully to the work of the Lord, because you know that your labor in the Lord is not in vain. Be on your guard; stand firm in the faith; be men of courage; be strong. Do everything in love" (I Corinthians 15:58; 16:13-14).

We discovered God's grace was sufficient for all things we faced as we committed our lives to Him and His will. It was His ministry and His will that was most important and we were committed to be faithful to the Lord wherever He called us to serve Him.

## God's Call To Bethel

Would God open another ministry for us? Would there be another church in need of a pastor? God can open and close doors that no one else can open or close. To the church in Philadelphia in Revelation 3:7, the Lord said, "To the angel of the church in Philadelphia, write: 'These are the words of Him who is holy and true, who holds the key of David. What He opens no one can shut, and what He shuts no one can open.'" Who is the angel of the church in this verse? Dr. John MacArthur, in the *MacArthur Study Bible*, says, "The word literally means 'messenger.' Although it can mean 'angel' — and does throughout the book — it cannot refer to angel here, since angels are never leaders in the church. Most likely, these messengers are the seven key elders representing each of those churches."[32] Another word for "elder" is "pastor" in the New Testament.

The Lord revealed Himself to Jacob in a dream at a place called Bethel. God said, "I will give you and your descendants the land on which you are lying. Your descendants will be like the dust of the earth, and you will spread out to the west and to the east, to the north and to the south. All peoples on earth will be blessed

---

[32] MacArthur, John, *MacArthur Study Bible* (Nashville: Word Publishing, 1997), *1993*.

through you and your offspring. I am with you and will watch over you wherever you go, and I will bring you back to this land. I will not leave you until I have done what I have promised you" (Genesis 28:13-15).

Jacob's dream encouraged and comforted him and led him to make a vow unto the Lord:

"When Jacob awoke from his sleep, he thought, 'Surely the Lord is in this place, and I was not aware of it?' He was afraid and said, 'How awesome is this place! This is none other than the house of God; this is the gate of heaven.' Early the next morning, Jacob took the stone that he had placed under his head and set it up as a pillar and poured oil on top of it. He called that place Bethel, though the city used to be called Luz. Then, Jacob vowed a vow, saying, 'If God will be with me and will watch over me on this journey I am taking and will give me food to eat and clothes to wear so that I return safely to my father's house, then the Lord will be my God and this stone that I have set up as a pillar will be God's house, and of all that You give me, I will give You a tenth'" (Genesis 28:16-22).

Jacob's encounter with the Lord at Bethel impacted his life so greatly that he was willing to tithe, or give a tenth back to God, of all that the Lord had given him. God had not commanded Jacob to tithe, but he voluntarily offered to do so out of gratitude because of God's revelation of Himself to him.

Bethel means, "the house of God." God would soon be leading us to a church called Bethel Baptist Church in Getzville, New York. How did the invisible hand of God work to lead us to Bethel? How did we know that God was calling us to a new ministry?

Pastor Nevin Korb, the pastor of my home church, Forest Baptist Church in Forest, Pennsylvania, had retired and became the interim pastor of Bethel Baptist Church. He had attended my ordination service at Green Street Baptist Church in Melrose, Massachusetts, and was aware of the theological differences and tensions we were experiencing in our ministry there. He told my parents that he could picture me as the pastor of Bethel Baptist Church, and if I were interested in considering another ministry, I should send a resume to the church.

We experienced the invisible hand of God at work when we first found out about this church. God guides His people in many different ways. Sometimes, His guidance comes through the Scriptures, or the still small voice of the Holy Spirit, or though His people, or through circumstances that He orchestrates. This time God worked through an unusual circumstance and His divine timing left us speechless.

## An Unusual Circumstance

Between Christmas and New Year's Day 1975, my parents came from Pennsylvania to Massachusetts to visit us. We were sitting in our living room at the parsonage when my parents told us about Bethel Baptist Church in Getzville, which is near Buffalo, New York. Sharon and I mentioned to my parents that if God called us to the Buffalo area we might be able to see our friends, Lee and Cathy Wood, who had moved to Buffalo just a few months prior. They had been attending our church in Melrose and we missed their friendship. I said, rather kiddingly, "Maybe they would even attend Bethel Baptist Church if God called us to that church."

We had received a Christmas card from Lee and Cathy and they wrote in the card that because of Lee's work schedule they would not be able to come back to the Melrose area over the Christmas holidays. As we were talking about Bethel Baptist Church and Lee and Cathy Wood, the doorbell and the phone rang at the same time. I went to answer the phone and Sharon went to open the front door. There was nothing significant about the phone call, but there was something very significant about who was at the door. Sharon and I were shocked. There stood Lee and Cathy at the door! What happened next had to be the invisible hand of God at work.

The first words out of Lee's mouth were, "We've come to get you to be the pastor of the church we've been attending in Buffalo." Knowing there are hundreds of churches in the Buffalo area, I said to Lee, "Surely you're not attending Bethel Baptist Church in Getzville, are you?" He responded, "Yes! how did you know?" Was this just an amazing coincidence or was it divine guidance and an example of God's perfect timing? To us this was far more than a coincidence. Only God could have orchestrated a scenario like this. Psalm 18:30 declares, "As for God, His way is perfect; the Word of the Lord is flawless. He is a shield for all who take refuge in Him."

Was God calling us to Bethel Baptist Church? We didn't know for certain, but after Lee and Cathy's unexpected visit, we knew we had to find out. I quickly submitted my resume.

In Acts 16:6-10, the apostle Paul was faced with an unusual circumstance: "Paul and his companions travelled throughout the region of Phrygia and Galatia, having been kept by the Holy Spirit from preaching the Word in the province of Asia."

Preaching in Asia was Plan A for Paul, but for some unknown reason the Holy Spirit would not let him go into Asia. If God closed that door, what was Plan B? "When they came to the border of Mysia, they tried to enter Bithynia, but the Spirit of Jesus would not allow them to." God again closed the door on Plan B, and they were unable to preach the Gospel in Bithynia. We might assume that Paul and his companions may have been quite confused about God's will. They may have been discouraged and thought, "Lord, we want to follow You wherever You lead us. We thought You were leading us to preach in Asia, but You closed that door. Then we thought You were leading us to preach in Bithynia, but You closed that door as well. Lord, we seem to be missing out on Your will, so please show us where You want us to preach."

How did God make His will known to Paul and his companions in this situation? Acts 16:8-10 gives the answer. "So they passed by Mysia and went down to Troas. During the night, Paul had a vision of a man of Macedonia standing and begging him, 'Come over to Macedonia and help us.' After Paul had seen the vision, we got ready at once to leave for Macedonia, concluding that God had called us to preach the gospel to them." In this particular situation God used a vision to communicate His will to Paul and his missionary companions.

We sent a resume to Bethel Baptist Church in early January of 1976. We didn't receive any response from the church and it had been two months since I sent my resume. We began to think that maybe God wasn't calling us to that church.

Meanwhile, tensions at Green Street Baptist Church had escalated since the January congregational meeting. It was extremely difficult to work with any number of the church leaders who strongly opposed my preaching and other things I tried to do in the ministry.

The church organist and I had many conflicts and it came to a point where I didn't think I could possibly go on much longer. I cried out to God in prayer, "Lord, I don't think I can go on beyond March 14th. Please, either bring a mighty revival, or let the organist resign." If God would do one of these two things, I thought I may be able to have enough grace and strength to continue in the ministry there.

God's plan is always best. Neither of the two things I prayed for came to pass, but God had a surprise in store. He was about to open a new ministry for us.

## A Surprise Visit

Sunday, March 7th was Girl Scout Sunday at our church. A Girl Scout troop held their weekly meetings in our facility, and one Sunday each year they invited their families to attend our morning worship service. It was a great Sunday. Our attendance that Sunday was probably 200 or more. I was very excited to preach the Word of God at the service. With many new people in attendance, I was thrilled to try to lead them to a personal relationship with Jesus Christ, if they didn't know Him as their Savior and Lord already.

After the worship service, I went to the back of the sanctuary to greet people as they were leaving. A man and woman that I had never seen before shook hands with me. I said to them, "Are you parents of one of the Girl Scouts?" They replied, "No, we're from Buffalo, New York, and just visiting today." I greeted another unfamiliar couple and I asked them, "Are you parents of one of the Girl Scouts?" They answered, "No, we're just visiting today. We live in Buffalo."

After greeting more people, the last man and woman to leave the sanctuary approached me. They introduced themselves, and the man said, "There are six of us here today who are part of a pulpit committee from Bethel Baptist Church in Getzville, New York. We'd like to take you and your wife out to dinner and talk with you."

I'm glad I had no advance notice that they were coming to our church that Sunday or I probably would have been extremely nervous. Now I made the connection and realized the other two couples I met who were from Buffalo were part of the pulpit committee as well. Since my wife's parents were visiting with us, we didn't go out to eat with the pulpit committee, but we were able to spend several hours with them later in the afternoon. The more we talked with the pulpit committee the more convinced we were that God had brought us together.

The pulpit committee invited us to visit their church. They wanted me to preach in their worship services and have us meet the congregation. They felt comfortable with us and we felt comfortable with them.

In God's perfect timing, which often amazes me, we had already been planning a week of vacation for the last week of March. We were planning to drive to Pennsylvania to visit our families. We now planned to spend the weekend in Getzville at their church and still have several days with our families, sensing clearly the invisible hand of God at work in bringing us together with the pulpit committee. Psalm 109:27 declares, "Let them know that it is Your hand, that You, O Lord, have done it." It was almost like the Lord took us by the hand and said, "Follow me and I will show you where I want you to serve Me over the next number of years." We were filled with overflowing joy and excitement as we trusted the Lord to lead us on a new adventure in serving Him.

## A Wonderful Church Family

The congregation at Bethel Baptist Church in Getzville, New York, a suburb of Buffalo, greeted us warmly when we arrived for the candidacy weekend. We could sense the love of Christ in the lives of the people. Jesus said, "A new commandment I give you:

Love one another. As I have loved you, so you must love one another" (John 13:34-35). The people had a genuine love for Jesus Christ and for one another. We also experienced their love for us as we got to know them in those few days.

One man from the congregation expressed his willingness to help us in a very practical way. I was embarrassed about the condition of our car. I had been in an accident a few weeks before and our car was so badly damaged in the front and the back that it looked more like an accordion than a drivable automobile.

A man named Ralph saw our car in the church parking lot and said, "Pastor, if God calls you to our church, I'd be willing to pound out some of those dents for you." I thanked Ralph for his generous offer and told him we had another car ordered and would be getting it in the near future.

We soon found out this congregation was hurting and needed encouragement. We were told that the previous pastor had been involved in moral failure, left the church, and a large number of people followed him and tried to start another church nearby. That church never succeeded and some of the people who left came back to Bethel in the coming months and years. God's Word says, "There should be no division in the body, but that its parts should have equal concern for each other. If one part suffers, every part suffers with it; if one part is honored, every part rejoices with it" (I Corinthians 12:25-26). The church was suffering because there had been a division in the body of believers.

On the Saturday night of our weekend visit to Bethel the church fellowship committee planned a dinner in the fellowship hall. It was to be an informal time so the congregation could get to know us and we could get to know them. I was asked to speak to the congregation after the dinner.

I believed the people needed some humor. The Bible says, "A cheerful heart is good medicine, but a crushed spirit dries up the bones" (Proverbs 17:22). I asked if I could test their Bible knowledge. "Does anyone know when the first baseball game took place in the Bible?" I can't remember if anyone responded to my question. I said, "The first baseball game in the Bible is recorded in Genesis 1:1. The Bible says, "In the big inning God created the heavens and the earth." Then I asked, "Does anyone know what happened in that game?" I explained, "Eve stole first; Adam stole second, and the Lord threw them both out. Then they raised Cain as they were able."

As the people were increasing their Bible knowledge I asked, "Who was the best tennis player in the Bible? It was probably Joseph because he served in Pharaoh's court." I had several more Bible questions for them. They laughed, but not heartily.

Later, after I had been their pastor for a year, I shared the same jokes with them again. This time the laughter came easily. Sharon and I believed that was a sign that God was bringing healing to their hurting hearts. "The Lord is close to the brokenhearted" (Psalm 34:18).

The candidacy weekend was a very positive experience for us as a couple and for the church as well. Now we all needed to pray and seek God's will for this important decision. Was God leading us to this church? We trusted in His divine guidance: "I will instruct you and teach you in the way you should go; I will counsel you and watch over you" (Psalm 32:8).

A few days after the candidacy weekend, the congregation voted to accept me as their pastor. Sharon and I believed God was leading us to accept their invitation as God's invitation. Like the apostle Paul in Acts 16:10, we "concluded that God had called us to preach the gospel to them." We were thrilled as we sensed the invisible hand of God leading us from Melrose, Massachusetts to Getzville, New York.

Within a few days, we returned to Melrose and I resigned from Green Street Baptist Church the following Sunday. When I announced my resignation, a lady in the congregation clapped. I never found out if she clapped because she was happy for us and our new future, or if she was just happy that we were leaving.

Two weeks later, we moved to Getzville to begin our new ministry. We had spent three and a half very challenging, difficult, and yet rewarding years at Green Street Baptist Church. We developed lasting friendships in those few years and we will always cherish those relationships. God taught us many valuable lessons and He was always faithful to keep His promises. Joshua said to the children of Israel, "You know with all your heart and soul that not one of all the good promises the Lord your God gave you has failed. Every promise has been fulfilled; not one has failed" (Joshua 23:14).

We soon discovered at Bethel that the Lord had led us to a wonderful church family. The congregation was united theologically and we felt loved and appreciated by the people whom God called us to serve. After the division and opposition we experienced in our first pastoral ministry, God was bringing healing and renewal to our spirits. The invisible hand of God was upon us, and, like David, we could say, "You give me Your shield of victory, and Your right hand sustains me" (Psalm 18:35). God had sustained us in the past and He would sustain us in the future.

In spite of our weaknesses, we knew God was with us. Missionary Hudson Taylor said, "All God's giants have been weak men, who did great things for God because they reckoned on His being with them."[33] We certainly didn't consider ourselves to be giants. We simply wanted to love and obey God and bring glory to Him.

I like to think of Bethel Baptist Church as our honeymoon church. The dictionary defines a honeymoon as "the early harmonious period of a relationship." What a joy it was to be in a harmonious church. I am not exaggerating when I say that in seven and a half years of our ministry at Bethel, I can only remember three incidents when someone got angry in a church meeting. We sensed the presence and power of God at work in the congregation and it seemed like the honeymoon never ended during our years at Bethel.

The people in the congregation invited us into their homes for meals and times of fellowship. An older couple, Bill and Esther, became like grandparents to our young children. Another couple, Harold and Shirley, took Sharon and me out to dinner and to a Christian concert at the Buffalo Christian Center about six times each year. This same couple invited us to share their cottage on the St. Lawrence River each summer. We enjoyed many memorable vacations there and even took other members of our family and friends with us on occasion. I have fond memories of

---

[33] Blackaby, Henry and Tom, *The Man God Uses* (Nashville: Broadman and Holman Publishers, 1999,), 111.

taking our two boys, Nathan and Evan, along with some of their friends on fishing trips on the St. Lawrence River in Cape Vincent, New York.

The Bible says, "Dear friends, let us love one another, for love comes from God. Everyone who loves has been born of God and knows God. Whoever does not love does not know God, because God is love" (I John 4:7-8). The people at Bethel were a wonderful church family. They loved God and they loved one another. My wife and I and our four young children were privileged to be recipients of their love, hospitality, and kindness.

## An Expanding Witness For Christ

When we went to Bethel in April 1976, there were about eighty people in the congregation. God began drawing people to Himself and to the church, the body of Christ. As the Word of God was preached from the pulpit and taught in Bible classes for all ages, the church began to grow. People were inviting their neighbors and friends. People felt loved and cared for when they visited the church. People were coming to know Jesus Christ as their Savior and Lord, and many confessed their faith and were baptized and became members of the church.

## Vacation Bible School

Vacation Bible School became a vital outreach ministry in the community. We rented a tent from a funeral home and when the weather was nice during the summer we held it outside. We were reaching children and young people for Christ. Even some eighth and ninth grade students who had such a positive experience wanted to come back the following summer.

God led a dedicated Christian couple, John and Alta, to Bethel and they were committed to serving the Lord. Alta was the director of our Vacation Bible School and led the program with great enthusiasm and joy. John became the chairman of the deacons and was a godly leader in the church. John and I met nearly every Thursday morning at 6:15 at his house for breakfast, fellowship, Bible study, and a time of prayer on our knees. The

Bible says, "Therefore, encourage one another and build each other up, just as in fact you are doing" (I Thessalonians 5:11). That's the kind of relationship John and I had in Christ, and the Lord blessed us as leaders in His church and our friendship has continued through the years.

### A Radio Broadcast

Our church began a weekly fifteen-minute radio broadcast on WDCX in Buffalo. The gospel message was reaching out to people in western New York and southern Ontario, Canada. "The Lord announced the Word, and great was the company of those who proclaimed it" (Psalm 68:11). We wanted to reach people and share the joy of the Christian life with them. I used my Sunday morning messages for the radio broadcast. I took my message manuscript to the radio station and somehow squeezed my twenty-five to thirty minute message into a fifteen-minute time slot. I never did figure out how that was possible, but it happened week after week.

When God called me into the ministry He gave me a burning desire to win souls for Christ. Proverbs 11:30 says, "He who wins souls is wise." People are lost in sin and darkness and if they do not come to know Jesus Christ as Savior and Lord they will be separated from Him for all eternity. This thought motivated me to share the good news of the gospel with as many people as possible.

### Ministry Beyond Our Local Church

I felt called by God to do the work of an evangelist. As invitations to speak at evangelistic or revival meetings were being offered to me beginning in 1979, the deacons at Bethel believed this was a way to expand our witness for Christ and be an encouragement to other churches. The church graciously gave me four weeks each year to do this ministry. I began travelling to churches in the United States and Canada to preach as God opened the doors for this new ministry. People were coming to Christ. Others were revived and I felt fulfilled in my calling to "do the work of an evangelist" as the apostle Paul instructed young pastor, Timothy in (II Timothy 4:5).

Bethel continued to grow and be blessed even as the church sent their pastor out to other churches as an ambassador for Christ. We were discovering that whenever we bless the greater kingdom of God, we are blessed in return. Jesus said, "It is more blessed to give than to receive" (Acts 20:31).

## Additional Staff

God began to expand our witness for Christ by adding staff to our church. My first assistant pastor was a young man named Dave. Dave ministered to our youth and also gave leadership to our Christian education ministries. His wife, Dena, also participated in Dave's ministry. After a few years, Dave and Dena left and God called Marc and his wife Sylvia to Bethel. Marc was an outstanding assistant pastor and we worked very well together. We were both graduates of Houghton College and Gordon-Conwell Theological Seminary, so we had much in common. God continued to expand our witness for Christ and we were thrilled to see people coming to Him and becoming part of His church at Bethel. Changed lives for the glory of God was what our ministry was all about.

## Changed Lives

Jesus changes lives. When Jesus began His public ministry, He "went into Galilee proclaiming the good news of God. 'The time has come,' He said. 'The kingdom of God is near. Repent and believe the good news'" (Mark 1:14-15). The two main points in Christ's message were to repent and believe. To repent means to have a change of mind that leads to a change of heart and behavior. It involves turning away from sin, (anything that displeases God), and turning to God by faith. When Jesus called people to believe, He wanted them to believe that He was the Christ, the Messiah, the sinless Savior and Lord who died on the cross to pay the penalty for their sins and was raised from the dead so they could be forgiven of their sins and be fully accepted by God. When people believed the good news of the gospel, their lives were eternally changed and they became children of God. Jesus said, "To all who received Him, to those who believed in His name, He gave the right to become children of God" (John 1:12).

## Terry And Faith

Terry and Faith became true followers of Jesus Christ and their lives were changed. They had become Christians before they came to Bethel. They wanted to serve the Lord and use their spiritual gifts and abilities for His glory. God began to use them in our youth ministry.

When I talked with Terry I sensed restlessness in his life like the troubled waves of the sea. He wondered if God was calling him into the ministry. If that were true, he had a great problem to deal with regarding his father. Terry worked with his father in his income tax and insurance business. His father wanted Terry to take over the business someday. Terry's father Ed was not a Christian at the time, and Terry was concerned that if God was calling him into the ministry his father would not understand.

Terry struggled with his decision, but the time came when he believed God was in fact calling him into the ministry and he needed to tell his father. When he broke the news, his father was upset with him and tried to persuade him to change his mind. Terry believed he had to obey God, go to seminary and prepare for the ministry.

Terry and his family left Bethel Baptist Church and his father's lucrative business and went to Grace Seminary in Winona Lake, Indiana. For several years, his father was very disappointed with Terry. He didn't want him to be so far away from him and his family in Buffalo. He wouldn't visit Terry, his wife Faith, or his grandchildren. They felt the intense pain of Terry's father's disappointment, but there came a time when they were reconciled and spent time together.

Terry's father rarely went to church or showed any interest in spiritual things. His wife, who was a Christian, invited Ed to a special Christmas service at the Metropolitan Chapel in Buffalo. Ed heard the gospel that night and realized how much God loved him and that he needed a Savior to forgive him of his sins. Before the service ended Ed prayed and invited Jesus Christ to come into his life as his Savior and Lord.

The invisible hand of God was at work in Ed's life, but he had no idea how merciful God had been to him. Ed only lived a few more days. He died while still in bed after a night's sleep, on December twenty-fourth. He had a massive heart attack and never recovered. He was fifty-four years old.

When I think of Terry and Faith, my faith is strengthened. Not only was Terry's wife's name Faith, but Terry's first church as a new pastor was called Faith Baptist Church, located in North Manchester, Indiana. As a couple they had great faith. The Bible says, "And without faith, it is impossible to please God, because anyone who comes to Him must believe that He exists and that He rewards those who earnestly seek Him" (Hebrews 11:6).

When Terry and Faith needed to replace their car, they prayed and asked God to supply their need. Someone totally unaware of their need gave them a check for $7,000 and specified that the money was for another car. On another occasion they prayed and believed God would meet their need for furniture, and He did. Through the years they prayed and trusted God to meet their needs and the Lord always provided for them in amazing ways. Things don't always happen in unusual and miraculous ways when God's people pray, but God rewards those who exercise genuine faith in Him and earnestly seek Him.

Faith Baptist Church was a church plant of about eighty to one hundred people. After the Lord provided the beautiful church property, the church family bought a double-wide to be used as their first building for worship. As people were becoming Christians and joining Faith Baptist Church the congregation outgrew their facility. Seven years later the Lord moved mightily and provided a beautiful new worship center, gym, and office space for the growing church.

The story of how God provided for this congregation is truly amazing. The church had a building fund and after the congregation had raised $30,000 to $40,000 the invisible hand of God began to work in unusual ways. On three separate occasions Terry received anonymous cashier's checks under the door of his office at the church. The checks were for $10,000, $15,000, and $20,000.

A lady sold a home in Florida and gave the proceeds of $86,000 to the building fund. A farmer sold a herd of cattle and gave the money to the church. (I think the farmer recognized that those cattle were not really his, but the Lord's since He owns "the cattle on a thousand hills" as Psalm 50:10 states clearly.)

Terry received an anonymous letter from "friends of Faith Baptist" who had heard what God was doing in Terry's congregation. The letter stated: "If you can raise up to $30,000 in the next six months, we will match that amount." The anonymous givers simply included an address with a post office box number to respond to. Within six weeks the congregation had raised over $36,000 and when they wrote back to share the joyous news, the anonymous givers sent the church a bank check to match the entire amount.

The church also received a gift for the building project for $100,000 from a man who the pastor was not sure was a Christian. The new facility was built totally debt free. God honored the faith of His people and kept His promise in Philippians 4:19 to "supply all your needs."

When the temple was being built, King David gave generously and so did the leaders. Then the people gave generously and willingly. They were, no doubt, inspired by the generosity of their leaders. David offered a prayer of thanks to God and in his prayer he said, "But who am I, and who are my people, that we should be able to give as generously as this? Everything comes from You, and we have given You only what comes from Your hand" (I Chronicles 29:14). As Christians we are only stewards of God's resources and He wants us to use His resources as He directs us to use them for His glory and the furtherance of the gospel around the world.

God did amazing miracles in Faith Baptist Church when the people trusted Him to provide for their needs and obeyed Him in giving what He put on their hearts to give. God's invisible hand was at work in the hearts of His people in North Manchester, Indiana, and He received great praise for what was accomplished in His church.

## Wanda

Wanda was a college student in North Manchester, Indiana. I met her when I was speaking at Faith Baptist Church for evangelistic meetings. The church had a dinner one night that was held in a large room at a local bank. After the dinner I preached the gospel and invited people to open their hearts to Jesus Christ and receive Him as their Savior and Lord, if they had never done so before. Wanda sat at the back of the room, tipped her chair back against the wall, and crossed her arms in front of her. The look on her face indicated she was not interested in anything I had to say. I thought perhaps God was speaking to her and she was resisting Him.

When I was finished speaking, Wanda left the room. While I was greeting people a man came to me and said Wanda was at his house crying. Wanda rented a room from this man and his wife while she was attending college. The man asked if I could come to his house and talk to Wanda.

When I arrived, Wanda was crying uncontrollably. Finally she calmed down enough so we could talk. When I asked her why she was crying she began to pour out her heart in anger and bitterness. She was mad at God because both of her parents had died at an early age, when she was a young girl. I listened to her for probably an hour or more, and then began to share with her how much God loved her, and that Jesus died on the cross for her sins. I tried to comfort her and explain how God could help her with her struggles and forgive her of her anger and bitterness, and come into her life.

Before the evening ended, Wanda prayed and turned her life over to Jesus Christ. The invisible hand of God had touched her and brought her into the family of God. Wanda's conversion to Christ reminds me of Acts 11:21 where the Bible says, "And the hand of the Lord was with them; and a great number believed, and turned unto the Lord." God's hand was not visible, but He was at work in drawing Wanda to His Son, Jesus Christ.

Wanda then told me she was from the Buffalo area. "What, are you kidding me? That's where we live!" I could hardly believe it. Was this a coincidence that we were both from the same area and yet we met hundreds of miles from where we lived? Did God have a divine purpose in bringing us together that day in North Manchester, Indiana? I chose to believe that this was another example of the invisible hand of God at work.

Wanda told me she was considering transferring back to the Buffalo area and attending the Amherst Campus of the State University of New York. "Are you kidding me? That's amazing! Our church is only a mile or two from the Amherst Campus!" I told Wanda that if she went to school at the Amherst Campus we would be happy to have her visit our church, which was just a short distance from the campus on Dodge Road.

At the end of the spring semester, Wanda moved back home near Buffalo. One Sunday she decided to visit our church with her boyfriend, Douglas. She had previously taken Douglas with her to other churches. He was not yet a Christian. He asked Wanda, "Why do pastors invite people to come forward to the front of the sanctuary at the end of the services?"

I had no idea that Wanda and Douglas would visit our church that particular Sunday. My message that day was entitled, "Why Give a Public Invitation?" The exact question Douglas was struggling with was answered in the message. When I was finished preaching, I invited anyone who wanted to receive Jesus Christ as Savior and Lord to come forward and I would pray for them.

Douglas decided he needed to be forgiven of his sins and wanted Christ in his life. He came forward and Wanda came with him. After the worship service, we went into a room to pray. Douglas prayed and invited Jesus Christ into his life. Was this just another coincidence, or did God lead Wanda and Douglas to Bethel Baptist Church that Sunday? Was it just a coincidence, or did God lead me to preach on the very subject Douglas had questions about? I chose to believe that God was the One who orchestrated the events of that day. "You are the God who performs miracles; You display Your power among the peoples" (Psalm 77:14).

Near the end of our conversation, Wanda told me that she would be attending the Amherst Campus for the fall semester. She then mentioned that she would be looking for an apartment in our area. "Are you kidding me? I know exactly where you can live!" I told her one of our deacons at our church just mentioned a couple days ago that he had an apartment that was vacant, and it was only about a mile from our church. Was this just another coincidence, or was the invisible hand of God at work again?

On their first visit to our church Douglas found Jesus Christ as his Savior and Lord and Wanda found an apartment. Sometimes when we think that it's just a coincidence, it's not; it's a divine appointment from God. "Help me, O Lord, my God; save me in accordance with Your love. Let them know that it is Your hand, that You, O Lord, have done it" (Psalm 109:26-27).

We saw many people come to know Jesus Christ as their Savior and Lord during the seven and a half years we were at Bethel Baptist Church. There were numerous divine appointments that the invisible hand of God had orchestrated. We were privileged to be part of a wonderful church family. It was thrilling to see the church grow and triple in size as the congregation expanded its witness for Christ. Changed lives is what the mission of Jesus Christ is all about.

## Think About It

- Are you part of a wonderful church family? If not, would you like to be? Ask God to lead you to a church where you can grow spiritually and serve Him joyfully.
- Is your witness for Christ expanding, stagnant, or diminishing? If it's not expanding, ask God to place His invisible hand upon you and give you a new touch.
- Has your life been changed through faith in Jesus Christ? If you answered no, He wants to change your life right now. Becoming a Christian is an act of faith. If you want Jesus Christ to save you, forgive you of your sins, change your life, and give you eternal life, then open your heart to Him in prayer. Pray the following prayer sincerely and trust God to keep His promises to you.

*Dear God, thank You for leading me to this moment in my life. I believe this is a divine appointment with You, and not just a coincidence that I am praying to You. Thank You for loving me so much that You allowed Your only Son, Jesus Christ, to die on the cross to pay the penalty for my sins. Thank You for raising Him from the dead so I could have eternal life with You. I am willing to repent and turn away from sin. Please cleanse me with the precious blood of Christ. Right now, I invite You, the resurrected Lord Jesus, to come into my life. Thank You for the gift of eternal life. Help me to live my life for You and serve You for the rest of my life. Thank You for hearing my prayer. In Jesus's name, I pray. Amen.*

If you just prayed to receive Jesus Christ into your life, I would be delighted to hear from you and to celebrate your decision to follow Him. Please note the contact information on the last page of this book.

CHAPTER 10

# THE INVISIBLE HAND OF GOD AT WORK IN MY MINISTRY AT CALVARY BAPTIST CHURCH

*"I have put My words in your mouth and covered you with the shadow of My hand – I who set the heavens in place, who laid the foundations of the earth, and who say to Zion 'You are My people'" (Isaiah 51:16).*

## God's Call To Calvary

"You have done what I sent you here to do." Those words were not spoken to me audibly, but I heard them in my mind and spirit. When I stood at the podium and looked at the congregation I dearly loved for the past seven years, I was shocked to think God may be calling me to another ministry. Was I hearing the voice of the Lord? I can't fully explain it, but I experienced it. Jesus said, "My sheep listen to My voice; I know them and they follow Me" (John 10:27).

I didn't want to leave Bethel Baptist Church in Getzville, New York. Seven years didn't seem long enough. I loved the people God called me to minister to, and I felt their love for me and my family. People were coming to know Jesus Christ as their Savior and Lord. Many had been baptized, joined the church as members, and were growing as disciples of Christ.

We had two Sunday morning worship services to accommodate the people God had led to Bethel. Our attendance had tripled from the eighty people we started with seven years prior.

God had called an outstanding assistant pastor, Marc Maffucci, to come along side me and help lead the ministry at Bethel. We had a weekly radio broadcast reaching out to a large area of western New York and southern Ontario, Canada. The

185

congregation had saved $130,000 toward an expansion of our facility.

The church had been sending me out at least four times a year to preach in other churches in the United States and Canada. The ministry of encouragement to pastors, church leaders, and congregations beyond our own was producing spiritual fruit for God's glory.

If someone had asked me, "Do you want to leave Bethel Baptist Church and no longer be their pastor?" I probably would have responded, "Absolutely not. God is doing amazing things in this church and I have no desire whatsoever to leave."

One day during the winter of 1983 I was reading in II Timothy chapter four. When I came to verse six, I read these words: "For I am already being poured out like a drink offering, and the time has come for my departure." I knew those words were written about the apostle Paul's approaching death, but I was troubled in my spirit by the phrase, "The time has come for my departure." It was almost like that phrase had been written in bold print. It caught my attention.

I questioned God, "Has the time for my departure come?" I began to experience a restlessness that drove me to prayer. "Lord, are You preparing me for a new ministry? If You want me to leave here, I am willing to obey and follow You. Please make Your will clear to me." I didn't really want to leave Bethel, but if God was calling me, I had to go. "Thy will be done."

During the summer of 1982, I met Pastor William Jeschke at a North American Baptist Conference held in Niagara Falls, New York. He invited me to conduct evangelistic meetings in April 1983 at Calvary Baptist Church in Bethlehem, Pennsylvania where he was the senior pastor. I stayed in his home during the days when the evangelistic meetings were being held.

Pastor Jeschke and his wife Elsie made me feel welcome and I appreciated their warm hospitality. As we sat at the table to eat dinner the first night, even before we prayed for the food, Pastor Jeschke said something that startled me. "Do you think you would like to be the pastor of this church?" It seemed strange that he asked me that question since I hadn't even preached yet, or met any of the people of the congregation.

Pastor Jeschke told me he had just received a letter from a pulpit committee regarding a church in Portland, Oregon, where he had been the pastor years ago. The congregation knew he was near retirement age, and they wanted him to return and be their pastor for a few years before he retired. He told me he would probably be leaving Calvary Baptist Church and that I should think and pray about the possibility of becoming the next senior pastor at Calvary.

Was this the invisible hand of God at work leading me to Bethlehem? For years I had desired to go to Bethlehem, but I was thinking about the Bethlehem in Israel, not the one in Pennsylvania. Had God misunderstood my heart's desire and sent me to the wrong Bethlehem? No, I knew God was perfect and that He didn't make mistakes. I also knew I was imperfect and I didn't want to make a mistake if God was calling me to Bethlehem in Pennsylvania. Ironically, two years later God did bless me with the opportunity to go to Bethlehem in Israel with a group of pastors and their wives.

Was God calling me to be the senior pastor of Calvary Baptist Church? I couldn't get the thought out of my mind—not that I wanted to, necessarily. What I wanted was to do God's will. The Bible says, "Show me Your ways, O Lord, teach me Your paths; guide me in Your truth and teach me, for You are God my Savior, and my hope is in You all day long" (Psalm 25:4-5).

I began praying that God would make His will clear to me if He was calling me to Calvary Baptist Church to become their next pastor if He was calling Pastor Jeschke back to Oregon.

One evening, before the evangelistic meeting started, the chairman of the deacon board, Bill Jackson, said something to me like, "Pray about whether God would want you to be our pastor someday." Had Pastor Jeschke told Bill Jackson about his possible departure? I didn't know, but I was challenged all the more to seek God's will on this matter.

God blessed the evangelistic meetings. His invisible hand was at work in drawing people to Christ and encouraging others in the church to have a closer relationship with Him. I thoroughly enjoyed the enthusiastic choir music, and the congregation showed a genuine interest in spiritual things. They listened intently as I preached about the death, burial and resurrection of Christ and called people to respond to Christ and His call upon their lives. I felt great freedom to preach the Word of God. In fact, one night I totally lost track of time and preached for an hour and twenty minutes. When I realized how long I had preached, I thought I had surely blown away any possibility that the congregation would ever call me as their pastor.

After the service that night I met my wife's cousin, Denise Coyle, who had sat through my exceptionally long message. She was pregnant and near her due date. She commented that if I had not stopped preaching soon, she felt like she could have had the baby before the service was over.

When the evangelistic meetings had ended I drove back to Getzville, New York. I continued to wonder, "Is God calling me to a new ministry?" Was it just a coincidence that Pastor Jeschke had received an invitation to return to Portland the same week I was scheduled to speak in his church? Was God's invisible hand at work in this situation?

I liked the people I had met and many things about the ministry at Calvary, but I decided to seek God's will, not my will. Proverbs 28:26 declares, "He who trusts in himself is a fool, but he who walks in wisdom is kept safe." I didn't want to trust in myself, but in the Lord and His wisdom.

Since God had been opening doors for me to preach at evangelistic and revival meetings, I wondered if He would call me to do the work of an evangelist/revivalist full-time. One of the leaders of the North American Baptist Conference had been talking to me about the possibility of being on staff with the conference as an evangelist/revivalist.

About a month had passed after I preached at Calvary Baptist Church and since I had not heard from Pastor Jeschke or from anyone at Calvary, I decided to write a letter to the North American Baptist Conference leader. I figured it couldn't hurt to inquire about other ministry possibilities while I waited to hear from Calvary.

However, as I was writing the letter something prevented me from completing it. It was almost like an unseen hand took hold of my pen and wouldn't let me write one more sentence. Now I was discouraged. I prayed, "What do you want me to do, Lord? You've been speaking to me through the Holy Spirit, through Your Word, and through the unusual circumstances of my visit to Bethlehem, but now I can't even finish a letter that I'm trying to write. Are you closing the door to a full-time evangelistic/revival ministry at this time in my life?" I was very restless and my mind was in turmoil. When I couldn't finish the letter, I told Sharon I was going out to get a haircut.

When I returned from the barber shop Sharon said Eric Beattie from Calvary Baptist Church had called while I was at the barber shop. He said he wanted to talk to me and would call back later. Eric was the chairman of the pulpit committee at Calvary Baptist Church. What amazing timing! He called on a day when I was really discouraged and confused about my future ministry. Maybe God was calling me to Calvary Baptist Church in Bethlehem, Pennsylvania after all.

The Bible says, "There is a time for everything, and a season for every activity under heaven" (Ecclesiastes 3:1). God's timing is always perfect. Eric called again in the evening. I was anticipating his call. I couldn't wait to talk to him because I began to believe God was answering my prayer concerning His will for my future ministry. Even though it is now thirty-three years later, I can still remember the essence of our phone conversation.

Eric said, "Our pastor has resigned and we are in need of a pastor. Since you were at our church in Bethlehem recently, we thought we would talk with you and see if you would be interested in considering a new ministry as pastor of Calvary Baptist Church? We met as a pulpit committee and decided that we are looking for several things regarding our next pastor. We hope to find a pastor between the age of thirty-five and forty-two who could appeal to the younger families in our church. We also desire to have a pastor who is strong in his preaching ministry, in evangelism, and who is a leader who can make decisions."

I couldn't do anything about my age, but I did meet their requirement since I was thirty-five years old at the time. The pulpit committee would have to decide if I met the other requirements, but I could affirm that their requirements were all important things I felt strongly about in my ministry.

During our conversation there was one question I wanted to ask Eric, but I was amazed how he answered my question before I even asked it. He said, "We wondered if you would like to continue doing evangelistic meetings if you became our pastor? We already discussed this and decided, if you wanted to do that, we would recommend to the church that you be given the same amount of time each year that your present church gives you." I was so excited at what Eric had just said that I felt like jumping up and down, but I restrained myself since we were still talking on the phone. I asked Eric if I could have a week to pray about what God wanted me to do before we went any further in our discussions. He agreed and said he would call back a week later. The day Eric was to call again, I set aside as a day of prayer.

Sometimes when I have spent a number of hours in prayer, I have felt very weak physically, but not that day. When I finished praying, I felt like I could lift our two-story house off its foundation. When Eric called that night I said, "Yes, I believe God wants me to accept the pulpit committee's invitation to be a candidate for the position of senior pastor at Calvary Baptist Church."

I had the wonderful joy of returning to Calvary Baptist Church in July 1983 along with my wife, Sharon, and daughter, Amy. The congregation voted to call me as their senior pastor and I began my ministry at Calvary the first week of September.

God's invisible hand was at work as He guided us to Bethlehem. It was only eighty-five days from the day Pastor Jeschke left Calvary until I arrived with my family. It is almost unheard of for a senior pastor position to be filled that quickly, unless the position is filled by another staff pastor who is already well known by the church.

### "He Does Not Lead Me Year By Year"
Barbara G. Ryberg

He does not lead me year by year
Nor even day by day,
But step by step my path unfolds;
My Lord directs my way.

Tomorrow's plans I do not know,
I only know this minute;
But He will only say, "This is the way,
By faith now walk ye in it."
And I am glad that it is so,
Today's enough to bear;
And when tomorrow comes, His grace
Shall far exceed its care.
What need to worry then or fret?
The God who gave His Son
Holds all my moments in His hand
And gives them, one by one.[34]

At our first Sunday worship service at Calvary Baptist Church, Eric Beattie, Chairman of the pulpit committee, invited Sharon, our four children (Nathan, Amy, Evan and Lisa) and me to join him on the platform as he formally introduced us to the congregation. Eric said some kind words about us, but then he said something that puzzled me. "There is one concern we have about our new pastor; we're not sure if he is a good speller or not. When the pulpit committee interviewed him, we asked him how he would spell the word 'farm' and he said, 'EIEIO,' just like the farmer Old McDonald had spelled it." Everyone laughed and I thought to myself, *I'll not get mad, I'll just get even.*

About three months after I began the ministry at Calvary we moved into a new house that we had built. Many people from the church helped us with painting, including Eric. It was now time for me to get even. The Sunday after the painting had been completed, I thanked everyone from the pulpit who had helped us paint our new house. I mentioned that everyone did a great job painting — well, except one man, Eric Beattie. I told the congregation we were using latex paint, but instead of going upstairs to get more paint, Eric went into the bathroom downstairs and simply added a little bit of water in his paint can. I felt I needed to speak to him about thinning the paint and so I

---

[34] Zuck, Roy B., *The Speaker's Quote Book* (Grand Rapids: Kregel Publications, 1997), 182.

went to him and said, "Repaint, you thinner, and thin no more." Eric and I were now even.

## Stay True To God's Word

Calvary had a long history of being a solid, evangelical, Bible-teaching, Bible-believing church. The church's strong stand on the inspiration and inerrancy of the Bible was one of the things that attracted me to the church. Jesus said, "Man does not live on bread alone, but on every word that comes from the mouth of God" (Matthew 4:4).

When the apostle Paul gave his farewell speech to the elders of the church in Ephesus, he said, "You know that I have not hesitated to preach anything that would be helpful to you, but have taught you publically and from house to house. I have declared to both Jews and Greeks that they must turn to God in repentance and have faith in our Lord Jesus Christ. For I have not hesitated to proclaim to you the whole will of God. Now I commit you to God and to the Word of His grace, which can build you up and give you an inheritance among all those who are sanctified" (Acts 20:20-21, 32).

Paul was committed to stay true to God's Word. He knew that it was the Word of God, preached in the power of the Holy Spirit, which God used to change lives.

Many churches today have fallen away from preaching the Word of God. Pastors who feed their people psychology, sociology, book reviews, and the philosophies of men — instead of God's holy Word — will not have God's power released in their lives nor in the lives of their people.

Dr. John MacArthur, in a message entitled "When God Abandons a Nation," wrote, "I would suggest that this is not a good time for weak men to be preaching weak messages in weak churches. This is a time for bold, powerful, strong, Biblical ministry that calls people to hear the Word of God and respond. This is the only hope for any people or individual."[35] I agree with Dr. MacArthur. I have no desire to be politically correct according

---

[35] Apprising.org/...text-of-when-god-abandons-a-nation-by john-macarthur

to our culture in what I preach and teach. I want to be biblically correct and stay true to God's Holy Word as long as I live.

While I was attending a revival conference in Lancaster, Pennsylvania, several years ago, Dr. Stephen Olford, former pastor of Calvary Baptist Church in New York City, was preaching a powerful, Spirit-anointed message. He challenged the pastors and Christian leaders in the audience to preach the Word of God and take a stand to remain true to Him, even if we had to take a bullet in the heart. Dr. Olford then asked for those who would make that commitment to stand up. I rose to my feet, along with many other pastors and Christian leaders.

Pastors and other leaders in our churches must not fear man, but only God. The Bible says, "Fear of man will prove to be a snare (a trap), but whoever trusts in the Lord is kept safe" (Proverbs 29:25). In I Chronicles 12:32 we read about the men of Issachar, "who understood the times and knew what Israel should do."

The leaders of our churches must be like the men of Issachar and help the people in our congregations understand the times in which we live and help them know what to do and what is right and what is wrong. Too many pastors and Christian leaders are afraid to take a stand on the moral issues of our day, like abortion, homosexuality, gambling, immorality, alcoholism, drug addiction, and a host of other issues.

Several years ago I preached a strong, Biblically-based message on the sin of abortion. After the service, a man said to me, "Pastor, if you keep preaching messages like that, you're going to drive people right out of the church." I replied, "I disagree. In fact, I think the opposite is true. People want to hear the truth. Parents tell me they want their children and teenagers to hear the truth." It's the truth of God's word that sets people free to be all that He created them to be.

It is my firm conviction that if people don't want to hear the truth they can find another church with a watered-down gospel and a message to tickle their ears. The Bible says, "For the time will come when men will not put up with sound doctrine. Instead, to suit their own desires, they will gather around them a great number of teachers to say what their itching ears want to hear.

They will turn their ears away from the truth, and turn aside to myths" (II Timothy 4:3-4).

If homosexuality, for example, is a sin and an abomination in God's eyes, and it is, then I refuse to call it an acceptable, alternative lifestyle. Leviticus 18:22 says, "Do not lie with a man as one lies with a woman; that is detestable." The King James Version refers to this sin as an "abomination." The word "abomination" means "loathsome, detestable, or repulsive." If God calls homosexuality an "abomination," how can Christians call it anything less if we want to stay true to God's Word?

Our American culture is in a moral and spiritual freefall. We are on a dangerous, slippery slide if we do not call sin "sin." If we accept homosexuality as an acceptable, alternative lifestyle, what will our culture recognize next as acceptable? Bestiality? In the very next three verses after homosexuality is written about in the book of Leviticus, we read, "Do not have sexual relations with an animal and defile yourself with it. A woman must not present herself to an animal to have sexual relations with it; that is a perversion. Do not defile yourselves in any of these ways, because this is how the nations whom I am going to drive out before you became defiled. Even the land was defiled; so I punished it for its sin and the land vomited out its inhabitants" (Leviticus 22:23-25). Should we love homosexuals, lesbians and transgender people and try to minister God's truth to them? Absolutely. We are commanded to love everyone. God's truth can set them free just as it can set anyone free from any sin. Jesus said, "Then you will know the truth, and the truth will set you free" (John 8:32).

With the way our American culture is deteriorating it is very possible that someday pastors will be required, by federal or state law, to perform wedding ceremonies for gays and lesbians. Pastors will have to choose whether they will bow down to man's law or obey God's law.

When the apostles of Christ were commanded not to preach in the name of Jesus, they refused to obey the authorities and were put in prison. The apostles said, "We must obey God rather than men!" (Acts 5:29). I told the congregation at Calvary that I would not perform a gay or lesbian wedding, even if I had to go to jail because of my refusal to do so. I am grateful to have a congregation committed to staying true to God's Word. Our elders have developed Biblical "lifestyle expectations" on the moral issues of our day. People who desire to become members of Calvary Baptist Church must agree to these lifestyle expectations.

The Bible says, "Shout it aloud, do not hold back. Raise your voice like a trumpet. Declare to my people their rebellion and to the house of Jacob their sins" (Isaiah 58:1). This verse motivated me to take a public stand against gambling when the political leaders in the city of Bethlehem were considering having a casino in our city. I spoke out numerous times at the city, county, and state level when public hearings were held. There were times when I was afraid, but I felt I had to speak out because it was the right thing to do. I wrote a letter to several hundred pastors in the Lehigh Valley, urging them to take a stand against gambling and to bring people from their churches to speak out at the public meetings. I am sad to report that very few pastors or Christians took a public stand against the casino. Perhaps Bethlehem would not have a casino today if more Christians had taken a stand against it. I believe gambling breeds greed, and greed breeds crime and corruption.

## The Power Of Prayer

Alfred Lord Tennyson recognized the significance of prayer when he said, "More things are wrought by prayer than this world dreams of."[36]

Jesus placed a priority on prayer. He arose early in the morning to pray and have fellowship with His Father in heaven. "Very early in the morning, while it was still dark, Jesus got up, left the house, and went off to a solitary place where He prayed" (Mark 1:35). Before Jesus chose His apostles, He held an all-night prayer vigil seeking His Father's will before making an important decision. "One of those days Jesus went out to a mountainside to pray, and spent the night praying to God. When morning came, He called His disciples to Him and chose twelve of them whom He also designated apostles" (Luke 6:12-13).

---

[36] Sweeting, George, *Who Said That?* (Chicago: Moody Press, 1994), 359.

Charles Spurgeon recognized the priority of prayer in his life and ministry. He said, "He who rushes from his bed to his business without first spending time with God is as foolish as if he had not washed or dressed, and as unwise as one dashing to battle without arms or armor."[37] Spurgeon also said, "I would rather teach one man to pray than ten men to preach."[38] He knew how powerful and effective prayer was in accomplishing God's work on earth.

Pastors will find very little power or anointing from the Holy Spirit to preach the gospel unless they are men of prayer. If I am weak in prayer, I am weak in every area of my Christian life. I have tried — and failed at times — to make prayer, personal Bible study, and fellowship with God my number one priority each day.

In 1982, I attended a "Change the World Through Prayer" seminar in a suburb of Buffalo, New York. I was deeply impacted and convicted that I needed to spend more time each day in prayer. The seminar leaders spent considerable time challenging those in attendance at the seminar with the words of Matthew 26:40-41. When Jesus was facing some of the most intense and sorrowful hours in the Garden of Gethsemane, He needed the support of His disciples. "Then He returned to His disciples and found them sleeping. 'Could you men not keep watch with Me one hour?' He asked Peter. 'Watch and pray so that you will not fall into temptation.'" Many pastors, church leaders, and people in our churches are weak in prayer and are falling into temptation and sin because they do not have the power of God in their lives to resist temptation.

Martin Luther feared himself more than anyone else. He knew that he was weak, and I know that I am weak. I need the power of God in my life to live as a Christian and to do the ministry that God has called me to do for His glory. I attempt to spend between two and three hours each morning in prayer and Bible study. I know I need this time with the Lord to stay on track with Him.

Since January 1, 1979 I have attempted to memorize a new verse of scripture each day. Dawson Troutman, founder of the Navigators ministry, said, "I know of no form of intake of the

---

[37] www.firstlings.com/web-exclusives/2014/12 Spurgeon-at-years-end
[38] Prayer-coach.com/2010/10/04/ prayer-quotes-Charles-Spurgeon

Word which pays greater dividends for the time invested than Scripture memory."[39] This quote by Dawson Troutman has motivated me greatly in my desire to memorize God's Word. Having His Word in my heart has helped me in preaching, counseling, and witnessing to people. I have experienced in my ministry the great dividends of Scripture memory that Dawson Troutman wrote about. Psalm 119:11 is also an encouragement for Christians to memorize God's Word: "I have hidden Your Word in my heart that I might not sin against You." God's Word in our hearts can keep us from sin, but unconfessed sin in our hearts can keep us from God's Word.

## Accountability Partners

Every Christian needs an accountability partner in their life. Ecclesiastes 4:9-10 declares, "Two are better than one, because they have a good return for their work: If one falls down, his friend can help him up. But pity the man who falls and has no one to help him up!"

Accountability partners can ask each other pointed questions. Someone gave me a list of the following questions and I have used them for many years with my accountability partner: "Have you been with a person of the opposite sex this week in an inappropriate way? Have you been completely above reproach in all your financial dealings? Have you exposed yourself to any sexually explicit material? Have you spent time in the Scriptures and in prayer each day? Have your spent time with your family? Have you controlled your anger? Have you monitored your time in front of the TV? Have you just lied to me?" Accountability partners must be honest with one another. Abraham Lincoln once said, "No man has a good enough memory to be a successful liar."[40]

Having an accountability partner has been extremely helpful to me through the years. I need someone to continually hold me accountable in many areas of my life. When I find myself struggling with something that I have confessed to my

---

[39] Newlife.godresources.org/growing/6-memorize-gods-word
[40] Cory, Lloyd, *Quotable Quotes*, (Wheaton: Victor Books, 1987), 227

accountability partner, I know he will ask me how I am doing in that area of my life the next time we meet. Knowing that my accountability partner will be praying for me gives me great encouragement to strive, by God's power, to be the husband, father, grandfather, and servant leader He wants me to be.

## Pastors Beware

Author Joel Rosenberg, in his book, *Implosion*, wrote: "All over the U.S., pastors continue to resign from their pulpits because they are having adulterous affairs. According to *Christianity Today's Leadership Journal*, 'four in ten pastors online have visited a pornographic website, and more than one-third have done so in the past year.' After assessing the increasing prevalence of such problems among pastors, the editors of the magazine warned, 'If you think that you can't fall into sexual sin, then you're godlier than David, stronger than Samson, and wiser than Solomon.'"[41] When are we most tempted? When we are Hungry, Angry, Lonely, or Tired— H.A.L.T. We would profit greatly by remembering the helpful acronym HALT.

## Corporate Prayer

Throughout the years of my ministry I have tried to make corporate prayer a priority in the churches where I have been privileged to be a pastor. I have experienced the amazing hand of God at work as His people have humbled themselves and prayed together. God does His greatest work when His people trust in Him and call upon Him in prayer.

The release of the movie "War Room" has helped many Christians recognize the mighty power of prayer and the need to realize that we are in a spiritual battle each day of our lives against the world, the flesh and the devil. Jesus said, "The thief [Satan] comes only to steal and kill and destroy; I have come that they may have life, and have it to the full" (John 10:10).

---

[41] Rosenberg, Joel C., *Implosion*, (Carol Stream: Tyndale House Publishers, Inc.,2012), 220.

The apostle Peter also reminded Christians of the battle they are facing all over the world. In I Peter 5:8-9 he wrote, "Be self-controlled and alert. Your enemy the devil prowls around like a roaring lion looking for someone to devour. Resist him, standing firm in the faith, because you know that your brothers throughout the world are undergoing the same kind of sufferings." The devil flees when he sees the weakest saint upon his knees.

When God's people make prayer a priority in their lives and in His church, they begin to experience the invisible hand of God at work in amazing ways. Dr. Martyn Lloyd Jones, in his book, *Preachers and Preaching* wrote, "Above all — and again this I regard as most important of all — always respond to every impulse to pray…It is the work of the Holy Spirit…So never resist, never postpone it, never push it aside because you are busy. Give yourself to it, yield to it, and you will find not only that you have not been wasting time with respect to the matter with which you are dealing, but that actually it has helped you greatly in that respect."[42] Prayer is the power that moves the hand of God.

In Luke 18:1 we read: "Then Jesus told His disciples a parable to show them that they should always pray and not give up." God taught me a valuable lesson on not giving up praying for someone. When I came to Calvary Baptist Church in 1983 I met a mother one Sunday who had three children with her. I asked her if she had a husband and she said she did, but that he was not a Christian. She asked me to pray for him. Her sincere and heartfelt request touched me deeply and I put her husband's name on my prayer list and for the past 33 years I continued to pray for his salvation. I did not give up praying for him and I am so grateful to God that shortly before this man died he confessed his faith in Jesus Christ as his Savior and Lord. Unless God releases us from praying about something we must never give up. God can save or transform anyone and, as I Thessalonians 5:17 exhorts us, we must remember to "pray without ceasing".

"Set us on fire, Lord, stir us we pray-
While the world perishes we go our way-

---

[42] Jones, Martyn Lloyd, *Preachers and Preaching* (Grand Rapids: Zondervan, 1971), 170, 171.

Passionless, powerless, day after day-
Set us on fire, Lord, stir us we pray."

*Unknown*

## Church Growth

Elijah and Elisha were mighty prophets of God. God planned to take Elijah to heaven without having him die first. The Bible says, "When the Lord was about to take Elijah up to heaven in a whirlwind, Elijah and Elisha were on their way to Gilgal. Elijah said to Elisha, 'Stay here; the Lord has sent me to Bethel.' But Elisha said, 'As surely as the Lord lives and as you live, I will not leave you.' So they went down to Bethel" (II Kings 2:1-2).

Wherever Elijah went that day Elisha insisted on going with him. When they reached the Jordan River, Elijah rolled up his cloak (his outer garment) and struck the water and the river parted so they could walk across on dry land. Surely the invisible hand of God was at work in the miracles God did through Elijah during the years of his ministry.

Elijah said to Elisha, after they crossed the river, "Tell me, what can I do for you before I am taken from you? 'Let me inherit a double portion of your spirit,' Elisha replied" (II Kings 2:9). Elijah told Elisha that if he saw him when he was taken from him his request would be granted. Elisha did see Elijah depart in a chariot of fire. Elisha began to experience a double portion of God's Spirit at work in his life and ministry.

When I left Getzville, New York, in 1983 to begin my ministry in Bethlehem, Pennsylvania, I asked the Lord for a "double portion" of His Spirit to be upon me. I wanted to experience the invisible hand of God at work in the ministry at Calvary and God has more than answered my prayers.

Church growth has taken place as the pastors, church leaders, and congregation at Calvary have lifted up Jesus Christ and exalted Him in the ministry. Friendship evangelism has proven to be one of the most effective means of church growth. We see this modeled in Scripture.

Andrew brought his brother, Simon Peter, to Jesus, right after he himself started to follow Jesus. "The first thing Andrew did was to find his brother Simon and tell him, 'We have found the Messiah' (that is, the Christ). And he brought him to Jesus" (John 1:41-42).

When Jesus healed a demon-possessed man, He said to him, "'Go home to your family and tell them how much the Lord has done for you, and how He has had mercy on you.' So the man went away and began to tell in the Decapolis (ten cities) how much Jesus had done for him, and all the people were amazed" (Mark 5:19-20). When Christians share with their family and friends what Jesus has done for them, there will be those who will come to Christ and also want to be a part of a local church. The vast majority of people, when asked how they came to Christ or to the church, have responded that they came because of a relative, friend, or word of mouth. As our congregation has taken friendship evangelism seriously, we have seen continuous church growth through the years.

I have been the senior pastor at Calvary for the past thirty-three years. We came to the church in 1983 when there were about 250 people in attendance. During the next year, the church grew to 312, and then the following year to 354. I shared with the deacons that church growth studies indicate that when a congregation grows to 80% of its seating capacity the church needs to either add additional services or expand its facility. After much prayer and consideration the deacons decided to add an additional worship service on Sunday mornings. This was a wise decision.

The church continued to grow in attendance to 400, 500, 600, 700, etc. In a few more years, we added a third morning worship service. A lady in our congregation told me many years ago that she believed there would come a day when 1,000 or more people would come to Calvary. I had a hard time believing that, but she was right. When we combine the worship attendance with our children's and youth ministry attendance there are well over 1,000 people being ministered to at Calvary each Sunday morning.

## Expanding Our Facility

In 1989, we were ready to expand our facility and add additional space to accommodate the people the Lord was leading to us. The deacons prayed and discussed the expansion project and wanted to do it debt-free. I said to the deacons that there was nothing wrong with taking out a mortgage. We all have a mortgage on our homes. A number of the deacons either spoke up or shook their heads to indicate that they did not have a mortgage. I could understand some of the men in their fifties and sixties not having a mortgage after paying on it for many years, but what amazed me was that two younger deacons in their thirties said they didn't have a mortgage.

I asked the younger deacons, "What did you do with your mortgage?" They replied, "We paid it off." I was truly amazed at the invisible hand of God at work in blessing them so much at such an early age to enable them to pay off their mortgage already.

I asked the deacons if we could wait another month before we voted on whether or not we should approach our building project on a debt-free basis. I wanted to seek the Lord on this matter and also research the scriptures about the building projects in the Bible. I also read books and other literature about building without borrowing. I spoke to pastors around the country who had built churches debt-free. I was thrilled to hear their miracle stories and I began to believe that it could happen at Calvary. I wanted God to show me His will on this matter.

The Lord opened a door for me to preach evangelistic/revival meetings in a small church in Oklahoma in April 1989. When I arrived at the pastor's house he mentioned that another pastor and his wife would be joining us for dinner. He told me the pastor had recently resigned from his church because of a controversy that developed over a debt-free versus mortgage approach to a building project. I said we were facing the same issue in our church. I believed it was far more than a mere coincidence that we were discussing this subject.

Then the pastor said he had a series of financial freedom videos that I could watch while I was there. I watched a number of the biblically-based videos and became deeply convicted that the Lord wanted us at Calvary Baptist Church to trust Him to supply all our needs and not borrow the money from the bank for our building project. This was a tremendous opportunity for us as a church to take God at His Word and watch what He would do. "And my God will meet all your needs according to His glorious riches in Christ Jesus" (Philippians 4:19). The Bible says, "And God is able to make all grace abound to you, so that in all things at all times, having all that you need, you will abound in every good work" (II Corinthians 9:8).

A conviction is a state of being convinced, a firm belief, or an assurance. As a Christian prays, reads the Word of God, seeks God's will with their whole being, and fasts as they are led by God, they become convinced and have an assurance of God's will and the direction He is leading them to go.

Tony Dungy was the coach of the National Football League Superbowl Champions, the Indianapolis Colts, in Superbowl XLI. He was the first African American coach to win a Superbowl. In his book, *Uncommon*, he wrote: "One of the things I have learned along the way is having the courage to stand by my convictions — those things that I know are right, those guiding principles that I know to stick with. Sometimes that means standing out from the crowd or not being popular, but sometimes that's the only responsible place to be. And that takes real courage — to do what you think is best even when you might be ridiculed for it. Stand by your convictions. Summon the courage to be uncommon. Remember that what you do when nobody is watching matters. Hang in there. Character is revealed through adversity. Don't rationalize your way around honesty. Don't blow your own horn. Some of the most rewarding times in life are when you have to stand alone, even if you are not comfortable doing so."[43]

Dr. Charles Stanley, pastor of First Baptist Church in Atlanta Georgia, is a man I admire greatly. I had the wonderful privilege of meeting Dr. Stanley and having a twenty minute private conversation with him in 2006 when he spoke at a leadership conference at Stabler Arena in Bethlehem, Pennsylvania. He is a man of deep biblical convictions. In his book, *In Step With God*, he wrote, "Don't ever compromise your convictions. Even if you are the last person standing; remain steadfast to what God has given

---

[43] Dungy, Tony, *Uncommon* (Carol Stream: Tyndale House Publishers, Inc., 2009), 29, 31, 35.

you to do because His way is the best way."[44] Good, better, best, never let it rest, until your good is better, and your better is best.

When my preaching ministry in Oklahoma was finished, I flew back to Bethlehem. I came back to Calvary with deep convictions in my heart and mind about trusting God to meet our needs as a church and not borrowing money to meet those needs.

Although we did not end up going totally debt-free in that stage of building, we saw many miracles in paying off the debt we incurred. My personal convictions did not change through this stage of building or in the next stage, but we did not allow this to be a church-splitting issue and we continued to use our expanded facility to reach out into our community and beyond for the glory of God and His kingdom.

The Bethlehem Christian School rents our facility for their ministry to children. God has had His invisible hand upon our relationship with the school for over thirty-five years. It's a marriage that furthers the kingdom of God. The school needs the facility when the church doesn't, and the church needs the facility when the school doesn't.

There is a plaque in one of the school classrooms with these words: "Never confuse the will of the majority with the will of God." We see this truth illustrated in the story of Joshua and Caleb.

Moses sent twelve spies to search out the Promised Land. God promised the land to His people. Numbers 13:1 says: "The Lord said to Moses, 'Send some men to explore the land of Canaan, which I am giving to the Israelites.'" Even though God promised the land to His people, ten of the spies came back with a negative report about the land and the many reasons why they couldn't conquer it. Only two spies, Joshua and Caleb, came back with a positive report and believed that the land could be conquered. Caleb said, "We should go up and take possession of the land, for we can certainly do it" (Numbers 13:30). Only Joshua and Caleb, of the twelve spies, were permitted to enter the Promised Land. This story teaches us that the majority may not always be right.

Our first expansion project was completed in 1991. The congregation at Calvary gave generously and our three-year line

---

[44] Stanley, Charles, *In Step With God* (Waterville: Christian Large Print, 2010), 12.

of credit was paid in full by the due date of June 6, 1993. The Sunday before the due date we still needed over $42,000, but the Lord's invisible hand was at work. He moved the hearts of the people in our congregation to give abundantly and the offering that day was over $53,000. In addition to the funds given to the expansion project, the congregation also gave generously to the ongoing budget of the church as well.

Our second expansion project at Calvary, which was much smaller, was accomplished debt-free and completed in 1994. We relocated to our current new facility in 2011, where we have more room to reach people for Christ. We purchased twenty-nine acres for our relocation. The cost for the land, construction costs, and other expenses exceeded $14 million.

God has mightily blessed the ministry at Calvary Baptist Church, and His people have generously given to pay off the debt on our new facility. At present, the indebtedness is under $2 million, and hopefully it will not be long before the church is totally debt-free again. Churches can save thousands and thousands of dollars, even millions of dollars, by paying off debt early rather than later. It can be done. "For nothing is impossible with God" (Luke 1:37).

Missionary Hudson Taylor said, "God's work done in God's way will never lack God's supply."[45] We must continually ask, "Are we doing God's work God's way?" We must base our ministry on the Word of God and trust Him to supply all our needs as He promised. God always keeps His promises. If the promise does not come to pass, the problem is not with God.

An unknown author wrote: "Somebody said it couldn't be done, but he with a chuckle replied-maybe it couldn't, but he would be one who wouldn't say so until he had tried. So he buckled right in with a trace of a grin on his face if he worried he hid it. He started to sing as he tackled the thing that couldn't be done and he did it." When we believe God for seemingly impossible things, He sometimes surprises us and His invisible hand brings the impossible to reality.

---

[45] www.goodreads.com/quotes/190685-god-s-work-done-in-god-s-way-will...

## Missions And Outreach

Missionary Henry Martyn said, "The Spirit of Christ is the spirit of missions, and the nearer we get to Him the more intensely missionary we must become."[46]

The Great Commission that Jesus Christ gave to His disciples involved the whole church taking the whole gospel to the whole world. Jesus said, "All authority in heaven and on earth has been given to Me. Therefore, go and make disciples of all nations, baptizing them in the name of the Father, and of the Son, and of the Holy Spirit, and teaching them to obey everything I have commanded you. And surely I am with you always, to the very end of the age" (Matthew 28:18-20).

Calvary Baptist Church has had a heart for missions for many, many years. God has raised up godly leaders to lead our missions team and to promote missions in our church. We presently support thirty-four missionary couples or individuals in Cameroon, Ethiopia, Guinea, India, Japan, Hungary, Canada, Brazil, Mexico, the United States, and two restricted access countries. The church invested more than $300,000 this past year in missions giving. It has been so exciting to see how God has moved on the hearts of His people at Calvary so that their generous giving to our special Easter and Thanksgiving Missions Offering goals have been exceeded year after year.

Each year we have short-term mission teams from Calvary who invest their time, talents, and treasures in reaching out to people in the name of Christ across the street and around the world. Missionary C. T. Studd declared, "Some want to live within the sound of church or chapel bell. I want to run a rescue shop within a yard of hell."[47]

Sharing the gospel with lost people and getting the message of Christ's redemptive love to the ends of the earth should be one of our greatest priorities as Christians. Witnessing about our faith in Jesus Christ should not be intimidating, but one of our greatest joys in life. Author Francis Chan said, "Our greatest fear should

---

[46] Sweeting, George, *Who Said That?* (Chicago: Moody Press, 1994), 325.
[47] Ibid, 325.

not be of failure, but of succeeding at things in life that don't really matter." [48]

An unknown author wrote, "Some men die in battle, some men die in flames, but most men die while playing silly games." All Christians should be involved in missions. There are a number of ways to participate: in going, when physically possible, even for a short term; in praying; and in giving. God has a special ministry for all His children. As we pray and seek to know His will, He will make known to us the specific ministry that He has planned for us.

In my earlier years of ministry I did not have a desire to do mission work in other countries. America was my country and even when God opened doors for me to minister His Word in Canada, I would pray, "Lord, I would be happy to stay in America for my ministry." I prayed for missionaries and was always willing to have them share their ministry in the church where I pastored. I was willing to financially support missionaries, but I had no desire to visit the mission fields. That changed in 1987.

## God's Call To The Nations

There were two specific times in 1987 when God captured my heart with His heart for the world. My heart was greatly stirred for the nations of the world on February 11, 1987, the day of my thirty-ninth birthday. With the realization that I was getting older and in looking back over my life and ministry, there was a definite gap when it came to missionary service.

On October 30, 1987, I was reading Luke chapter twenty-four when suddenly verse forty-seven seemed to be magnified and raised from my Bible in large, bold print. "And repentance and forgiveness of sins will be preached in My name to all nations, beginning at Jerusalem." When I read that verse, I got into a little debate with God, which is not a good idea because I never win in a debate with Him. My argument went like this: "Lord, there is no way I could ever go to all the nations of the world. That's

---

[48] www.goodreads.com/quotes249877-our-greatest-fear-should-not-be-of...

impossible for one person to accomplish, even in the span of an entire lifetime."

Then, I sensed the Lord speaking to my heart. It was as if He said, "Let's go over to Mark 16:15 and consider what I said there." I read these words, "Go into all the world and preach the good news to all creation." I concluded that He was calling me to go into some parts of the world and preach the gospel to people who lived there. That seemed possible to me so I began to pray about it.

I wrote these words in my Bible: "I pray for the privilege of preaching the gospel on every continent before I die." I made a list of the seven continents in my Bible and put a check mark after North America, since God had already given me the privilege of preaching in the United States and Canada. I began to pray daily for an open door to preach the gospel on the other six continents. If it was God's will for me to preach in other countries, I was willing to obey Him. It was thrilling to experience God answering my prayers and expanding my vision for world-wide missionary service. His invisible hand was at work.

Over the past twenty-nine years God opened doors for me to preach the gospel on six continents. I have not yet preached the gospel on the continent of Antarctica, but I pray nearly every day for the privilege of proclaiming Christ there as well. My four children have kidded with me over the years and have said, "Dad, who are you going to preach to in Antarctica, the penguins?"

Psalm 2:8 declares, "Ask of Me, and I will make the nations your inheritance, the ends of the earth your possession." In Acts 1:8 Jesus said, "But you will receive power when the Holy Spirit comes on you; and you will be My witnesses in Jerusalem, and in all Judea and Samaria, and to the ends of the earth." The King James Version of the Bible says, "unto the uttermost part of the earth." I think Antarctica is perhaps the "uttermost part of the earth" and therefore, I pray for the privilege of preaching the gospel somewhere on the continent of Antarctica. I want to obey my Lord and Savior Jesus Christ and glorify Him in helping to fulfill the Great Commission wherever He leads me throughout the world.

God has amazing ways of changing our desires when we desire what He desires for us. When I was struggling to surrender to God's will regarding the ministry, I remember fearing that God would call me to Africa and ask me to live in a mud hut. In the winter of 1988 God did just that. He called me to speak at a missionary retreat in Cameroon, West Africa. I believed God had opened the door for this ministry and I accepted the invitation to minister His Word in Cameroon. Ironically, for several days I actually stayed in a mud hut in the bush village of Mfe. Other than having to sleep with a mosquito net around me and occasionally having primitive sanitary facilities, I had a very positive experience in Africa.

In addition to preaching in the local village church at Mfe, I was asked to preach at a funeral service for a government official. I only had about ten minutes to prepare my thoughts while the pastor of the village church and I climbed a steep hill to the home where the man was buried in his front yard. Being called on to preach without notice happened several times while I was in Africa. It has been said, "A pastor must be ready to preach, pray, or die at any moment," and that was certainly true for me while ministering in Africa.

Before I preached at the government official's funeral service, the JuJus, several witch doctors who looked and acted like they were demon possessed, performed a ceremony. It was one of the scariest experiences I've had in over forty-three years of ministry.

I ate fufu in Cameroon, which is like a cornmeal mush. People asked me when I came back from Africa what fufu tasted like. I told them it was like a combination of mashed potatoes, cream of wheat, and wallpaper paste. After eating fufu and njamma jamma, a bitter spinach-like vegetable, for four weeks, I lost nine pounds.

I preached thirty-six times in various places in Cameroon and also spoke several times on the radio. I had the joy of giving twenty-six haircuts to our missionaries — something I learned to do while I was in college.

## Meeting A Man Named Harry

One of my most memorable experiences while travelling to Cameroon was meeting a man named Harry Rich who was from Sydney, Australia. We sat together on a plane from New York City to Zurich, Switzerland. I had prayed that God would open doors for me to share my faith in Jesus Christ as I travelled. God's invisible hand was at work in our conversation. Harry mentioned several things that convinced me our meeting was not a coincidence, but a divine appointment. Harry told me that his mother had died recently. I tried to comfort him by quoting several key verses of Scripture that I often found helpful in sharing with people when they were grieving.

Harry then said that he had been reading an interesting book about the Jewish people. How amazing is God's divine planning and timing! I had just recently finished a series of messages about the Jewish people in Bible prophesy. What a coincidence? No, another amazing example of the invisible hand of God at work.

When I told Harry that the Old Testament and New Testament of the Bible had much to say about the Jewish people, he wanted to hear more. At this point I got my Bible out of my briefcase and began sharing with my new friend numerous verses about the Jewish people. I also shared my personal testimony with Harry and explained to him how Jesus Christ became real to me when I was seventeen years old.

When our Swiss Air flight attendant served us a delicious meal, I discovered that I was more interested in sharing the "bread of life" with Harry than I was in eating. Almost our entire flight time to Europe was taken up with spiritual conversation. I explained to Harry how God loved him and Christ died on the cross for his sins as well as for my sins and the sins of the whole world. John 1:29 states clearly, "Look, the Lamb of God, who takes away the sin of the world." I also explained that Jesus was resurrected from the dead so that Harry could have eternal life in heaven someday. I explained the need to repent, to turn away from sin, and receive Christ by faith.

The time passed quickly and we were soon ready to land in Zurich. It was December 26, 1988 when Harry and I met. As our

747 jumbo jet was landing, Harry said, "My goal for 1989 is to find inner peace." I replied, "Harry, yesterday was Christmas day, the day Christians celebrate the birth of the Prince of Peace." After sharing several more verses of Scripture about peace I said, "Harry, you don't have to wait until 1989 to find inner peace. Jesus can give you the inner peace you desire right now."

I asked Harry if he wanted to open his heart to Jesus Christ and begin to experience His peace in his life. Harry said, "yes," and I led him in a prayer to receive Jesus Christ into his life as his Savior and Lord. There were tears of joy in our eyes as we prayed together. According to Luke 15:10, "There is rejoicing in the presence of the angels of God over one sinner who repents."

Harry and I spent a couple of enjoyable hours together in Switzerland before we parted. That was the beginning of a long-term friendship. Even though we lived thousands of miles apart, we corresponded with one another and our friendship has grown over the years.

In May 2013, Harry and his wife Shirley traveled to Pennsylvania to visit with us in our home. What a wonderful time we had together. Their visit was a gift from God. There is no doubt in my mind that the invisible hand of God was at work in bringing Harry and me together on the plane that day in December 1988. I had prayed that the Lord would give me someone to share my faith with as I traveled to Cameroon, West Africa, and He answered my prayer in a marvelous way. Sharing Jesus Christ with people is one of the most exciting things Christians can possibly do to advance the Kingdom of God on earth.

Through the many years when Harry and I kept in contact with one another via Christmas cards, letters, and emails, Harry would often write: "When are you coming to Australia? I want to hear you preach in Sydney." After praying for twenty-eight years, God heard and answered my prayers and gave me the privilege of preaching the gospel in Australia, and specifically in Sydney, in February, 2015. I had the great joy of ministering the gospel for two weeks alongside missionaries Marco and Cybelle Liporoni, who are affiliated with Heaven Sent Ministries in Virginia.

I conducted revival meetings in the city of Hornsby at the New Diamond Music school, which is a ministry led by very gifted musicians and recording artists, George and Linda Tassone. I also preached the gospel in three churches where the pastors were from Portugal, Egypt and Pakistan. Using translators is always challenging but also rewarding, especially when people respond to the gospel message the Lord has led me to share with them.

## Preaching The Gospel In Other Nations

God continued to answer prayer outside the U.S. and Canada and open doors for me to preach the gospel in many countries: Cameroon in 1989; Philippines in 1993; Japan in 1993, 2016; Brazil in 1994, 1996, and 2005; Albania in 1995; Russia in 1998; Mexico in 1999, 2008 and 2014; Ukraine in 2000; Kenya in 2003; Romania in 2004; South Africa in 2007; India in 2010; Australia in 2015; and in China in 2016.

I had prayed for years that someday, if God opened the door and I could minister for His glory, I would like to preach at least once in a large venue like a stadium. God gave me that opportunity in India. Pastor Joseph Thomas, a pastor friend and native of India, and I were invited to speak at a conference held in Assam, India in February 2010. It was the annual conference of the Boro Baptists. At the time I did not know how many people were expected to be at the conference. I thought perhaps a few hundred people would attend or maybe even a few thousand. The Sunday morning before Joseph and I left for India, I found out through an email that Stacy Gabrielle, the leader of our Missions Team, read to the congregation that the Boro Baptists were expecting 30,000-40,000 attendees at the conference.

Preaching the good news of the gospel to that many people was certainly challenging. I experienced great anxiety, especially knowing that I was scheduled to speak on Saturday night when attendance was likely to be at its peak. Many questions raced through my mind: *Did I have the right message for the evening service? Would my interpreter and I be able to work well together? Would God give me the strength and wisdom that I needed to preach the gospel? Would I rely completely on the Lord for His anointing by the Holy Spirit as I preached?*

I found myself becoming very anxious and burdened about this awesome responsibility to preach to so many people. I cancelled my plans to attend the Boro Baptist cultural event during the afternoon so that I could spend more time in praying and going over my message notes before I was to meet with my interpreter later in the afternoon.

I was so nervous about preaching the gospel that night that I called my friend and prayer partner, Scott Weldon, back in Pennsylvania and asked him to pray for me. God answered prayer and gave me the power of the Holy Spirit to preach.

At the end of the service I challenged those who had never put their faith in Jesus Christ to trust Him as their Savior and Lord. I asked them to stand up if they were willing to repent of their sins and put their faith in Jesus Christ to save them and give them eternal life. All over that vast audience people began to stand up and I led them in a prayer of commitment. Only God knows how many people came to a saving knowledge of His Son during that service. I offered to God all the praise, glory, and honor for the awesome moving of His Holy Spirit that night. Psalm 115:1 expressed my praise to the Lord for what He did. "Not to us, O Lord, not to us but to Your name be the glory."

My heart overflowed with joy as the invisible hand of God was at work in touching lives and drawing people to Jesus Christ. The Bible tells us what happened in Antioch when the good news about the Lord Jesus was preached. "The Lord's hand was with them, and a great number of people believed and turned to the Lord" (Acts 11:21). I, too, experienced the Lord's hand at work in India. We cannot see the hand of the Lord, but we can certainly see the evidence of His mighty hand at work.

## Unusual Opportunities To Share The Gospel

I have often prayed that God would open unusual doors for me to witness for Christ. People have asked me, "How did you ever get an opportunity to do that?" I tell them, "God opened the door. That was of God, not of me. I only prayed and asked Him to use me for His glory." I will mention just four unusual doors that God opened. "What He opens, no one can shut, and what He shuts, no one can open" (Revelation 3:7).

In 1990 I was invited to preach at the Northern California Association of North American Baptist Churches. I was also invited to preach in two congregations in northern California.

It was February and the Chicago O'Hare Airport was closed because of ice and snow. I sat in the Allentown-Bethlehem-Easton airport in Pennsylvania praying that God would open the airport in Chicago so I could catch my flight for Sacramento. During the delay of a couple hours, I was reading a magazine produced by the Slavic Gospel Association. I read how God was tearing down the walls of communism in Russia and Eastern Europe. My heart was so stirred by what I read that I turned to the back of my Bible where I record long-term prayer requests. I wrote this request: "That I may be enabled to preach the gospel in Eastern Europe (Russia, the Soviet Union), or wherever God opens the doors. I have a burden for this."

A couple hours later the Chicago airport opened and when I landed in Chicago I changed planes. A man was sitting in the aisle seat. I excused myself as I walked in front of him to the window seat. I wanted to talk to him about the Lord, so I said, "I am grateful to the Lord that the ice melted and I was able to get to Chicago." When I mentioned "the Lord," he said, "You must be a Christian." I replied, "I am." He reached out his hand to shake hands with me and said, "My name is Andrew Semenchuk. I'm the assistant director of the Slavic Gospel Association here in Wheaton, Illinois."

I said, "You're kidding me! Let me show you what I've been reading for the past several hours." I reached into my briefcase and pulled out the Slavic Gospel Association magazine. I told him how my heart was stirred in reading about what God was doing in Russia and Eastern Europe, and I showed him the prayer request that I had recorded in the back of my Bible not more than two hours before I arrived in Chicago.

Andrew said he had just been in Russia for eighteen days and he shared with me firsthand what God was doing in Russia and Eastern Europe. He encouraged me and said, "You pray, and God will open a door for you to minister there." I did pray, and over the next fourteen years God opened unusual doors for me to preach the gospel in Albania, Russia (Omsk, in Siberia), Ukraine, and Romania.

## Sharing Christ At 39,000 Feet

In 1996 when I was ministering in Brazil, I met a pilot who worked for a Brazilian airline. I asked many questions about flying and he asked me what flight I would be on when I returned to the United States from Brazil. He knew the pilot of my flight and made arrangements for me to meet him when I boarded the plane. When I met the pilot, he was busy preparing for takeoff but said that I should come back to the cockpit in an hour. I was stunned and couldn't believe what he just said. I quickly responded, "Okay, but we'll be in the air in an hour, won't we?" He replied, "You couldn't do this in the U.S., but you can sit with me in the cockpit."

I went back to my seat and kept an eye on my wrist watch. When the hour was up, a flight attendant took me to the cockpit. The pilot explained how the radar system worked and many other things about the plane as we flew at 39,000 feet at night. I could hardly believe that I was actually sitting in the cockpit of a jumbo jet while we were in flight!

After about half an hour, the pilot excused himself and said that he had to make ground connections. I silently prayed, "Lord, you didn't get me into this cockpit simply to learn about flying. Please open a door for me to share my faith in Christ with the pilot."

Within a few minutes I was sharing my personal testimony of how Jesus Christ changed my life and how He spared my life just six months prior when I had prostate cancer surgery. The pilot had many questions about spiritual matters that I tried to answer. Near the end of our seventy minute conversation, the co-pilot turned and said to me, "I'm a Christian, and my favorite hymn is 'Amazing Grace.'"

Only God could have opened such an unusual opportunity for me to share my faith in Christ. This is another example of the invisible hand of God at work. Even though the pilot did not invite Jesus Christ into his life that moment, the gospel message was presented to him. I cannot save anyone, but I am grateful to God that I can be used by Him to plant the seeds of the gospel in the hearts of people He leads me to, even in very unusual circumstances.

## Ministering At Ground Zero

When Islamic terrorists attacked the World Trade Center Twin Towers in New York City on 9/11, the whole world was in turmoil. A member of our church, who was the wife of an FBI agent, came into our church office and told our staff that her husband was on duty near Ground Zero where the attacks had taken place. I said to her, "If I, or any of our pastors, could help at Ground Zero, please let your husband know of our willingness to help."

On Sunday night, just five days after the tragic event, she called and asked if I wanted to go with them to Ground Zero the next day. Her husband had the day off, but felt compelled to go back. After being cleared through several extremely tight security check points, we arrived inside "the pit" at Ground Zero.

I will never forget the sights, sounds, and smells at Ground Zero that day. I was wearing a collarless white shirt, and shortly after arriving in the pit I heard someone hollering, "Father, come and pray! We just removed a body." I knelt in several inches of dust and prayed with two rescue workers as they placed a heavy cardboard box on the ground in front of me. This was an awesome moment that I will long remember. Even in the pit of Ground Zero the presence of God was very evident. Psalm 139:7-8 declares, "Where can I go from Your Spirit? Where can I flee from Your presence? If I go up to the heavens, You are there; if I make my bed in the depths (or even in the pit at Ground Zero), You are there."

The FBI agent, his wife, and I prayed with many rescue workers and gave them printed copies of scripture verses about comfort and strength. Only the invisible hand of God could open a door for the gospel at Ground Zero, which He did. It was an unusual opportunity to minister to people who were hurting beyond words. I praise God for the privilege of being there that day.

## The Living Truth TV Ministry

I have also had the privilege of reaching people with the gospel through our weekly television program called *The Living Truth*, which Calvary Baptist Church sponsors. The program is broadcast on thirteen cable stations and also on Direct TV and on the Dish Network of stations. What started as a three-month experiment has now been broadcast for over eleven years. Over 400 people have been interviewed and have shared powerful testimonies about how Jesus Christ has changed their lives.

We've heard testimonies about people who were flipping through channels on their TV remote and began to watch our program. I interviewed Dr. James McGuire, an OB/GYN doctor from our church, who shared touching stories about how he experienced the invisible hand of God at work numerous times when he was faced with difficult situations in delivering babies.

When Dr. McGuire's interview was being aired, the former assistant dean of Temple Medical School in Philadelphia just happened to be flipping channels and recognized Dr. McGuire who had been a medical student at Temple years before. Within two hours after the interview aired, the former assistant dean received two phone calls from two other doctors in the Philadelphia area who just happened to catch the interview as well. Was that a coincidence or was it the invisible hand of God at work?

When our TV programs are being recorded a team of godly prayer warriors are in the studio praying. They pray that God will anoint the programs with His Holy Spirit and that He will cause people to watch the programs when they are aired. God hears and answers those prayers.

Calvary Baptist Church has also sponsored one minute radio messages on secular stations over the past thirty or more years. We view these radio spots and our TV ministry as outreach ministries. God has led people to our church through these ministries.

The pastors, elders, and leaders of various ministries at Calvary desire to experience the invisible hand of God at work in all our missions and outreach ministries. God has worked mightily through Christmas and patriotic concerts, drama events including "Heaven's Gates and Hell's Flames," seminars, redemption groups, care groups, and community groups that meet in homes. The ministry of Grief Share and Divorce Care has helped to bring comfort and healing to many hurting people in our congregation and community. Our children's ministry outreach in public schools through Child Evangelism Fellowship clubs and Vacation Bible School, and our youth ministry's service projects and short-term mission trips have touched many lives.

The founder of modern missions, William Carey, once said, "Attempt great things for God, and expect great things from God."[49] As a body of believers in Jesus Christ we have seen God do amazing things as we have moved out of our comfort zones and have attempted great things for God. God has far exceeded our expectations time and time again as we have trusted in Him to guide us to accomplish His purposes for His glory.

As stated before, I have had the wonderful privilege of being the senior pastor of Calvary Baptist Church for the past thirty-three years. God has led many of the finest Christ-centered people in the world to Calvary. What a joy it has been to preach the Word of God to the congregation and to have sensed the presence of God at work in many lives. The words of the Lord in Isaiah 51:16 have been a reality in my life as I have ministered His Word at Calvary: "I have put My words in your mouth and covered you with the shadow of My hand."

My prayer, thirty-three years ago, that I would experience a double portion of God's Spirit and blessing in the ministry at Calvary Baptist Church, has been answered in marvelous ways. I have experienced the invisible hand of God at work in ways that I would have never dreamed possible.

---

[49] www.wmcarey.edu/carey/expect

## Think About It

- Are you willingly serving God where He has called you to serve Him?
- Are you committed to stay true to God's Word, regardless of the cost or consequences to you personally or to your family?
- Are you experiencing growth in your spiritual life and are you part of a growing church family?
- How are you investing your talents, treasures and time in missions and outreach ministries?

CHAPTER 11

# *THE INVISIBLE HAND OF GOD AT WORK IN PROVIDING*

*"Jabez cried out to the God of Israel, 'Oh, that You would bless me and enlarge my territory! Let Your hand be with me, and keep me from harm so that I will be free from pain.' And God granted his request" (I Chronicles 4:10).*

## God Promises To Provide

We must believe God's promises if we want to experience the fulfillment of them in our lives. The Bible says, "And my God will meet all your needs according to His glorious riches in Christ Jesus" (Philippians 4:19). Some Christians believe that God will meet some of their needs, but it is very difficult for them to believe God will meet *all* their needs. Did God really mean what He said? When God said, "all," did He really mean "all"? All means all, and that's all that all means.

God keeps all His promises because God is God and He cannot and will not lie. "God is not a man, that He should lie, nor a son of man, that He should change His mind. Does He speak and then not act? Does He promise and not fulfill" (Numbers 23:19)? We may not always keep our promises as human beings, or even as Christians, but God always keeps His promises. But we must remember that many of God's promises are conditional upon our faith and obedience. For example, God said, "If we confess our sins, He is faithful and just and will forgive us our sins and purify us from all unrighteousness" (I John 1:9).

God is always faithful and just, even when His people are not. If we want our sins to be forgiven, we must confess them as God said. Our sins are not automatically forgiven. When we repent and turn away from of our sins and by faith receive Jesus Christ into our lives as Savior and Lord, He forgives us on the basis of His shed blood on the cross. We are justified in God's sight as Romans 5:1 indicates: "Therefore, since we have been justified through faith, we have peace with God through our Lord Jesus Christ."

When we sin after becoming a Christian we need to apply I John 1:9 and ask for His forgiveness, not because we have somehow lost our salvation, but so we can remain clean in God's sight and experience His sanctifying work in our lives. In this way Christians become "an instrument for noble purposes, made holy, and useful to the Master and prepared to do any good work" as II Timothy 2:21 indicates.

God made many promises to His people, the Israelites. Obedience led to blessing, but disobedience led to consequences, and sometimes the consequences were severe. Joshua said to the Israelites, "You know with all your heart and soul that not one of all the good promises the Lord your God gave you has failed. Every promise has been fulfilled; not one has failed. But (notice this transitional word) just as every good promise of the Lord your God has come true, so the Lord will bring on you all the evil (disaster) He has threatened, until He has destroyed you from this good land He has given you. If (notice this conditional word) you violate the covenant of the Lord your God, which He commanded you, and go and serve other gods and bow down to them, the Lord's anger will burn against you, and you will quickly perish from the good land He has given you" (Joshua 23:14-16).

God delights in the faith and obedience of His people. Those who believe God and obey God experience the fulfillment of His promises. What God says in His Word He requires His people to believe. If they do not have faith in God and in what He said, they will never experience what He promised them. "For we also have had the gospel preached to us, just as they did; but the message they heard was of no value to them, because those who heard did not combine it with faith" (Hebrews 4:2). Faith pleases God and leads to great blessing for those who exercise faith in Him. Hebrews 11:6 clearly states: "And without faith it is impossible to please God, because anyone who comes to Him must believe that He exists and that He rewards those who earnestly seek Him."

God's invisible hand works in amazing ways to provide for His children. The story of God's provision for a seminary illustrates this point. The following story took place in Texas in 1924.

Lewis Sperry Chafer was the founder of a seminary originally known as The Evangelical Theological College, but was later named Dallas Theological Seminary. The seminary started with only thirteen students, but today it is one of the largest seminaries in the United States. Shortly after the seminary opened for classes, it was nearly bankrupt. Creditors wanted their money, or they would foreclose on a certain day at noon. The board of directors met that day in President Chafer's office to pray. Even though the board of directors believed it was God's will to start the seminary, the financial crisis seemed impossible; however, "Nothing is impossible with God" (Luke 1:37). They needed great faith to trust God that He would do the impossible and keep the seminary open. The minutes were passing and the noon deadline was approaching.

Harry Ironside was in the prayer meeting. He was a well-known Bible teacher who later became the pastor of Moody Memorial Church in Chicago. "Ironside was known for his down-to-earth style in both preaching and praying. He prayed, 'Lord, we know that the cattle on a thousand hills are thine. Please sell some of them and send us the money.'"[50]

God's invisible hand was at work in the prayer meeting, and also in the life of a Texas cattleman. He had just sold two carloads of cattle and felt that God wanted him to give the money to the seminary. When he came to the seminary business office, he gave a check to the secretary. She looked twice at the check and, after thanking the cattleman, she took it to the president's office. She wasn't sure if she should interrupt the prayer meeting, but she knew the noon deadline was fast approaching. She gently tapped on the door and President Chafer opened it. She gave him the check and explained how the cattleman wanted the seminary to have it. President Chafer recognized the name on the check and knew it was legitimate. When he looked closely at the check, he was flabbergasted. It was exactly the amount of money the

---

[50] Hendricks, Howard, *Standing Together* (Sisters: Multnomah, 1995), 154-155.

seminary needed to pay the creditors. President Chafer said to Harry Ironside, "Harry, God sold the cattle."[51]

The Bible says, "And God is able to make all grace abound to you so that in all things at all times, having all that you need, you will abound in every good work" (II Corinthians 9:8). Ralph Waldo Emerson, the nineteenth century poet, said, "All I have seen teaches me to trust God for all I have not seen."[52]

God knows all our needs, and He promised to "meet all our needs according to His riches in Christ Jesus," as Philippians 4:19 clearly states. God met the needs of the Israelites in the wilderness. He provided manna, water, meat, clothes, shoes, protection, and everything they needed.

God provided resources for a poor widow when the creditor of her deceased husband was planning to take her two sons to be slaves. All she had was a little oil. Elisha the prophet told her to ask her neighbors for empty jars. When she began pouring oil into the jars, the oil did not stop flowing until every jar was filled. She was told by Elisha to sell the oil and pay her debts. The widow and her sons were able to live on what she had left after paying all her bills. This miracle story of God's provision is found in II Kings 4:1-7.

Miracle stories of God's provision are also recorded in the New Testament. In Mark chapter six, Jesus took five loaves of bread and two fish, and blessed and multiplied them and fed five thousand men, plus women and children. "They all ate and were satisfied, and the disciples picked up twelve basketfuls of broken pieces of bread and fish" (Mark 6:42-43). Jesus continually met the needs of His disciples.

Jesus asked His disciples a question: "When I sent you without purse, bag, or sandals, did you lack anything? 'Nothing,' they answered'" (Luke 22:35). If Jesus met all their needs, and if He is the same yesterday, today, and forever — as Hebrews 13:8 states clearly — then Jesus will meet all our needs as well. We must trust and obey Him and wait for His perfect timing. He will keep His promises to us, just as He did for others in the past. Henry Blackaby said, "God can do anything He wants with one person

---

[51] Ibid, 155.
[52] www.quotationspage.com/quote34329.html

who believes Him and will obey Him."[53] The key question is: "Will we believe God and obey Him?"

## Lord, Increase Our Faith

The disciples of Christ had a need for more faith. On numerous occasions Jesus rebuked His disciples for their lack of faith. Jesus said, "And why do you worry about clothes? See how the lilies of the field grow. They do not labor or spin. Yet I tell you that not even Solomon in all his splendor was dressed like one of these. If that is how God clothes the grass of the field, which is here today and tomorrow is thrown into the fire, will He not much more clothe you, O you of little faith?" (Matthew 6:28-30). God knows our need for clothes and we should not worry about where our clothes will come from for He will supply them for us in one way or another.

Jesus rebuked the disciples for their lack of faith when they were in a storm on the Sea of Galilee. It was a furious storm, but Jesus calmly slept in the boat and was at peace. "The disciples went and woke Him, saying, 'Lord, save us! We're going to drown!' He replied, 'You of little faith, why are you so afraid?' Then He got up and rebuked the winds and the waves, and it was completely calm" (Matthew 8:25-26). If Jesus could calm a mighty storm on the Sea of Galilee then surely He could calm the storms we face in our lives as His children. The key question is: "Will we trust Him in the storms of life?"

Jesus was teaching His disciples to believe that He could and would meet all of their needs if they would have faith in Him. This was a very difficult hurdle for the disciples to overcome. If they could learn to focus on what was most important, they would discover that all their needs would be met. Jesus said to them, "But seek first His kingdom and His righteousness, and all these things (what they would eat, drink, wear, etc.) will be given to you as well" (Matthew 6:33). The disciples, like most people today, had a strong tendency to focus on material things and not

---

[53] Blackaby, Henry and King, Claude, *Experiencing God* (Nashville: LifeWay Press, 1990), 33.

on the kingdom of God and His righteousness. They needed to learn this valuable lesson of making eternal things their focus.

"The apostles said to the Lord, 'Increase our faith'" (Luke 17:5). They knew they lacked faith, but they also knew Jesus could increase their faith.

The prayer of Jabez was a faith-increasing prayer. Praying this prayer has increased my faith and desire to see God do amazing things in my life, family, and ministry. "Jabez cried out to the God of Israel, 'Oh that you would bless me and enlarge my territory! Let your hand be with me and keep me from harm so that I will be free from pain!' And God granted his request" (I Chronicles 4:10). Even though Jabez could not see the Lord's hand at work in his life, he prayed that God's hand would be with him.

One of the most popular books published in the year 2000 was *The Prayer of Jabez*, by Bruce Wilkinson. I have read this little book numerous times, and each time I have been stirred in my mind and heart to trust God to do greater things than I have ever experienced before.

In the preface of the book, the author writes, "This petition has radically changed what I expect from God and what I experience every day by His power. In fact, thousands of believers who are applying its truths are seeing miracles happen on a regular basis."[54]

Jabez wanted God to bless him. He wanted to experience God's presence, power, and provision for his every need. He wanted God to enlarge his territory, which probably meant more than expanding his land holding, but increasing his influence for the kingdom of God. He also wanted to be free from harm and from the pain it could bring into his life.

Bruce Wilkinson wrote, "A miracle is an intervention by God to make something happen that wouldn't normally happen. Do you believe that miracles still happen? Many Christians I've met do not."[55]

I believe in miracles, and I have experienced God's invisible hand at work in my life accomplishing things I could never do on my own. Bruce Wilkinson states, "That is what your Father's hand is like. You tell Him, 'Father, please do this in me because I can't

---

[54] Wilkinson, Bruce. *The Prayer of Jabez* (Sisters: Multnomah Publishers, 2000), 7.
[55] Ibid, 43.

do it alone! It's too big for me!' And you step out in faith to do and say things that could only come from His hand. Afterwards, your spirit is shouting, 'God did that, nobody else.' God carried me, gave me the words, gave me the power and it is wonderful! I couldn't recommend more highly living in this supernatural dimension! Tragic as it might sound, the hand of the Lord is so seldom experienced by even mature Christians that they don't miss it and don't ask for it."[56] It is the deepest longing of my heart to have God's invisible hand upon my life accomplishing things that can only be explained as "an act of God" that He did for His glory alone.

Bruce Wilkinson explains what it is like to have God's invisible hand upon a person's life. "You could call God's hand on you 'the touch of greatness.' You do not become great; He becomes great through you."[57] God must always receive the glory for anything great He does in and through a person's life. "I am the Lord; that is My name! I will not give My glory to another or My praise to idols" (Isaiah 42:8).

## God's Provision For George Mueller

I have been encouraged, strengthened in my faith, and thrilled to read about the life and ministry of George Mueller. Henry Blackaby wrote, "He was a pastor in England during the nineteenth century. He was concerned that God's people had become very discouraged. They no longer looked to God to do anything unusual. They no longer trusted God to answer prayer. They had so little faith."[58]

"God began to lead George to pray. George's prayers were for God to lead him to a work that could only be explained by the people as an act of God. George wanted the people to learn that their God was a faithful, prayer-answering God. He came upon the verse in Psalm 81:10, 'Open wide your mouth, and I will fill it.'

---

[56] Ibid,53.
[57] Ibid, 49.
[58] Blackaby, Henry and King, Claude, *Experiencing God* (Nashville: LifeWay Press, 1990), 33.

God began to lead him in a walk of faith that became an outstanding testimony to all who hear his story."[59]

God did many miracles in providing for up to 2,000 orphans who lived at George Mueller's orphanage at one time. George was a mighty man of faith and prayer. He took God at His Word, and God kept His promises, as He always does. "And without faith, it is impossible to please God, because anyone who comes to Him must believe that He exists and that He rewards those who earnestly seek Him" (Hebrews 11:6). George Mueller believed God and spent time earnestly seeking Him, His will, His way, and His provisions.

In his book, *George Mueller: Man of Faith and Miracles*, Basil Miller wrote about how George would seek to know God's will. "I never remember in all my Christian course, a period now (in March 1895) of sixty-nine years and four months, that I ever sincerely and patiently sought to know the will of God by the teaching of the Holy Ghost, through the instrumentality of the Word of God, but I have been always directed rightly. But if honesty of heart and uprightness before God were lacking, or if I did not patiently wait upon God for instructions, or if I preferred the council of my fellow men to the declarations of the Word of the Living God, I made great mistakes."[60]

I have experienced the invisible hand of God at work in providing for my needs. I trusted God to supply the funds for tuition, room and board, books, and all fees for my college and seminary expenses. God provided every dollar. I didn't borrow any money and was able to graduate debt-free from college and seminary.

## God Provided Money For A Conference

Someone said, "Little is much when God is in it." Even though God can and does supply very large needs, He also supplies little needs as well. Two examples come to mind that happened when I was a student at Houghton College from 1966 to 1970. I desired to

---

[59] Miller, Basil, *George Mueller: Man of Faith and Miracles* (Minneapolis: Bethany House, 1941), 51.

[60] Ibid.

attend the Urbana Missionary Conference in Illinois at the end of December 1967. The registration fee was seventy dollars. I didn't have the money.

Several people in Mankato, Minnesota owed me money for dictionaries that I delivered to them during the previous summer, but they did not pay me at the time of delivery. They promised to send me a check, but no checks came in the mail. I contacted them several times during the fall months, but they still did not send me any money. When I decided to go to the Urbana Conference, I prayed that God would cause them to send me the money they owed me. I can't explain it apart from God answering prayer, but checks began to arrive in the mail and I had all the money I needed to go to the conference.

## Money For Snow Tires

Houghton College is located in western New York in the Snow Belt. We had many huge snowstorms when I was a student at Houghton. One weekend my wife and I were driving to Buffalo in a snowstorm. We were travelling to the church where I was a youth pastor. I needed snow tires for my car. I only had thirty dollars in my wallet. I prayed that God would supply our need. When we got to Buffalo, I pulled into a gas station and asked the attendant if he had any used snow tires for sale. He asked me what size tires I had on my car. When I told him, he said, "Do you see those two tires leaning against the building? I just took them off an elderly lady's car. I tried to tell her she didn't need new snow tires, yet she said she wanted them. Those tires are the size you need. You can have them for thirty dollars." Sharon and I were so happy with God's provision, we could have shed tears of joy.

## Money For A Baby Carriage And Bills

When our first child Nathan was born, we had extra expenses and I needed an additional forty-five dollars to pay several bills that were due. Ironically, if I didn't write out a check for my tithe, which was forty-five dollars, then I would have exactly enough to pay all my bills. What should I do? Should I just pay the bills and skip giving my tithe to the Lord that week? That didn't seem right to me. How could I get ahead by putting God behind? I prayed and asked God what I should do. Immediately He brought to my mind Proverbs 3:9-10: "Honor the Lord with your wealth, with the first fruits of all your crops; then your barns will be filled to overflowing, and your vats will brim over with new wine." These verses showed me that I should honor God and give to Him first. That's what I decided to do. I trusted God to meet our needs and I wrote out a check for forty-five dollars for my tithe. God would soon surprise me and teach me a valuable lesson about honoring Him and trusting Him to meet our needs as a family.

My wife's parents drove from Pennsylvania to Massachusetts and arrived at our house around noon the same day I had the financial need. It was not unusual for my father-in-law to give us ten or twenty dollars when they visited us, or when we were home in Pennsylvania visiting them. He almost always mentioned what he wanted us to do with the money he gave us. "You can use this to buy gas for your trip back to Massachusetts," or "Here's a few dollars to take Sharon out to eat."

What happened this day was very unusual. When my in-laws arrived, my father-in-law gave me a fifty-dollar bill and said, "You can get a baby carriage with this money." I thanked him for his generous gift, but the thought went through my mind, *I can use this fifty dollars to pay the bills that are due and get a baby carriage in a couple of weeks when I have more money.*

After we visited for a little while, it was time for lunch. As we sat at the table, my father-in-law handed me another fifty-dollar bill and said, "You can do whatever you want with this." My eyes began to fill with tears, and I asked to be excused for a moment. I went into my office and knelt in prayer. I prayed, "Oh, Lord, you are so good. Not only did you give me the forty-five dollars I needed to pay my bills, but you gave me an extra five dollars so I could give a tithe back to you." Jesus said, "Therefore I tell you, whatever you ask for in prayer, believe that you have received it and it will be yours" (Mark 11:24).

## A Boat, Trailer, And Motor

When I was the pastor at my first church in Melrose, Massachusetts, my wife and I were invited to a home for dinner. During the meal, the husband and father of the family, Dave, and I were talking about boating. I mentioned that someday I hoped to have a small boat so that I could go flounder fishing in the ocean. Dave replied, "I'll give you a boat; I have three of them."

Dave gave me a wooden boat that was about twelve feet long and needed work done on it. I repaired the boat and painted it, but I needed a trailer to tow the boat to the ocean. If God could supply a boat, He could supply a trailer as well. I prayed that the Lord would provide a trailer, if it was in His will to do so. I John 5:14,15 says, "This is the confidence we have in approaching God: that if we ask anything according to His will He hears us. And if we know that He hears us-whatever we ask-we know that we have what we asked of Him."

I happened to be driving through Dave's neighborhood one day, and he happened to be outside, so I stopped to talk to him. I told him that I now had the repairs done on the boat and that I was now praying for a trailer. With excitement in his voice Dave said, "My neighbor across the street, Goldberg, just told me the other day he has a trailer for sale. He put new lights on it and he'll sell it for fifteen dollars." I quickly went to Mr. Goldberg's house and bought the trailer.

God supplied the boat and the trailer, but now I needed a small motor. I decided to pray and see what God would do. James 4:2 says, "You do not have, because you do not ask God."

I conducted a funeral for a man whose wife was a member of our church and lived on our street. After the funeral service, I was invited to the lady's house for lunch with other people who attended the funeral. I was sharing with the lady's brother-in-law how God provided a boat and a trailer for me, and now I was praying for a motor. I was using this story about how God had answered my prayers as a witness to the man. I shared my faith in Christ with him. After the luncheon, I returned home.

What happened next amazes me to this day, even though it has been about forty years since this incident took place. A Jewish friend of mine, Gary, stopped for a visit shortly after I arrived home from the funeral luncheon. I was now trying to share the good news of the gospel with Gary. He enjoyed fishing, so I told him how God provided a boat and trailer for me, and that I was now praying for a motor. During this brief conversation, the telephone rang. It was my neighbor who called. I had just left her house not more than thirty minutes ago. Gary could hear my phone conversation, which went something like, "Really, you have a motor in your basement that you want to give me? That's great, I'll be right over!"

Gary thought I was joking with him, but I wasn't. I said, "Gary, let's walk over to my neighbor's and get the motor she wants to give me." I had no idea that my neighbor's husband who died had a small motor in his basement. The man I had been sharing my faith with at the luncheon knew that his brother-in-law had a motor, but he didn't feel free to say anything to me about it. After I left the house he mentioned to his sister-in-law that I could use the motor her husband had stored in the basement. When my friend, Gary, saw the motor and realized that this was not a joke, he was so moved emotionally that he went outside to wait for me.

God provided a boat, trailer, and motor all for the total cost of fifteen dollars. For many years God has provided numerous opportunities for me to share this story and to use it as a springboard to talk with people about Jesus Christ and His wonderful plan for their lives.

### God Provided For Greater Needs

God hears and answers the prayers of His people when they call upon Him. God is pleased when we pray and bring our needs to Him. "The prayer of the upright pleases Him" (Proverbs 15:8). Jesus said, "Ask and it will be given to you; seek and you will find; knock and the door will be opened to you. For everyone who asks receives; He who seeks finds; and to Him who knocks the door will be opened. If you, then, though you are evil, know how to give good gifts to your children, how much more will your Father in heaven give good gifts to those who ask Him!" (Matthew 7:7-8,11) Just as parents delight in giving good things to their children when they ask, God delights in giving to His children even more.

God promised to meet all our needs, but not all our wants. Sometimes we get needs and wants mixed up. That's why it's important to ask for God's wisdom when we make our requests to Him. He wants us to make our needs and requests known to Him even though He already knows them. "Do not be anxious about anything, but in everything, by prayer and petition with thanksgiving, present your requests to God and the peace of God, which transcends all understanding, will guard your hearts and minds in Christ Jesus" (Philippians 4:6-7). There is a wonderful peace to be experienced when we make our requests known to God and express our thankfulness to Him for hearing our prayers.

### God Supplied To The Dollar

I purchased some clothes at a men's clothing store. Apparently, the corporate office of the store appreciated my purchase and sent me a gift card and two coupons totaling $120. The next time I went into the store a salesman greeted me and said, "If you need a new suit we have some good quality suits on sale for $199 and if you buy one we'll give you a dress shirt and necktie for free." I did need a new suit, so I decided to look at the suits.

I try to remember to pray about what I purchase, especially larger items. "Lord, is this something I need, or not?" I've learned that if I don't have peace about a decision I'm making, I try to say no. The policy, "if in doubt, don't" has been helpful to me on many occasions. I have turned down numerous offers through the years if I didn't have peace about any given decision.

I did have peace about buying the suit, and having $120 in gift cards and coupons gave me even greater peace. The suit needed alterations, which cost $20. Therefore, the total for the suit and alterations was $219, and when the $120 from the gift card and coupons was deducted, the final cost came to $99. Getting a new suit, dress shirt, and necktie all for $99 made me as happy as a little kid in a candy store. But that's not the end of the story.

The ministry of Focus on the Family has designated October as Pastor Appreciation Month. When I arrived at the church, after leaving the men's clothing store, I checked my mailbox and discovered that someone sent me a pastor appreciation gift. Enclosed in a card was a check for $110. At first, it seemed like an unusual amount. But I like to give God a tithe (10%) of what He gives to me. It was Jacob who said to the Lord, "Of all that You give me, I will give You a tenth" (Genesis 28:22). A tithe of $110 is $11. When I deducted the $11 from the $110, I had $99 left. What a coincidence? I just paid $99 for a suit, and also received a dress shirt and necktie free. God supplied my need to the dollar. To me, this was another example of the invisible hand of God at work. God was so good in providing for my needs, and I gave Him all the praise, honor, and glory for what He did. I've discovered it is exciting to trust God to meet my needs and then watch to see how He will provide, sometimes in the most unusual ways.

## House Closing Costs

Just a few weeks before we moved from Getzville, New York to Bethlehem, Pennsylvania in the summer of 1983, a letter arrived addressed to the church. The letter was from a lawyer's office. My secretary handed me the letter and said I should open it.

The letter stated that the church would be receiving $1,000 from the estate of an elderly lady who recently died. How wonderful that she remembered the church in her will, especially since she was not a member of the church, although she did attend worship services regularly.

Then my secretary said, with a smile on her face, "Pastor, I just put a letter from the same lawyer's office in your mailbox. It's addressed to you." She was standing right near the church mailboxes, so I said, with excitement in my voice, "Get it!" She handed the letter to me, and when I opened it and read it I was more excited than a teenager who had just gotten a driver's license.

The letter stated that, if I was the pastor when the lady died and performed her funeral service, I would receive $1,000. I shouted, "I was the pastor when she died, and I did perform her funeral service!" Wow, I was entitled to the money! What perfect timing. Within a few weeks, I would be leaving that church to begin my new ministry in Bethlehem. If I had left the church a few weeks earlier, I would not have been entitled to the money according to the way the will was written.

Estates can sometimes take a long time to be settled. I prayed, "Lord, please send us that money when we need it most." Again, God's timing is perfect. We received the check on the Saturday before the following Thursday when we had the closing on our new house that we had built in Bethlehem. We really needed extra money for the closing costs. God's invisible hand had provided again.

## Purchasing Cars

The manager at a car dealership informed me, "I can't sell you that car for that price." I replied, "Your salesman made a deal with me last night, and here's the paper with the price he quoted to me." I said to the manager, "This is the kind of thing that gives some car dealers a bad reputation. You need to honor the deal your salesman made with me last night." The sales manager may not have appreciated hearing that from a twenty-five-year-old, but it was true and he needed to hear it.

The manager said he would go back to his office and work on the figures. What he didn't know was that I had prayed about what I could afford for a used car in 1970, and that was no more than $60 a month. I believe the Lord gave me peace about that amount for a monthly car payment as my wife and I were heading off to seminary, and I wasn't going to pay one penny more. The manager went back and forth into his office several times. "How about this amount?" I said, "No." He continued to come back to me with figures, until he said, "How's $59.97?" I said, "I'll take it, but if you charged me four cents more per month, I wouldn't buy the car."

If I remember correctly, I think the car manager said, "You're crazy." He may have thought I was crazy, but I wasn't about to change what I believed God put in my heart concerning the monthly payment for the car. God gave me courage and conviction, and I drove off the dealer's lot with the car. Psalm 104:28 says, "When You [God] open Your hand, they [the creatures of the sea] are satisfied with good things." If God can open His hand and provide for the creatures of the sea, think of how much more He can provide for you and me.

## An Offer Refused

Several years ago, a man approached me after a funeral service and said, "Pastor, I'm going to sell my car, and if you would like to buy it, I'll sell it to you for $5,000." The car I had been driving had high mileage, and his offer was very generous and appealing. I asked the man if I could pray about it for a week or so. I looked up the value of the car in the Kelly Blue Book, and it was $10,000. What a great offer I had received from a very kind man.

I asked the Lord that, if He wanted me to buy the car, would He please provide the $5,000, because I did not have the money to buy it. I had learned to trust God to meet my needs, and I did not want to borrow the money to purchase the car. Proverbs 22:7 says, "The rich rule over the poor, and the borrower is servant to the lender." I did not want to be in a servant position, so when God did not provide the money for the car, I concluded that it was not His will for me to have it. I turned down the offer, and thanked the man for his generosity in offering me the car at such a great price. I was at peace with my decision.

God had a better plan, and I'm so thankful that I trusted Him for His provision and guidance regarding another car, if it was His will for me to replace my high mileage car.

God's timing is always best and I have been amazed through the years how perfect His timing really is. It wasn't long after I turned down the offer to buy another car that my father died. My brother and sister thought that I should have my dad's low-mileage, like new Park Avenue Buick to replace my high mileage car. God's plan is always far better than my plan, and He was teaching me to wait upon Him for His perfect timing and provision. "As for God, His way is perfect; the Word of the Lord is flawless. He is a shield for all who take refuge in Him" (Psalm 18:30).

## God Confirmed His Will

Vince Lombardi, the famous National Football League coach once said, "We would accomplish many more things if we did not think of them as impossible."[61] God specializes in doing seemingly impossible things. The Bible is a book of miracles from Genesis to Revelation. Those who believe that the Bible is the divinely inspired Word of God must believe in miracles, because the Bible is filled with miracles. *Who wants to follow a God who can't do miracles?*

Abraham and Sarah were well past the age of child bearing. The Lord spoke to Abraham and told him that his wife was going to give birth to a son. Sarah overheard the conversation between the Lord and Abraham, and she laughed. "Then the Lord said to Abraham, 'Why did Sarah laugh and say, Will I really have a child now that I am old?' Is anything too hard for the Lord? I will return to you at the appointed time next year, and Sarah will have a son" (Genesis 18:13-14). God performed a miracle in a seemingly impossible situation, and Sarah had a son. They called him Isaac, which means, "laughter." God confirmed His will to Abraham and Sarah and gave them the son He promised to give them.

God delights to do miracles when His people step out by faith and take Him at His word. When two blind men came to Jesus, they asked Him to have mercy upon them. Jesus said to them, "Do you believe that I am able to do this?" "Yes, Lord," they replied. Then He touched their eyes, and said, 'According to your faith will it be done to you'" (Matthew 9:28-29). They put their faith in Jesus and He healed them of their blindness.

When Jesus visited his hometown of Nazareth, the people were amazed at His teaching. They said, "Where did this man get this wisdom and these miraculous powers?" (Matthew 13:54) They only recognized Jesus as the carpenter's son, and not the Son of God. Their unbelief caused them to be offended by Him. Their unbelief prevented Jesus from performing many miracles in His own hometown. Matthew 13:58 summarizes the unbelief that Jesus encountered: "And He did not do many miracles there,

---

[61] Impossiblehq.com/25-impossible-quotes

because of their lack of faith." Jesus doesn't do many miracles today where He finds a lack of faith.

## God Performs Miracles

Psalm 77:14 is a bold statement about miracles: "You are the God who performs miracles; You display Your power among the peoples." God delights to display His miracles and power when people believe in Him and take Him at His Word.

In 1989 I became deeply convicted that God wanted me to lead our family to become debt-free. As I studied the scriptures I learned about financial freedom and what the Bible teaches about finances. I longed to obey the Lord and to get our financial house in order according to His Word. A statement by missionary Hudson Taylor seemed to be burned into my heart and mind: "God's work, done in God's way, will never lack God's supply."[62] I began to believe this powerful quote, to share it with others, and to put it into practice in my personal life and in our family. I was responsible before God for what I did and how I lead my family. Others may believe that God is leading them in another direction, but I had to believe God and live by the convictions I had in my heart and mind based on His Word and the leading of the Holy Spirit.

Joshua and Caleb were men of great faith, courage, and whole-hearted commitment to obey God. They were men with convictions and were unwilling to compromise what God said to them. Caleb said to Joshua, "You know what the Lord said to Moses, the man of God at Kadesh Barnea about you and me. I was forty years old when Moses, the servant of the Lord, sent me from Kadesh Barnea to explore the land. And I brought him back a report according to my convictions, but my brothers who went up with me made the hearts of the people melt with fear. I, however, followed the Lord my God wholeheartedly. So in that day, Moses swore to me, 'The land on which your feet have walked will be your inheritance, and that of your children forever, because you have followed the Lord my God wholeheartedly'" (Joshua 14:6-9).

---

[62] www.goodreads.com/quotes/190685-god-s-work-done-in-god-s-way...

Joshua and Caleb were blessed mightily by God. When ten of their fellow spies brought back a negative report about the Promised Land, Joshua and Caleb gave a positive report. Even though they were in the minority, they chose to believe God and live by their convictions wholeheartedly.

God wanted to bless Israel and make His people an example to all the earth. Moses said, "If you fully obey the Lord your God and carefully follow all of His commands I give you today, the Lord your God will set you high above all the nations on earth. All these blessings will come upon you and accompany you if you obey the Lord your God" (Deuteronomy 28:1-2).

God places a high premium on obedience. He is God, and we are not. We are commanded to obey Him because He is God and He knows what is best for us. Jesus said, "If you love Me, you will obey what I command" (John 14:15).

Dietrich Bonhoeffer (1906-1945) was committed to obeying God. He was a Lutheran pastor who believed that Hitler's Nazism was an anti-Christian movement. In his uncompromising love and obedience to God he stood against the government of his day. "Arrested in 1943, for smuggling Jews into Switzerland, he pastored his fellow prisoners until he was executed for treason on April 9, 1945. His writings have inspired many to be faithful to Jesus's teachings."[63] He was willing to die for his faith in Jesus Christ. Bonhoeffer once said, "Only he who believes is obedient; only he who is obedient believes."[64] He believed and obeyed the truth that he preached from the word of God.

## No Need To Borrow

Deuteronomy chapter twenty-eight lists the blessings and curses that God would bring upon His people if they obeyed or disobeyed Him. Obedience brought blessing, but disobedience brought cursing. Deuteronomy 28:12-14 were verses of Scripture, along with many others, that spoke to me about becoming debt-free and not borrowing money to meet my needs or the needs of

---

[63] Rusten, Michael E. and Sharon, *When and Where in the Bible and Throughout History* (Wheaton: Tyndale House, 2005), 443-444.

[64] Cory, Lloyd. *Quotable Quotations* (Wheaton: Scripture Press, 1985), 266.

my family. Among God's many blessings to Israel was the promise that, if they obeyed God, they would not need to borrow. God would be their ultimate source to meet all their needs.

"The Lord will open the heavens, the storehouse of His bounty, to send rain on your land in season and to bless all the work of your hands. You will lend to many nations but will borrow from none. The Lord will make you the head, not the tail. If you pay attention to the commands of the Lord your God that I give you this day and carefully follow them, you will always be at the top, never at the bottom. Do not turn aside from any of the commands that I give you today, to the right or to the left, following other gods and serving them" (Deuteronomy 28:12-14).

Could God actually meet all our needs, not just some of our needs, and bless us so that we wouldn't need to borrow? I knew that God *could* do that, but *would* He? The only way I could find out was to trust Him. Could I go to the bank of heaven instead of the local bank to meet my needs? Borrowing money is so common, so much a part of our American culture. Doesn't everyone borrow money? The vast majority of people seem to have trouble even thinking about how they could possibly live without borrowing money. But debt is one of the greatest problems in America today.

Debt has caused many problems in marriages, families, churches, and businesses, as well as in our government. Alice Rivlin, who has served on President Obama's Debt Commission, said before the Senate Budget Committee in 2011, "The United States cannot go on borrowing at projected rates. Without major policy changes, we risk a debt crisis that could severely damage our economy and weaken our influence in the world... We face the prospect of debt crisis and economic disaster if we do not act."[65]

When I made the commitment in 1989 to stop borrowing, to trust God to meet our needs as a family and become debt free, I knew it wouldn't be easy. I knew that it would take a number of years to accomplish this goal, but I was willing to trust God to

---

[65] Hearing Before the Senate Budget Committee, United States Senate, Calling for Debt Reduction as an Opportunity to Make Government Work More Fairly and Effectively, March 15, 2011, (statement of Alice Rivlin, Senior Fellow, Economics Studies).

help me. I immediately started adding more money to my bimonthly mortgage payments, and increased the amount as much as possible. It was exciting to watch the mortgage principle decrease every two weeks. It was also very motivational to realize that I could save thousands and thousands of dollars of interest by paying off my mortgage early.

If I had to use my credit card, I tried to pay the balance off every month. Providing for the many needs of a family, with a wife and four children, as well as paying expensive college tuition payments was challenging and seemed impossible at times. But God does the impossible and He delights to provide for His people when they trust in Him. Luke 18:27 declares, "What is impossible with men is possible with God."

My wife Sharon went back to work when our youngest child started school. I will always be grateful to the Lord for the wonderful wife He gave me and for her willingness to sacrificially and faithfully help pay for household expenses so we could save more for college tuition. We were committed to doing all we could to help our children get through college debt-free.

## A Financial Crisis

One year we had two of our children attending two different Christian colleges. That year the tuition payments were extremely expensive, but God was faithful to supply every dollar we needed. I can't explain it, but every month we had just enough to cover all our expenses.

When our oldest daughter changed her major in college that meant she had to add an extra semester in order to graduate. Her scholarships ended after four years and she also got engaged and was planning to be married the following summer.

At this point I faced a major financial crisis. How could we possibly pay for all the tuition payments and also save for an upcoming wedding? Was I tempted to go to the bank and borrow money or take out college loans? Yes, I was greatly tempted to do that. But God had been so faithful in hearing our prayers and supplying all our needs. Would God continue to supply all the resources we needed to pay those high tuition bills along with all the other expenses we had as a family? Would He supply all we needed for our daughter's wedding the following summer? I believed God *could*, but did I believe God *would*?

## The Need To Fast

Ezra, the Old Testament scribe, faced a crisis in a time of need. Several times he spoke about "the hand of God" being upon him. Ezra proclaimed a fast so the people might humble themselves and ask for God's help. He wanted God to intervene and not just get help from the king. Ezra said, "I was ashamed to ask the king for soldiers and horsemen to protect us from our enemies on the road, because we had told the king, 'The gracious hand of our God is on everyone who looks to Him, but His great wrath is against all who forsake Him'" (Ezra 8:22).

I discovered by reading about the life and ministry of Ezra, that fasting can be helpful, especially in a time of great need. When I fast I often sense a closeness to God and become more sensitive to His guidance and will.

When I faced a financial crisis because of overwhelming college tuition payments and the additional expenses of an upcoming wedding, I spent five days fasting and seeking God's will. I had no idea how God might intervene or confirm His will to me during this time of crisis, but He did. He used an ordinary event during one of the days of the fast to increase my faith, to strengthen me, and give me the assurance that He would indeed meet my every need.

I went to the Today's Man Store near the Lehigh Valley Mall in Whitehall, Pennsylvania, to buy a pair of corduroy slacks. When I walked into the store I saw a large sign near a rack of clothes that had "75% OFF" written on the sign. That was an incredible sale. I was in need of some new clothes, so I looked at the sale items. What I found was a $160 London Fog raincoat for $39.99, a London Fog car coat for $39.99, two shirts for $5 each, a scarf for $5, and a pair of corduroy slacks for $7. I paid $102 for $408 worth of clothes.

As I was driving home from the store, I suddenly felt overwhelmed with God's presence as I reflected on the blessing of how God had just provided all these clothes at such a great sale price. It was a holy moment. I remember praising God and praying something like, "Oh Lord, You are so great. You provided all these clothes for me at such an unbelievable price." Then I suddenly felt like a surge of faith was welling up inside of me. At that moment, I made a conscious decision that by faith I was going to trust God to provide every penny we needed for tuition payments, for my daughter's wedding expenses, and for everything else we needed. I continued praising the Lord and prayed, "Lord, I'm not going to the bank. I'm not going to borrow any money. I believe You will supply all our needs as You promised. I trust in You."

God used this time of fasting to confirm in my heart that He could be trusted. All tuition bills were paid in full. All the wedding expenses for our older daughter's wedding the following summer, and our younger daughter's wedding two years later, were paid in full. God supplied all our needs and we did not borrow a penny. When God says He "will meet all your needs according to His glorious riches in Christ Jesus" (Philippians 4:19), He means exactly what He says.

If God's children do not trust in Him and believe His promises, they will never experience the blessings of seeing how abundantly He would have met all their needs. An elderly lady once quoted these meaningful words to me: "Yesterday He helped me. Today He did the same. How long will this continue? Forever, praise His name."

## Becoming Debt-Free

February 25, 2002 was a day I will never forget. After chipping away at our debt for a number of years, we became totally debt-free that day. No more mortgage payments, loan payments, tuition payments, car payments, wedding expenses, or credit card bills. Becoming debt-free was such a joyful experience. I gave God all the praise, honor, and glory for what He had done. Becoming debt-free was not easy, but every sacrifice God enabled us to make was worth the effort in achieving the goal.

God was faithful to His promises, and He supplied all our needs. Jesus said, "Then you will know the truth, and the truth will set you free" (John 8:32). After many years of financial bondage and debt, we were financially free, free indeed. What God did for us He has done for many other people who have trusted Him and stood firmly on His promises.

As a pastor, it has been thrilling to have people from our church family come to me and say, "Pastor, we are debt-free." I long to see more and more of God's people experience the joy of financial freedom. I long to see our church become debt-free again, so we'll have more resources to expand the kingdom of God and fulfill the Great Commission of our Lord to go into all the world and make disciples.

## Building A New House Debt-Free

After our four children were all married and established in their own families, it was a new season for my wife Sharon and me. What did God have in store for us as a couple? For years we had talked about building another house someday. If it was God's will, we wanted to do it; and if it wasn't His will, we didn't want to do it. As we prayed about it, we sensed God's leading to proceed in the direction of finding a lot and building a new house. We met several times with a Christian builder to get more ideas and to discover what would be involved.

God had been so faithful in meeting all our needs in the past, but those needs were much smaller than what would be needed to build a new house. The thought of getting older and building a one-story house was appealing to us. We didn't want to build a mansion; we'll be living in a mansion for all eternity. John 14:2 in the King James Version of the Bible says, "In My Father's house are many mansions." But the New International Version of John 14:2 interprets this verse in this way: "In My Father's house are many rooms." I'll stick with the King James Version on that verse. I much prefer a mansion over a room, especially when I plan to live there for all eternity.

Would it be possible to buy a lot and build a new house debt free? Our God owns the cattle on a thousand hills (Psalm 50:10); in fact, He owns everything according to Psalm 24:1. "The earth is the Lord's, and everything in it, the world, and all who live in it." If God owns everything—and He does—and if He led us to build a new house, then it actually wouldn't be our house, but His house. The key question and prayer for us as a couple was: "Lord, do you want us to build another house for You and for Your glory?" Whatever we did, or did not do, we wanted our decision to glorify our Lord and Savior Jesus Christ.

Our commitment to get out of debt and not go into debt again was strengthened when we looked at a model house in a development where many new houses were being built. We got to know the builder, who was a Christian.

One day the builder said to me, "Pastor, I spoke with my boss and he said we could build a house for you and your family at our cost. Whatever it costs us, that's what it will cost you." I was shocked when I heard what he said. I couldn't believe what I was hearing. An offer like that was unheard of. We could gain instant equity in the value of the house which could amount to perhaps $30,000 to $50,000. Some people may conclude, "You would be crazy to pass up an offer like that." We did pass up this incredibly generous offer because we were committed to living debt-free and we did not have enough equity in our present house or in savings to build a new house at that time. Even though we could have built the new house at the builder's cost, we would still have had to take on debt to build it, and we were not willing to do that. God did not lead us in that direction.

If we were to build a new house, my wife wanted to have public water, not a well, and I wanted to live in the country where I could see deer from our back porch. Those two requirements were difficult to meet, but after looking at many lots over a period of six years, God led us to a lot in the country where public water was available and deer could be seen from our back porch. Actually, two lots that met our requirements came available at the same time. Which lot did God want us to buy?

A few months before we made our decision to sign an agreement of sale for one of the building lots, Sharon and I had just finished giving a major commitment to our church building fund. Our church was in the process of buying a lot and building a new facility at the exact same time we were in our personal search for a lot and desiring to build a new house. It was amazing to see the parallels in the two projects.

As a pastor, I was challenging our congregation to sacrifice for our new facility. As I was asking our congregation to sacrifice for the Lord's work at Calvary, I knew that we had to sacrifice as well.

There is a great difference between giving out of reason and giving out of revelation. Reason says, "What do I think I can give?" Revelation says, "Lord, what do you want me or us to give?" By reasoning I had an idea of what I thought we could give, but when I began to fast and pray and desire to obey God, I believe He revealed what He wanted us to give.

I believe the secret to success in any ministry capital campaign or building project is to challenge God's people to *fast, pray, and obey* God regarding what He wants them to give to the capital campaign or building project. As we did this personally, God led my wife and me to commit two-thirds of a year's salary to our church building project. I had always wondered what it would be like to really sacrifice for the Lord. I was soon to find out. The joy of sacrificial giving was overwhelming.

God continued to meet all our needs throughout that year even though we were living on much less income each month. I have believed for the past forty-three years that I cannot out-give God. I have a little shovel and He has a big scoop. I also have forty-three years of records that indicate that I cannot out-give God. Jesus said, "Give, and it will be given to you. A good measure, pressed down, shaken together and running over, will be poured into your lap. For the measure you use, it will be measured to you" (Luke 6:38).

God blesses in amazing ways, and not just materially. Those who are generous in giving to Him and the work of His Kingdom are spreading the good news of the gospel around the world. I once heard it said, "There was a man, though some did call him mad, the more he gave away, the more he had." Giving to God is an eternal investment and the rewards are out of this world.

Of the two lots that we were considering, God led us to purchase the less expensive one. I really liked it even more than the more expensive one. It had a tree line with many mature trees. It was a flat lot and the other lot was on a hill, which would have made mowing the lawn a challenge.

The amazing invisible hand of God was at work in blessing us when we bought our lot. The amount of money the Lord enabled us to save by buying the less expensive building lot was even more than the amount my wife and I had given to the Lord in our church building fund commitment. On May 5, 2008, the day we purchased our building lot debt-free, it was like God gave us back all that we had given Him plus even more. Again, I discovered that I could not out-give God. Only God could have done something this wonderful. "To God be the glory, great things He has done."

Now that we had purchased a lot, we needed to sell our existing house before we could begin building a new one. We had our house on and off the market for three years. The economy was in a great downturn beginning in 2008 and in many ways it was the worst time to try to build a new house. House values were dropping, but God was at work. He often does great things during difficult times.

I had prayed that God would be glorified in the timing of the sale of our house. I wanted Him to be glorified in the whole process, desiring to have a testimony of what God did. In I Corinthians 10:31 the Bible says, "So whether you eat or drink or whatever you do, do all to the glory of God."

We bought our building lot on May 5, 2008, and exactly two years later (May 5, 2010), God brought a young family who made an offer to buy our house. How absolutely incredible was God's perfect timing. "There is a time for everything, and a season for every activity under heaven...a time to build" (Ecclesiastes 3:1, 3).

We now had a reasonable offer to sell our house, but Sharon was concerned about all the stress of moving. She was hesitant to sell the house. If it had been up to me alone I would have signed the papers to sell the house that day. I am so glad I didn't do that. God had a great surprise in store for us.

I wanted to be sensitive to Sharon's concerns and said to her, "We don't have to accept the offer today. Let's pray about it for one more day." The next day was the National Day of Prayer.

Sharon and I attended a prayer rally at city hall in Bethlehem. After the rally we returned to the church parking lot and sat in our car and prayed again for God's guidance and perfect will as to whether He wanted us to sell our house and build a new one. Amos 3:3 says, "Can two walk together, except they be agreed?" The answer to that question is no, they cannot walk together except they be agreed. It was very important that whatever decision we made about selling our house, we had to be agreed.

After we prayed Sharon agreed to sell the house at the price we were offered the previous day. When I called our realtor to tell him we would accept the offer on our house he said, "Guess what? I just received another identical offer on your house, which puts you in a great position. I'll contact both prospective buyers and tell them you are willing to sell the house to whoever gives the highest offer." By waiting on the Lord for one more day, the final offer on the house increased significantly. God heard and answered our prayers and surprised us with the additional increase in the selling price of the house.

I was so excited that I didn't ignore Sharon's hesitation about accepting the offer to sell our house the day before. God was teaching me to be more sensitive to what my wife thinks and this was a lesson I needed to learn.

Within three hours after we accepted the offer to sell our house, God provided a condo for us to live in until our new house could be built. When I called our builder to tell him we had sold our house and were ready to start building the new house, he said that the timing in his schedule was "perfect."

On February 13, 2011, Calvary Baptist Church in Easton, Pennsylvania, moved into our new facility at 5300 Green Pond Road. What a tremendous joy it was for the congregation to move into our new facility, especially because it was the year of our 100th anniversary since the church had been founded in 1911.

Two weeks later, on February 25, 2011, my wife and I began moving into our new debt-free house, which was the exact ninth anniversary of the day we became debt-free on February 25, 2002. God's timing is so amazing. Was this just a coincidence or was it another example of the invisible hand of God at work?

In the prayer of Jabez, as recorded in I Chronicles 4:10, Jabez prayed, "Let your hand be with me..." God's invisible hand is with us to provide for all (not just some, many, or most) of the needs of His children who will trust in Him and believe His promises. Our God is awesome, and He is the greatest of all promise keepers.

## Think About It

- Do you trust God to meet all (or just some, many, or most) of your needs?
- Do you feel a need for an increase in faith to believe God and His promises? If so, ask God to increase your faith.
- Do you have amazing testimonies to share for God's glory of how He has provided for you? Share some of those testimonies with someone this week.
- Do you believe God will provide for your smallest needs and your greatest needs as well?
- Do you desire to be debt-free? If so, what steps will you begin taking today?

CHAPTER 12

# *THE INVISIBLE HAND OF GOD AT WORK IN HEALING*

*"Stretch out Your hand to heal and perform miraculous signs and wonders through the name of Your holy servant Jesus"(Acts 4:30).*

## A Cancer Diagnosis

"Your colon looks fine, but I don't like the way your prostate gland feels. If I were you I'd see a urologist and I wouldn't wait. If you would like me to get an appointment for you, I will." My colon doctor called a urologist while I was still in his office. He said, "I have a forty-seven year old male who needs to see you right away." I went to my colon doctor for a routine checkup and left his office wondering if I had prostate cancer. I was grateful for the doctor's persistence and concern. He was certainly serious when he wanted me to see a urologist as soon as possible.

When I came home from the colon doctor's appointment I shared with my wife what he recommended about seeing a urologist and how he made an appointment for me. I wasn't expecting to hear news like this. My wife was very concerned as well. I didn't share this news with our children or anyone else just yet. I wanted to wait until I saw the urologist and had further tests done before I shared it with other people.

The thought of possibly having cancer was on my mind continually as I went about my daily activities and ministry responsibilities. My wife and I were praying together and seeking to trust God and asking for His help. We knew He was with us, but we felt the need to draw closer to Him in this time of crisis. I Peter 5:7 says, "Cast all your anxiety on Him because He cares for you" and that was exactly what we were seeking to do. As a pastor I had counseled with many people over the years who had cancer, but now I was sitting in the patient's seat waiting for more answers. This was a very different experience for me.

I remember reflecting on the fact that I felt more tired than usual. Mowing the grass the past summer seemed like a much greater task than it normally did, although I really enjoyed working outside in the yard. Was my tiredness a symptom that something was wrong? I would soon know the answer to that question.

During my visit with the urologist, he assured me that he didn't think I had cancer. My blood test (PSA) came back normal. The doctor decided to do an ultrasound, which also didn't show anything unusual. A few weeks later I went back to the urologist for another physical exam. This time when the doctor did the prostate exam, I had pain. When he examined me it felt like he touched an open sore. He said to me, "I really don't think you have cancer, but we better do a biopsy to make sure." He told me to call his office the following Thursday morning to get the results from the biopsy.

There are certain days in everyone's life that will always be remembered. December 12, 1995 was one of those days in my life. My wife, Sharon, was at a ladies' meeting at the church and my son, Evan, and I were at home. When the telephone rang, Evan answered it and said, "Dad, it's Dr. Lennert. He wants to talk to you."

If my doctor was calling me at home during the evening, two days earlier than when I was to call his office, I thought, "This can't be good news." My doctor got directly to the point. "We have the results from your biopsy, and we discovered you have a malignant tumor on your prostate gland. Because you are producing testosterone that will feed the cancer, we must be aggressive in our approach. I recommend we put you on two hormone drugs, shrink the tumor and then do surgery to remove it. You'll also need more tests to see if the cancer has spread anywhere else in your body." I only had one question: "Dr. Lennert, when you did the biopsy you took six little snips to be tested. In how many snips did you find cancer?" He answered, "In all six."

The word "cancer" is one of the most frightening words a person can ever hear, especially when it is spoken to you personally from your doctor. I was shocked when I heard it. A cold numbness gripped my heart, and many thoughts raced through my mind. "What will happen to me as a result of having cancer? Will I live or die? What about my wife and four children? What about my ministry and all the dreams and goals I have for my life?"

"How will I ever be able to tell my children that I have been diagnosed with cancer?" Our two oldest children were in college and my diagnosis came just at the time when they were facing their final exams. My wife was certainly aware of the possibility that I may have cancer, but telling our four children that their dad had cancer was one of the most difficult things I have ever had to do. My wife and I would need God's strength to tell them and He gave us His strength as we called upon Him. Psalm 29:11 assured us that "The Lord gives strength to His people; the Lord blesses His people with peace."

Immediately after the phone conversation with my doctor I went to my bedroom to pray. As I knelt by my bed, I cried out to God about my problem. I remember praying for healing, but I also told God there was one thing I wanted more than anything else, even more than healing, and that was His perfect will for my life. I surrendered my life to Him regardless of what that may involve. I had learned to trust God during difficult times in the past, and I resolved to trust Him with the problem of cancer as well.

Later that evening my wife came home and I shared the news with her. She was a tremendous support to me. She cried with me, read the Word of God with me, prayed with me, and went with me to my doctor appointments. She was by my side at all times and I was very grateful to God for a loving wife.

I had faith that my life was in God's hands and peace calmed my fears. I knew God was with me and would help me. Jesus said, "Peace I leave with you; My peace I give you. I do not give to you as the world gives. Do not let your hearts be troubled and do not be afraid" (John 14:27). The Lord told His people what to do in a time of crisis. "Call upon Me in the day of trouble; I will deliver you, and you will honor Me" (Psalm 50:15).

My mother died from lung cancer in 1992. At the time of her cancer diagnosis in 1989, my pastor friend, Scott Weldon, told me to read Psalm 112. I found this Psalm to be exceptionally helpful during this difficult time in my life. The seventh verse of Psalm 112 seemed to leap off the page of my Bible and penetrate into my heart and mind. "He will have no fear of bad news; his heart is steadfast, trusting in the Lord." I had just received bad news from my doctor, but this verse told me not to fear bad news. I determined right then not to be afraid, but to be steadfast and trust in the Lord. How comforting God's Word was to me. I could trust Him with all my fears, anxieties, and concerns. I could trust Him with my whole life. I could trust Him to give me courage and strength to face the future. I could trust Him to heal me, if it was His will, and I could trust Him to help me if it was not His will to heal me.

I don't think it is wrong to question God. Even Jesus, when He was dying on the cross for the sins of the world questioned His Father by asking, "My God, my God, why have You forsaken Me?" (Matthew 27:46). I chose not to question God as to why He allowed me to have cancer.

Ruth Graham, the late wife of Dr. Billy Graham, wrote: "Oh Lord, I would not ask you why, these trials come my way, but what is there for me to learn of Your great love, I pray? I lay my whys before Your cross in worship kneeling. My mind too numb for thought, my heart beyond all feeling, and worshiping You, realize that I in knowing You don't need a why."[66]

The words of Ruth Graham have helped me focus more on the "what" question rather than on the "why" question when I face difficulties in life. I seem to gain far more insight when I ask God what He wants me to learn in a situation rather than questioning Him as to why He allowed this circumstance to come into my life.

All five members of my immediate family have had cancer. Both of my parents died from cancer. My mother had lung cancer; although she never smoked, she worked in an office where others smoked. She died on July 22, 1992. My father died with prostate cancer on December 12, 2001. Ironically, my father's death was on the sixth anniversary of my cancer diagnosis, which was on

---

[66] Lotz, Anne Graham, *Why?* (Nashville: Thomas Nelson, 2004), forward XVII

December 12, 1995. The day before my father died, my older brother, Dennis, told me he had just been diagnosed with prostate cancer. A few years later my sister, Rosalie, was also diagnosed with uterine cancer. God chose to take my parents to heaven as a result of having cancer, but He chose to heal my brother, sister, and me. All three of us have been cancer survivors for many years. God used my brother and sister to be a great support to me when I had cancer and I tried to support them when they had cancer as well. We loved one another and prayed for each other and God brought us through some very difficult days.

The invisible hand of God was at work in healing us. Acts 4:30 says, "Stretch out Your hand and heal and perform miraculous signs and wonders through the name of Your holy servant Jesus." It was through the power and name of Jesus Christ that we were healed. Jeremiah 17:14 declares, "Heal me, O Lord, and I will be healed; save me and I will be saved, for You are the One I praise."

Cancer has certainly taken the lives of millions of people, but cancer is limited in what it can do. An unknown author wrote

## "WHAT CANCER CAN'T DO"

"It cannot cripple love. It cannot destroy confidence. It cannot invade the soul.

It cannot shatter hope. It cannot kill friendship. It cannot reduce eternal life.

It cannot corrode faith. It cannot shut out memories. It cannot quench the Spirit.

It cannot eat away peace. It cannot silence courage. It cannot lessen the power of the resurrection."

Cancer cannot separate a genuine Christian from God's love in Jesus Christ. "No, in all these things we are more than conquerors through Him who loved us. For I am convinced that neither death nor life, neither angels nor demons, neither the present nor the future, nor any powers, neither height nor depths, nor anything else in all creation, will be able to separate us from the love of God that is in Christ Jesus our Lord" (Roman 8:37-39).

## An Expiration Date

God has given each person a certain amount of time on this earth. When our expiration date arrives our earthly life will end. It doesn't matter how young or old we may be, what color our skin is, or what our family background or heritage may be. When our allocated time is passed, we will die.

David and Jesus both died, but Jesus was resurrected from the dead. "For when David had served God's purpose in his own generation, he fell asleep, he was buried with his fathers and his body decayed. But the One whom God raised from the dead did not see decay. Therefore, my brothers, I want you to know that through Jesus the forgiveness of sins is proclaimed to you. Through Him everyone who believes is justified from everything you could not be justified from by the law of Moses" (Acts 13:36-39).

When David had fulfilled God's purpose he died. He accomplished what God sent him to do on the earth and he didn't stay one day longer than God had planned for him. It was in God's plan that Jesus would accomplish His Father's will in thirty-three years. Why didn't God let Jesus stay on the earth longer? Couldn't He have performed more miracles, preached the good news in more places, and touched the lives of many more people if He had stayed on the earth longer? Certainly He could have done many more mighty works, but that simply was not in God's plan for His life. When Jesus was dying on the cross He said, "It is finished" (John 19:30). He completed God's plan of redemption. He fulfilled His Father's will. The payment for sin was paid in full. Jesus said, "I have brought You (God the Father) glory on earth by completing the work You gave Me to do" (John 17:4).

Even if God chooses to heal us from many different illnesses in this life, we are still going to die someday. Jesus raised Lazarus from the dead. What a great miracle that was, but Lazarus died the second time as well. It's difficult enough to face physical death once, but poor old Lazarus had to go through it twice. Knowing we must face death someday, we must be prepared for that day. Amos, the Old Testament prophet said, "Prepare to meet your God" (Amos 4:12). Jesus also said, "So you also must be ready, because the Son of Man will come at an hour when you do not expect Him" (Matthew 24:44).

There is a greater miracle than being healed physically. No matter how great the physical miracle may be, the miracle of the new birth is the greatest miracle anyone, anywhere could ever experience. Jesus said, "I tell you the truth, no one can see the kingdom of God unless he is born again" (John 3:3). When a person repents, turns away from sin, and believes that Jesus Christ died on the cross for their sins and was resurrected for their justification, they are born again into a new life.

If we are only born once (physically), then we will face two deaths - a physical and a spiritual death. The spiritual death separates a person from God for all eternity, even in a terrible place called hell. A person who has been born again spiritually will only die once- a physical death. If Jesus Christ returns in the rapture before a Christian dies, then that person will not face physical death, but will be raptured (caught up) directly to heaven to be with the Lord as I Thessalonians 4:17 indicates. When physical death occurs for Christians they go immediately to be with the Lord. "Therefore we are always confident and know that as long as we are at home in the body we are away from the Lord. We live by faith, not by sight. We are confident, I say, and would prefer to be away from the body and at home with the Lord" (II Corinthians 5:6-8). Those who are in Christ will never experience spiritual death or separation from God.

In Psalm 90:12 Moses wrote these inspired words: "Teach us to number our days aright, that we may gain a heart of wisdom." Knowing that God has prepared a certain number of days for each one of us to live on this earth, we need His wisdom to live each day in a way that pleases Him.

## Why Is There Suffering In The World?

One of the oldest questions mankind has ever asked is, "Why is there suffering in the world?" I do not pretend to have all the answers to this age old question, but I would like to suggest a few answers that I hope will be helpful.

## Suffering Came Into The World As A Result Of Sin

Adam and Eve, the first man and woman, lived in a perfect world, a perfect environment and a perfect garden, called the Garden of Eden. God put His seal of approval on everything He made. "God saw all that He had made, and it was very good" (Genesis 1:31). If everything God made was perfect, then something must have happened to make it imperfect. What happened? Adam and Eve messed up big time. God told them not to eat of a certain tree in the garden. "The Lord God took the man and put him in the Garden of Eden to work it and take care of it. And the Lord commanded the man, 'You are free to eat from any tree in the garden; but you must not eat from the tree of the knowledge of good and evil, for when you eat of it you will surely die'" (Genesis 2:15-17).

Eve was tempted by the serpent, who was actually Satan, in a subtle, physical form. He had been cast out of heaven because of his pride, arrogance, and rebellion against God. He wanted to be like God. "You said in your heart, I will ascend to heaven; I will raise my throne above the stars of God; I will sit enthroned on the mount of assembly, on the utmost heights of the sacred mountain. I will ascend above the tops of the clouds; I will make myself like the Most High. But you are brought down to the grave, to the depths of the pit" (Isaiah 14:13-15).

Just as Satan wanted to be like God, he tempted Eve to eat of the forbidden fruit, so she could be like God. "You will not surely die," the serpent said to the woman. "For God knows that when you eat of it your eyes will be opened, and you will be like God, knowing good and evil." (Genesis 3:4-5). Eve chose to listen to Satan rather than God and she also gave some of the fruit to

Adam. Someone said, "The problem in the Garden of Eden was not the apple on the tree, but the pair on the ground."

Eve chose to listen to Satan because she, like Satan, wanted to be her own boss and was tempted to do things her way and not God's way. As human beings we think we are smart enough and can know what is best for us. We are easily deceived. As creatures designed by God, we need the Creator Himself to tell us the right path to take, the path that leads to life and righteousness and not to death.

When Adam and Eve sinned against God, they brought shame, guilt, fear, and death into the world. "Therefore, just as sin entered the world through one man, and death through sin, and in this way death came to all men, because all sinned" (Romans 5:12). Eve tried to blame the serpent and Adam tried to blame Eve. They tried to pass the buck, but as President Harry Truman said, "The buck stops here."[67] God held Adam and Eve accountable for their own sin just as He holds everyone accountable for their own sin today. "So then, each of us will give an account of himself to God" (Romans 14:12).

Suffering came into the world as a result of sin. If we don't want the fruits of sin in our lives then we must stay out of the devil's orchard. Sin sees the bait, but not the hook. Adam and Eve got hooked and brought great suffering upon themselves and upon all mankind. Because God is holy, righteous and just He must punish sin, and He did severely. God cursed the serpent (Genesis 3:14-15). God brought pain and suffering into Eve's life. "I will greatly increase your pain in childbearing; with pain you will give birth to children. Your desire will be for your husband, and he will rule over you" (Genesis 3:16).

Adam also faced great pain and suffering. "To Adam He said, 'Because you listened to your wife and ate from the tree about which I commanded you, 'You must not eat of it,' Cursed is the ground because of you; through painful toil you will eat of it all the days of your life. It will produce thorns and thistles for you, and you will eat the plants of the field. By the sweat of your brow you will eat your food until you return to the ground, since from it you were taken; for dust you are and to dust you will return"

---

[67] www.trumanlibrary.org/buckstop.htm

(Genesis 3:17-19). The curse of suffering and death that Adam and Eve experienced passed on to their children and to all future generations. We live in a fallen, sin-cursed world and our environment in every way has been tainted by sin resulting in suffering. We are all going to face various forms of suffering, simply because we are part of the human race–and infected with a fatal disease called sin.

## Suffering Can Bring About Good

God uses suffering for our good. Joseph suffered at the hands of his brothers and he also suffered in Egypt. Four times (in Genesis 39: 2,3,21,23) we read "The Lord was with Joseph" or "the Lord was with him." God did not abandon him in his suffering. God used his suffering for good. When his brothers came to Egypt, Joseph showed them kindness. He said to them, "You intended to harm me, but Got intended it for good to accomplish what is now being done, the saving of many lives" (Genesis 50:20).

The New Testament teaches that God uses all things for good in the life of Christians. "And we know that in all things God works for the good of those who love Him, who have been called according to His purpose" (Romans 8:28). Sometimes we question how God brings good out of evil. We may even lose heart when we see wars, crime, immorality, greed, and evil all around us. We must believe that God is working all things for good, and keep our eyes on Him rather than on the world around us. When we can't see God's invisible hand at work, we must trust His heart.

God has used suffering in my life to bring about good. C.S. Lewis said, "God whispers to us in our pleasures, speaks to us in our conscience, but shouts in our pains: it is His megaphone to rouse a deaf world."[68] God used pain to get my attention when I was seventeen years old and not walking with the Lord. If I had not had so much pain when I had my tonsils removed, I may not have recognized my need for a personal relationship with God through faith in Jesus Christ. My pain drew me to the Lord and

---

[68] www.searchquotes.com/quotation/God_whispers_to_us_ in_ our_ pleasures

set my feet on the right path in life. "Before I was afflicted I went astray, but now I obey your Word" (Psalm 119:67).

God used hardship and suffering to bring about good when I was a pastor in my first church in Massachusetts. If I had bailed out of that painful situation before God called me to Getzville, New York, I would have missed out on His perfect timing and perhaps not been called to Getzville at all. I am grateful for the difficult years in my first ministry because God taught me many valuable lessons there.

God has used physical suffering in my life on numerous occasions to bring about good and draw me closer to Him. During a recent eighteen-month period, I had four surgeries including carpal tunnel surgery on my right hand, rotator cuff surgery on my left shoulder, and two surgeries on my back. I had such intense sciatic nerve pain down my back and left leg to my ankle that I could hardly walk at times. I couldn't stand to sing during our worship services or to shake hands with people after the services, but by God's amazing grace and strength I didn't miss one Sunday of preaching. When I have struggled through times of great pain and distress, it drew me closer to the Lord. The Lord taught me to depend more upon Him for my strength, wisdom, and all I needed to keep going and accomplish His will.

During my most recent back surgery, my surgeon fused three vertebrae and put three titanium rods and eight screws in my back. Some people were already aware that I was missing some screws, but I didn't realize I needed eight screws.

God used my three month recovery time following my last back surgery and a one-month sabbatical after my recovery from back surgery to give me the time to write this book. If I had not had back surgery, I may have never written this book. God uses suffering, trials, setbacks, and afflictions to accomplish His good purposes.

I have sensed the invisible hand of God at work in my life far more during the difficult times than when things were going well according to my perspective. God's ways and my ways are often very different. "For My thoughts are not your thoughts, neither are your ways My ways, declares the Lord. As the heavens are higher than the earth, so are My ways higher than your ways and

My thoughts than your thoughts" (Isaiah 55:8-9). Suffering can bring about good in a person's life in ways that person would have never imagined. God's good purposes are brought to pass for His glory.

## Suffering Can Refine Us

There is an old Chinese proverb that says, "The gem cannot be polished without friction, nor men perfected without trials." God uses trials to perfect His children and make them more like His Son, Jesus Christ.

When the apostle Peter wrote the epistle of I Peter, the Christians he wrote to were facing great trials and times of suffering. Peter wrote to encourage them in their faith. "In this you greatly rejoice, though now for a little while you may have had to suffer grief in all kinds of trials. These have come so that your faith of greater worth than gold which perishes even though refined by fire - may be proved genuine and may result in praise, glory and honor when Jesus Christ is revealed. Though you have not seen Him, you love Him; and even though you do not see Him now, you believe in Him and are filled with an inexpressible and glorious joy, for you are receiving the goal of your faith, the salvation of your souls" (I Peter 1:6-9).

Madam Guyon said, "It is the fire of suffering that brings forth the gold of godliness."[69] Very few people will ever suffer as much as Job suffered. He lost his seven sons and three daughters in a terrible wind storm, possibly a tornado. His oxen, donkeys, sheep, camels and servants were stolen or destroyed when "the fire of God fell from the sky" (Job 1:16). He was afflicted "with painful sores from the soles of his feet to the top of his head" (Job 2:7). Job's wife told him to "curse God and die" (Job 2:9). But Job said to her, "You are talking like a foolish woman. Shall we accept good from God, and not trouble? In all this, Job did not sin in what he said" (Job 2:10).

God was refining Job as a result of all the suffering he experienced even though at the time Job did not realize what God was doing. Sometimes our suffering does not make sense to us,

---

[69] www.azquotes.com/Quote1345841

but we must trust in the sovereignty of God and believe that He is a loving Father who always has our best interest in His plan for our lives.

Job said, "But He knows the way that I take; when He has tested me, I will come forth as gold" (Job 23:10). Someone said, "Satan may turn up the heat, but God keeps His hand on the thermostat." God knows what He is doing when He allows suffering to come into the lives of His children. His purposes are always good even if we do not understand them or even like them.

When Christians face trials and times of suffering, the invisible hand of God is at work in their lives. God is at work purifying, refining and burning away the dross in our lives.

An unknown author wrote about the valley we experience when we face trials and suffering. God is always with us even though we cannot see Him. Even in the darkest valley He is there with us to comfort and sustain us.

## The Valley

I have been through the valley of weeping,
The valley of sorrow and pain;
But the "God of all comfort" was with me,
At hand to uphold and sustain.

As the earth needs the clouds and the sunshine,
Our souls need both sorrow and joy;
So He places us oft in the furnace,
The dross from the gold to destroy.

When He leads through some valley of trouble,
His powerful hand we can trace;
For the trials and sorrows He sends us
Are part of His lessons of grace.

Oft we shrink from the purging and pruning,
Forgetting the Vine Keeper knows
The deeper the cutting and paring,
The richer the cluster that grows.

Well He knows that affliction is needed;
He has a wise purpose in view,
And in the dark valley he whispers,
"Hereafter you'll know what I do."

As we travel through life's shadowed valley,
Fresh springs of His love ever rise;
And we learn that our sorrows and losses
Are blessings just sent in disguise.

So we'll follow wherever He leadeth,
Though pathways be dreary or bright;
For we've proof that our God can give comfort,
Our God can give songs in the night.[70]

### Suffering Can Mature Us

God desires that His children be mature, or complete in Christ. He often uses trials and times of suffering to bring about maturity. Dr. John MacArthur, in the MacArthur Study Bible, comments on the word "trials" in James 1:2: "This Greek word connotes trouble, or something that breaks the pattern of peace, comfort, joy, and happiness in someone's life. The verb form of this word means 'to put someone or something to the test', with the purpose of discovering that person's nature or that thing's quality. God brings such tests to prove–and increase the strength and quality of one's faith and to demonstrate its validity."[71]

James wrote to the twelve tribes of Jews that had been scattered abroad. The ten northern tribes were called Israel, and the two southern tribes were called Judah. James wrote to encourage the brethren who were faithful to the Lord. "Consider it pure joy, my brothers, whenever you face trials of many kinds, because you know that the testing of your faith develops perseverance. Perseverance must finish its work so that you may be mature and complete, not lacking anything" (James 1:2-4).

---

[70] http://www.Hymnal.net/en/hymn/h/728
[71] MacArthur, John, *The MacArthur Study Bible (Nashville: Word Publishing, 1997)*,1926.

Many of God's choicest servants, both men and women, have suffered greatly and yet remained faithful to the Lord. The prophets and apostles faced great persecution, beatings, and imprisonments; it made them stronger and more committed to love and obey the Lord.

Joni Eareckson Tada was paralyzed as a result of a diving accident. God has since taken her around the world to share her story of suffering and finding victory in Christ. Joni said, "When life is rosy, we may slide by with knowing about Jesus, with imitating Him and quoting Him and speaking of Him. But only in suffering will we know Jesus."[72]

Following my surgery for prostate cancer I experienced the most intense physical pain I have ever known. My catheter got plugged up and I felt like I was going to burst. I also experienced bladder spasms which my doctor said was very unusual. Sometimes for thirty to forty minutes I would be in excruciating pain. Tears rolled down my cheeks. The only thing that gave me comfort was focusing on Jesus suffering on the cross for me. His pain was far greater and intensely more excruciating than any pain I ever experienced. Just knowing this fact helped me endure when my pain seemed unbearable.

Isaiah the prophet spoke of the suffering Messiah. "Surely He took up our infirmities and carried our sorrows, yet we considered Him stricken by God, smitten by Him, and afflicted. But He was pierced for our transgressions, He was crushed for our iniquities; the punishment that brought us peace was upon Him, and by His wounds we are healed" (Isaiah 53:4-5). Jesus did this for each one of us, even though we are so unworthy of such love.

### Suffering Can Produce Perseverance And Character

God is far more interested in who we are than in what we do. Character matters to God. D. L. Moody said, "Character is what you are in the dark."[73] Peter the Great declared, "I have conquered an empire but I have not been able to conquer myself."[74]

---

[72] www.azquotes.com/quote/804929
[73] www.beliefnet.com/.../character-is-what-you-are-in-the-dark.aspx

The apostle Paul expressed God's heart regarding perseverance and character when he wrote to the Christians in Rome. "We also rejoice in our sufferings, because we know that suffering produces perseverance; perseverance, character; and character, hope. And hope does not disappoint us, because God has poured out His love into our hearts by the Holy Spirit, whom He has given us" (Romans 5:3-5).

Perseverance and character reveal our true nature in Christ. When people observe us suffering they can experience the invisible hand of God at work in a Christian's life. We learn far more about God and His nature when we go through times of suffering than when things are going well. Some of the most wonderful and intimate times we will ever experience in our relationship with God will take place when we go through suffering. The Psalmist said, "It was good for me to be afflicted so that I might learn your decrees" (Psalm 119:71). Only a mature believer in Christ could say "it was good for me to be afflicted." Affliction is good because it produces so much good in us and makes us more like Christ in our daily lives and witness for Him.

Dr. Erwin Lutzer, pastor of Moody Memorial Church in Chicago, said, "God has a program of character development for each one of us. He wants others to look at our lives and say, 'He walks with God, for He lives like Christ.'"[75]

## God Knows What He's About

When God wants to drill a man
And thrill a man
And skill a man.
When God wants to mold a man
To play the noblest part;
When He yearns with all His heart
To create so Great and bold a man
That all the world shall be amazed,
Watch His methods, watch His ways!
How He hammers him and hurts him,

---

[74] Quotationsbook.com/quote/6029
[75] Sweeting, George, *Who Said That?* (Chicago: Moody Press, 1994), 81.

And with mighty blows converts him
Into trial shapes of clay which
Only God understands;
While his tortured heart is crying
And he lifts beseeching hands!
How He bends but "never breaks"
When his good He undertakes;
How he uses whom He chooses
And with every purpose fuses him;
By every act induces him
To try His splendor out--
God knows what He's about![76]

## Suffering Can Discipline Us

God's invisible hand at work in the lives of His people, Israel, sometimes brought them into severe discipline. When His people rejected His Word, Isaiah said, "Therefore the Lord's anger burns against His people; His hand is raised and He strikes them down. The mountains shake, and the dead bodies are like refuse in the streets. Yet for all this, His anger is not turned away, His hand is still upraised" (Isaiah 5:25).

Would God ever purposely hand His people over to their enemies to discipline them? Yes, God did it numerous times. God's people were taken as captives into Assyria and into Babylon. The Babylonian captivity lasted for 70 years. Ezra, the scribe said, "But because our fathers angered the God of heaven, He handed them over to Nebuchadnezzar the Chaldean, King of Babylon, who destroyed this temple and deported the people to Babylon" (Ezra 5:12). God also turned His people over to their enemies, the Philistines. "Again the Israelites did evil in the eyes of the Lord, so the Lord delivered them into the hands of the Philistines for forty years" (Judges 13:1).

God disciplines His people because He loves them and wants them to share in His holiness. "My son, do not make light of the Lord's discipline, and do not lose heart when He rebukes you, because the Lord disciplines those He loves, and punishes

---

[76] www.mhmcintyre.us/god-knows-what-hes-about

everyone He accepts as a son. Endure hardships as discipline; God is treating you as sons. For what son is not disciplined by his father? If you are not disciplined (and everyone undergoes discipline), then you are illegitimate children and not true sons.

Moreover, we have all had human fathers who disciplined us and we respected them for it. How much more should we submit to the Father of our spirits and live. Our fathers disciplined us for a little while as they thought best; but God disciplines us for our good, that we may share in His holiness. No discipline seems pleasant at the time, but painful. Later on, however, it produces a harvest of righteousness and peace for those who have been trained by it" (Hebrews 12:5-11). God disciplines His people because He loves them and wants to shape them into the image of His Son.

God has disciplined me many times through the years. When I was attending Gordon-Conwell Theological Seminary (1970-1973) in South Hamilton, Massachusetts, I had a part-time job as a janitor at a post office which was located in an old building that needed repairs.

One morning, the toilet in the men's room was blocked up and when I told the owner of the building, Christine, who ran a bar next to the post office, she was furious. She said, "I'll tell you why the toilet is blocked up. When the men in the post office use the restroom and wash their hands they throw their paper towels into the toilet and not into the wastebasket." I told her that was not true. No one was throwing paper towels into the toilet. Of course I couldn't verify what the men did or didn't do with their paper towels, but I was angry at Christine because she refused to fix up the old building. Shortly after my conversation with Christine, I went back to work in the post office and a convicting thought came into my mind. My anger had blinded me to the truth. I was the guilty person. When I cleaned the toilet in the men's room I used wet paper towels. And where did I throw them when I was finishing cleaning? I threw them into the toilet and flushed them. I didn't purposely lie to Christine, but when the Holy Spirit convicted me and made me aware of what I had done, I knew I had to humble myself and confess my sin to her, but I didn't want to do it that day.

Psalm 38:2 says, "For Your arrows have pierced me, and Your hand has come down upon me." I felt like the heavy hand of God had fallen upon me. I was miserable in my guilt and I knew God was disciplining me, especially when I arrived at our apartment later that day. My wife greeted me with the words, "Our toilet is blocked up and sewage is emptying into our neighbor's bathtub in their apartment downstairs." I said to my wife, "I'm the guilty one. I sinned and God is disciplining me." I had to explain to my wife what had happened at the post office earlier that day.

Was the invisible hand of God disciplining me? I couldn't see His hand upon me, but the circumstances of the two blocked up toilets was too uncanny to not make a connection. My guilt troubled me for two days, and on Monday morning I humbled myself, went to Christine and told her that it was my fault that the toilet was blocked up. I also told her that I was sorry for what I had done.

Christine responded with an angry, "I told you so" attitude and was not very understanding or accepting of my apology. Although I thought she would react the way she did, that was no excuse for me to not go to her and apologize. She made me go into the basement of the post office and clean out the sewage pipes. After I had confessed my sin to Christine and also to God, and the sewage pipes were cleaned out, I felt clean in my heart as well. "Create in me a clean heart, O God, and renew a right spirit within me" (Psalm 51:10). Sometimes God uses suffering to discipline us. His hand of discipline produces much good in the lives of His children, and when we as Christians seek to make things right with those we have wronged, it is a testimony of His amazing grace at work in our lives.

## Suffering Can Glorify God

Sometimes suffering is a direct result of sin. When people break the law and are caught, they usually have to suffer in one way or another. "If you suffer, it should not be as a murderer or thief or any other kind of criminal, or even as a meddler" (I Peter 4:15).

Many people in the Corinthian church were sinning before the Lord and partaking in the Lord's Supper or communion in an unworthy manner. "A man ought to examine himself before he eats of the bread and drinks of the cup. For anyone who eats and drinks without recognizing the body of the Lord eats and drinks judgment on himself. That is why many among you are weak and sick, and a number of you have fallen asleep (or died). But if we judged ourselves, we would not come under judgment. When we are judged by the Lord, we are being disciplined so that we will not be condemned with the world" (I Corinthians 11:28-32). Here we see there is a direct correlation between sin and suffering, but that is not always the case. Sometimes, suffering has nothing to do with sin, as we'll see in John chapter nine.

Jesus healed a man who was born blind. Some people, including Christ's disciples, thought the man was blind because either he or his parents had sinned, but that was not the case. "As He went along, He saw a man blind from birth. His disciples asked Him, 'Rabbi, who sinned, this man or his parents, that he was born blind?' 'Neither this man nor his parents sinned,' said Jesus, 'but this happened so that the work of God might be displayed in his life'" (John 9:1-3).

God had a purpose in the man's blindness. By healing him, Jesus displayed God's mighty healing power which was always displayed for the purpose of glorifying God. In His high priestly prayer, Jesus prayed, "Father, the time has come. Glorify Your Son, that Your Son may glorify You" (John 17:1). There are times when suffering is simply to glorify God and has nothing to do with sin.

## Jesus Can Heal Instantaneously

There are numerous examples in the gospels—the books of Matthew, Mark, Luke and John—where Jesus healed someone instantaneously. "A man with leprosy came and knelt before Him and said, 'Lord, if you are willing, you can make me clean.' Jesus reached out His hand and touched the man, 'I am willing,' He said, 'Be clean!' Immediately he was cured of his leprosy" (Matthew 8:2-3). Leprosy is a terrible disease. Lepers were considered unclean and were outcasts from society. They lived apart from their family and friends. Jesus didn't hesitate to touch the leper and heal him instantaneously.

When I was ministering in Cameroon, West Africa, in 1989, I visited a leper colony called New Hope Village. Leprosy had destroyed fingers, toes, ears, and other body parts of the residents at the leper colony. It was sad to see the effects of this terrible disease upon human bodies. Those affected with leprosy also had the added emotional pain and shame of being cast off as untouchable in society. Jesus came to remove the shame and stigma of people like these lepers. These people were treated as unlovable, untouchable, and almost less than human. Jesus not only chooses to sometimes heal us physically like he did that leper in Matthew 8:2-3, but He removes our shame. Not only the shame that stems from our own sins, but also the shame caused by things outside of our control (like physical deformities, mental illness, social awkwardness, etc.). Jesus tenderly moved toward a sufferer like this leper and loved him perfectly and completely.

Although the lepers at New Hope Village were not healed and made whole like the leper in Matthew chapter eight, they were some of the happiest people I have ever met. They had "new hope" because of the transforming power of Jesus Christ in their lives.

One of my fondest memories of my four weeks of ministry in Cameroon was my visit to New Hope Village. As our mission vehicle pulled away from the leper colony, many of the lepers were clapping their hands, some without fingers, as they shouted, "Happy, happy, happy." Happiness that came from their faith in Jesus Christ.

Their faces were radiant with His glory shining through them. "Those who look to Him are radiant; their faces are never covered with shame" (Psalm 34:5). This experience at New Hope Village left a lasting impression on my life. Although these lepers were extremely poor and had suffered greatly from the effects of this terrible disease upon their bodies, their joy in the Lord was unforgettable.

## Examples Of Jesus Healing People

Another example of healing took place when Jesus instantaneously healed Peter's mother-in-law. "When Jesus came into Peter's house, He saw Peter's mother-in-law lying in bed with a fever. He touched her hand and the fever left her, and she got up and began to wait on Him" (Matthew 8:14-15). I have often wondered what it would have been like to have lived and actually observed Jesus doing His miracles on earth.

There is no doubt in my mind that Jesus can and does heal instantaneously when it is in His plan and purpose to do so. Many people can bear witness to Christ's healing power in their lives. I, too, have experienced His healing power in my life on numerous occasions, and on one occasion it was an instantaneous healing.

When I was in seminary, I was having severe pain in one of my legs from my knee to my ankle. The pain intensified over a weekend, and I was planning to go to a doctor on Monday if the pain persisted. When Monday morning arrived I still had intense pain, but now I was also having pain in my other leg, from my knee to my ankle. I was alone in our apartment. Bending down and wrapping my two hands around my ankles, I cried out to God and asked Him to touch me and take away the pain.

Something like a heat wave passed through my body and I was instantaneously healed of the pain in both legs. I jumped up and down, actually trying to create the pain, but it was gone. *Totally gone.* I could hardly believe it. I had prayed for healing and that is exactly what I experienced. I believe the invisible hand of God was at work in healing me not only in this incident, but on several occasions throughout my life.

Over the past forty-three years of my pastoral ministry I have seen many miracles of healing in the lives of people I have known personally or have heard of healing miracles from people I knew and respected. Following are two specific examples.

## Lorin

As I write today, there is a man in our congregation named Lorin who nearly eight years ago was told by his doctor he only had weeks or months, at most, to live. He was diagnosed with several forms of cancer, a heart condition that was inoperable, diabetes, and several other problems. He had two stem cell transplants and more blood transfusions than he would want to count—until about a year ago when he suddenly no longer needed continual blood transfusions. He is a walking miracle. Everyone who knows him has heard his miracle stories and his radiant testimony of what Jesus Christ has done in his life. He bears witness to the power of answered prayer and praises God for all the love and support he has received from the Body of Christ.

## Jamie

Two years ago Jamie, who is a wife and mother, was diagnosed with a tumor on her pancreas the size of a lemon. Jamie's husband, Jerry, works with one of our church members, Joe, who related Jamie's story to me in an email.

A week after Jamie's diagnosis, the doctor planned to do a biopsy of her tumor. He reviewed the scans he had taken the week before in preparation for the biopsy. The doctor told Jerry and Jerry's daughter who was with him, that Jamie would be back with them in thirty to forty minutes. When an hour and thirty-five minutes passed the doctor came back to the room to speak to Jerry and his daughter.

According to Jerry's email: "The doctor, still in scrubs came in. He just stood there and stared at us. I put my hand on my daughter's hand. She was visibly shaking. I could feel my heart pounding in my head. The doctor reached over, took a chair, and pulled it over to us. He sat down and then dropped his head again as to not make eye contact. *I can't lie*, I thought to myself. Regardless of what he says next I have to hold it together for my daughter. Tears refused to yield and found their way down my cheeks. The doctor looked at us as if dazed and said, 'I usually send out a report with one of my assistants but this time I thought I would just come myself'. We sat there just glued to his every word. Then in a very weak, timid voice came the two words I was truly not expecting to hear at that moment, 'It's gone. The tumor is just gone. I made numerous passes, looked back at last week's test several times to confirm the location. Then looked at the records to make sure I had the right patient. It's gone??'"

Jerry wrote, "At that point I couldn't hold it back another second, I yelled out, 'Oh Great Physician, thank you.' I scared the poor doctor to death I'm sure. I looked back at him and said in a loud voice, 'It's gone!!' I'm sure the fact that my daughter jumped up and just held me had nothing to do with comfort and everything to do with keeping me from running and screaming up and down the hospital hallways." God can and does heal miraculously when it is in His will to do so.

## When Jesus Doesn't Heal

Jesus healed many people during the days of His earthly ministry. People through the ages have experienced the invisible hand of God at work in divine healing and miracles. Thousands of people alive today can bear witness to the healing touch of Jesus Christ in their lives. I believe in divine healing and have experienced it in my own life and in the lives of others, but what do we say to people when Jesus doesn't heal them? Are we to say, "You didn't have enough faith or you didn't pray enough about it. You should have fasted more and gotten more people to pray for you."

I believe we desperately need "a balanced view" of healing in the church of Jesus Christ today. We certainly should fast, pray and believe God for miracles of healing. There are no doubt miracles waiting to happen if God's people would take Him at His Word and receive what He has to offer them.

Think with me for a moment. Did God love Peter more than James, the brother of John? Why did God allow James to be killed, but Peter to be miraculously freed from prison, even by an angel, as seen in Acts 12:1-19? Is it possible that God had a different plan for each of their lives and yet He loved them both the same?

What about the great missionary statesman, the apostle Paul? Didn't he have enough faith to be healed of his "thorn in the flesh" from II Corinthians 12:7-10? Didn't he pray enough or fast enough? Why would God withhold divine healing from this man who was used by God so mightily? Didn't Paul lead people to a saving knowledge of Jesus Christ, disciple them and even start many churches? Didn't Paul write the majority of the New Testament Scriptures? If Paul did all these things and many more, why didn't God heal him as well?

I would suggest this simple answer to all these questions: God had a better plan. God's plans are perfect and His plans are different for every person. God is sovereign. God is in control. God knows what He is doing, even though we may not know what He is doing or why. Someone said, "If God were small enough to be understood, He wouldn't be big enough to be worshipped." We must let God be God and have His way in our lives—even when His way is the way of suffering, pain, death, and even death by brutal martyrdom.

Hebrews chapter eleven contains the names of many great men and women of faith. They had mountain-moving faith and accomplished exploits for the glory of God, but did they all escape suffering and pain? No, some did and some didn't. In the first thirty-four verses there are many listed who escaped the lions, the fire, the sword, and were victorious in battle or in life's circumstances.

Beginning in verse thirty-five, we read about those who were tortured and didn't escape, but were mocked, beaten, imprisoned, stoned, sawed in two, persecuted, and mistreated. God had a better plan for them. "These were all commended for their faith, yet none of them received what had been promised, since God had planned something better for us so that only together with us would they be made perfect" (Hebrews 11:39-40).

Some Christians are repulsed by a god who would allow or even cause pain and suffering for anyone. If that's our view of God, then how do we explain the suffering and death of God's only Son, Jesus Christ? God stopped Abraham from taking the life of his son, Isaac, but no one stopped God from taking the life of His Son, Jesus Christ. Why would God let Jesus be brutally whipped with strands of leather that had pieces of metal or bone attached to them so they would tear chunks of flesh from His body? Why would God permit Jesus to be spit upon, have hair from His cheeks savagely ripped out, have a crown of thorns, no doubt shoved upon His head and have spikes driven through His hands and feet? Why would God let Jesus die such a cruel and inhumane death?

*Why?* Because that was God's plan for Jesus. We may not fully understand it or even like it, but that is how God expressed His love for us. "But God demonstrated His own love for us in this: While we were still sinners Christ died for us" (Romans 5:8). The more we understand Christ's pain and suffering for us, the more we will realize how much God loves us. "For Christ also hath once suffered for sins, the just for the unjust, that He might bring us to God, being put to death in the flesh but made alive by the Spirit" (I Peter 3:18).

## The Promise Of Sufficient Grace

God does heal miraculously and instantaneously when it is in His plan to do so. Since we cannot fully understand the mind and plan of God, we should pray for healing. We should pray that God would touch us with His invisible and powerful hand, and heal us for His glory. We should confess our sins to God and to one another and be certain there is no unconfessed sin in our lives that could block God's divine channel of healing from flowing into us. "Therefore confess your sins to each other and pray for each other so that you may be healed. The prayer of a righteous man is powerful and effective" (James 5:16).

When God did not heal Paul of his "thorn in the flesh" (II Corinthians 12:7) even though he pleaded with the Lord three times to remove it, God had a better plan. God said to Paul, "My grace is sufficient for you, for My power is made perfect in weakness." When Paul accepted God's sufficient grace for his "thorn in the flesh," he responded by saying: "Therefore I will boast all the more gladly about my weaknesses, so that Christ's power may rest on me. That is why for Christ's sake, I delight in weaknesses, in insults, in hardships, in persecutions, in difficulties. For when I am weak, then I am strong" (II Corinthians 12:9-10). God's better plan for Paul was the promise of sufficient grace in the midst of his suffering and pain.

We should rejoice that we do not know what Paul's "thorn in the flesh" was. Perhaps it was the very form of suffering that you, me, or anyone else experienced when it was in God's plan for us to suffer. Yes, sometimes God permits us to suffer for His name sake and for His glory. The key verse to summarize a balanced view on suffering is I Peter 4:19. "So then, those who suffer according to God's will should commit themselves to their faithful Creator and continue to do good." God's best plan for His children is to surrender to His perfect will, which may include divine healing or sufficient grace for a time of suffering. Whether God miraculously heals us or allows us to suffer in this life, His children should seek to glorify Him in all things. We must always remember that suffering and healing are only temporary. We are not home yet.

## Think About It

- Have you experienced miraculous healing in your life? If you have then share your testimony with others so they can be encouraged by what God has done for you.

- How would you explain to someone why there is suffering in the world?

- Do you believe God can and does heal instantaneously when it is in His plan to do so?

- If God doesn't heal you when you ask to be healed, are you willing to accept His sufficient grace and bring glory to Him through your suffering?

CHAPTER 13

# THE INVISIBLE HAND OF GOD AT WORK IN SPIRITUAL REVIVAL

*"Humble yourselves, therefore, under God's mighty hand, that He may lift you up in due time" (I Peter 5:6).*

## God's Invisible Hand Upon America

God's invisible hand was at work in the founding of America. Our first president, George Washington, recognized the hand of God and His role in the birth of our nation. In his inaugural address to Congress he said, "No people can be bound to acknowledge and adore the invisible hand which conducts the affairs of men more than the people of the United States. Every step by which they have advanced to the character of an independent nation seems to have been distinguished by some token of providential agency... We ought to be no less persuaded that the propitious (favorable) smiles of heaven cannot be expected on a nation that disregards the eternal rules of order and right, which heaven itself has ordained."[77]

George Washington clearly acknowledged God's blessing and His providential hand at work in establishing our nation. Washington also gave us a warning that God's blessing and smiles could be taken from us as a nation.

America was established upon godly, biblical principles. President Thomas Jefferson did not claim to be a Christian. Although he was a deist he still recognized that our liberties as a nation came from God. Jefferson said, "And can the liberties of a nation be thought secure when we have removed their only firm basis, a conviction in the minds of people that these liberties are

---

[77] *The Rebirth of America* (The Arthur De Moss Foundation, 1986), 32.

the gift of God? That they are not to be violated but with His wrath? Indeed I tremble for my country when I reflect that God is just: that His justice cannot sleep forever."[78] These words by Jefferson are inscribed on the wall at his memorial in Washington, D.C.

President Abraham Lincoln acknowledged God and the Holy Scriptures and their role in our nation. He said, "It is the duty of nations, as well as of men, to own their dependence upon the overruling power of God and to recognize the sublime truth announced in the Holy Scriptures and proven by all history, that those nations only are blessed whose God is the Lord."[79] Psalm 33:12 is the basis of what Lincoln said. "Blessed is the nation whose God is the Lord, the people He chose for His inheritance."

Anyone who visits Washington, D.C. can read these words etched on the walls of the Lincoln Memorial, "That this nation, under God, shall have a new birth of freedom, and that government of the people, by the people, for the people, shall not perish from the earth."[80] The words of Lincoln on the north wall of the memorial are taken from his second inaugural address and refer to God, the Bible, providence, the Almighty, and His divine attributes. His words include this statement: "As was said 3,000 years ago, so it still must be said, 'The judgments of the Lord are true and righteous altogether.'"[81]

Evidence of America's godly heritage is recorded in many places in Washington, D.C. Those who have climbed the scores of stairs inside the Washington Monument saw biblical phrases such as, "Search the Scriptures, holiness to the Lord, and train up a child." Engraved on the metal cap of the Washington Monument are these words: "Praise be to God." The Ten Commandments are displayed on the wall above the Chief Justice in the United States Supreme Court building.

The words, "under God" are part of our Pledge of Allegiance, and our coins and paper currency include our national motto, "In

---

[78] https://www.monticello.org/site/jefferson/quotations-jefferson-memorial
[79] http://www.nytimes.com/1863/04/30/news/the-national-fast-proclamation-by-the-president-of-the-united- states.html
[80] http://www.nps.gov/linc/index.htm
[81] http://avalon.law.yale.edu/19th_century/lincoln2.asp

God we trust." The Declaration of Independence, that was signed on July 4, 1776, concludes with these words, "With a firm reliance on the protection of Divine Providence, we mutually pledge to each other our lives, our fortunes, and our sacred honor."[82]

Benjamin Franklin, like President Thomas Jefferson, did not claim to be a Christian, but he certainly acknowledged the importance of prayer when our Constitution was being written during the summer of 1787. A group of representatives were meeting in Philadelphia to draft the constitution. After several weeks of struggling to find the right words and being divided on various issues, it seemed like the constitutional convention could be dissolved in complete confusion.

Did the invisible hand of God guide the framers of the U.S. Constitution? What could unite them when they were so divided? Where would they get the wisdom and perseverance they needed and not give up in utter frustration? This was a crucial moment in the history of America. How could this dilemma be resolved?

Benjamin Franklin, who was eighty-one years old at the time, rose to his feet and addressed the constitutional convention. He remarked, "In the beginning of the contest with Britain, when we were sensible of danger, we had daily prayers in this room for Divine Protection. Our prayers, Sir, were heard and they were graciously answered. All of us who were engaged in the struggle must have observed frequent instances of a superintending Providence in our favor... Have we now forgotten this powerful Friend? Or do we imagine we no longer need His assistance?"[83]

Franklin recognized the vital role God played in their deliberations. He made a motion to the delegates of the convention. He declared, "I have lived, Sir, a long time, and the longer I live, the more convincing proofs I see of this truth: that God governs in the affairs of men. And if a sparrow cannot fall to the ground without His notice, is it probable that an empire can rise without His aid? We have been assured, Sir, in the Sacred Writings that except the Lord built the house, they labor in vain

---

[82] http://www.archives.gov/exhibits/charters/declaration_transcript.html

[83] The Records of the Federal Convention of 1787 : Farrand's Records, Volume 1. (MADISON: Thursday June 28th. in Convention), 451.

that build it. I firmly believe this... I therefore beg leave to move that, henceforth, prayers imploring the assistance of Heaven and its blessing on our deliberation be held in this assembly every morning."[84] The Constitution was completed and is still the foundation of our form of government in the United States 240 years later. Many evidences of the invisible hand of God at work were experienced during the founding of our nation.

Is it just a coincidence that the three branches of our government, the judicial, legislative, and executive are identical to what Isaiah, the Old Testament prophet, wrote about in Isaiah 33:22? "For the Lord is our judge, the Lord is our lawgiver, the Lord is our king; He will save us." Is there any doubt, with the biblical knowledge many of the framers of the Constitution had, that they based the three branches of our government on this text in the book of Isaiah? Many of our laws are based on the Ten Commandments and other texts in the Scriptures. There are so many biblical references in the historical records of our government that if they were all to be removed, our government would collapse like a house of cards. Abraham Lincoln recognized this truth when he said, "All the good from the Savior of the world is communicated through this Book; but for the Book we could not know right from wrong. All the things desirable to man are contained in it."[85] George Washington also said, "It is impossible to rightly govern the world without God and the Bible."[86] Many of the early leaders of America had a great respect for the Bible and they recognized the need for God if our nation was to prosper and be protected from foreign enemies. They often referred to various Scriptures in their writings and deliberations. This can readily be observed as we read the official documents, records of meetings, and letters of many of our nation's greatest leaders.

---

[84] Ibid, 451-452.

[85] Basler, Roy P., *Collected Works of Abraham Lincoln*, *Volume VII* (1864), 542.

[86] Walker P. Whitman, *A Christian History of the American Republic: A Textbook for Secondary Schools* (Boston: Green Leaf Press, 1939,1948), 42.

## Israel And America

I recognize that Deuteronomy chapter eight was written by Moses specifically for Israel, but all of Scripture has something to teach us. The apostle Paul said, "For everything that was written in the past was written to teach us, so that through endurance and the encouragement of the Scriptures we might have hope" (Romans 15:4).

Whenever I read Deuteronomy chapter eight, I think about how God's hand of blessing has been upon America through the years. God has not only blessed the people of America, but also the land itself. America is a beautiful and fruitful land; I recognize this as a precious gift from God. People who visit America from around the world acknowledge what a beautiful and prosperous nation America has been for many years.

Moses wrote about Israel, which in many ways is like America. "Observe the commands of the Lord your God, walking in His ways and revering Him. For the Lord your God is bringing you into a good land–a land with streams and pools of water, with springs flowing in the valleys and hills; a land with wheat and barley, vines and fig trees, pomegranates, olive oil and honey; a land where bread will not be scarce and you will lack nothing; a land where the rocks are iron, and you can dig copper out of the hills. When you have eaten and are satisfied, praise the Lord your God for the good land He has given you" (Deuteronomy 8:6-10).

God's blessing on the land of Israel was so abundant that His people had all their needs met so they could be truly satisfied. God delighted to bless His people and prosper them. His blessing in Deuteronomy chapter eight is similar to Psalm 128:1-2: "Blessed are all who fear the Lord, who walk in His ways. You will eat the fruit of your labor; blessings and prosperity will be yours."

When I think of the beauty and fruitfulness of America it reminds me of the song, "America the Beautiful," written by Katharine Lee Bates.

> O beautiful for spacious skies,
> For amber waves of grain,
> For purple mountain majesties

Above the fruited plain!
America! America!
God shed His grace on thee,
And crown thy good with brotherhood
From sea to shining sea![87]

## America Must Not Forget God

When God blesses people, who in reality are unworthy of His blessing, there is always a danger that they will forget the source of their blessings and become proud in themselves. Moses warned God's people of this danger: "Be careful that you do not forget the Lord your God, failing to observe His commands, His laws and His decrees that I am giving you this day. Otherwise, when you eat and are satisfied, when you build fine houses and settle down, and when your herds and flocks grow large and your silver and gold increase and all you have is multiplied, then your heart will become proud and you will forget the Lord your God, who brought you out of Egypt, out of the land of slavery" (Deuteronomy 8:11-14).

Pride is an extremely subtle sin that can lead people away from God quicker than all other sins of human nature. "Pride goes before destruction, a haughty spirit before a fall" (Proverbs 16:18). Because God has blessed America greatly, there is a strong tendency in her people to become proud and forget God. When we are blessed we sometimes want to take credit for what has happened. We feel good about ourselves and soon believe we can accomplish whatever we want without God's help, guidance or wisdom. This is a dangerous way of thinking. We must take heed to God's warning in Proverbs 16:5: "The Lord detests all the proud of heart. Be sure of this: They will not go unpunished." God does not tell us how or when He will punish our foolish pride, but if we do not repent and humble ourselves, the day of punishment will come sooner or later.

God is far more interested in the character of His people than He is in the level of their material prosperity. "Better a little with

---

[87] Bates, Katherine Lee. "America the Beautiful." (http://www.gilderlehrman. org/history-by-era/art-music-and-film/resources/"america-beautiful, 1893).

the fear of the Lord than great wealth with turmoil. Better a meal of vegetables where there is love than a fatted calf with hatred" (Proverbs 15:16-17). Having God's blessing in our lives is far better than having great wealth and material prosperity. Proverbs 10:22 tells us, "The blessing of the Lord brings wealth." The kind of wealth God offers us is far more than just more "things or toys" for us of all ages to enjoy. True wealth is often more of a spiritual blessing from God and that is what we as individuals need as well as our nation.

Thomas Chandler Haliburton said, "The happiness of every country depends upon the character of its people, rather than the form of its government."[88] The greatness of a nation is not measured only by the beauty and fruitfulness of its land, or by the culture, education, or influence of its people. The greatness of a nation comes from the blessing of God and the godly character of its people. "Righteousness exalts a nation, but sin is a disgrace to any people" (Proverbs 14:34).

Alex De Tocqueville, the French political philosopher of the nineteenth century, wanted to discover the secret to America's greatness. He traveled throughout America and saw the beauty and prosperity of the land. He became acquainted with the American form of government. He observed our educational system and America's businesses. What was the secret to America's greatness? "Not until he visited the churches of America and witnessed the pulpits of this land 'aflame with righteousness' did he find the secret of our greatness. Returning to France, he summarized his findings; "America is great because America is good; and if America ever ceases to be good, America will cease to be great." [89]

The fact that millions of people have immigrated to America throughout the years of our existence as a nation shows how blessed and special this nation is. The invisible hand of God at work in the founding and history of America is evident to any serious inquirer. God's hand upon a nation and the desire of its people to be under His hand is the secret to its greatness, but what if that nation slips out from under God's hand? What then?

---

[88] http://www.quotes.net/quote/59512
[89] "Queries and Answers." *New York Times* (30 August 1942), BR27.

## God's Hand Lifted From America

More than 150 years ago, President Abraham Lincoln observed the greatness of America. He also observed something about this nation that troubled him greatly. What Moses had warned the people of Israel about was happening in America—the people were becoming prideful and forgetting God.

On April 30, 1863 President Abraham Lincoln's Proclamation for a National Day of Fasting, Humiliation, and Prayer drew the nation's attention to what Lincoln saw happening in America:

> "We have been the recipients of the choicest bounties of heaven. We have been preserved, these many years, in peace and prosperity. We have grown in numbers, wealth and power, as no other nation has ever grown. But we have forgotten God. We have forgotten the gracious hand which preserved us in peace, and multiplied and enriched and strengthened us; and we have vainly imagined, in the deceitfulness of our hearts, that all these blessings were produced by some superior wisdom and virtue of our own. Intoxicated with unbroken success, we have become too self-sufficient to feel the necessity of redeeming and preserving grace, too proud to pray to the God that made us! It behooves us, then to humble ourselves before the offended Power, to confess our national sins, and to pray for clemency and forgiveness."[90]

Could the invisible hand of God that mightily blessed a nation also be lifted from that nation? What would cause God to lift His hand from a nation or an individual? What could happen to a nation if God lifted His hand from it?

---

[90] http://www.nytimes.com/1863/04/30/news/the-national-fast-proclamation-by-the-president-of-the-united-states.html

## God's Solemn Warning

In Deuteronomy chapter eight we see not only God's blessing upon a nation and His solemn warning to a nation, but we are also told what could happen to a nation that is proud and forgets God:

> "You may say to yourself, 'My power and the strength of my hands have produced this wealth for me.' But remember the Lord your God, for it is He who gives you the ability to produce wealth, and so confirms His covenant, which He swore to your forefathers, as it is today. If you ever forget the Lord your God and follow other gods and worship and bow down to them, I testify against you today that you will surely be destroyed. Like the nations the Lord destroyed before you, so you will be destroyed for not obeying the Lord your God" (Deuteronomy 8:17-20).

There is a principle in the Bible that bears witness to the fact that God is just and that He punishes sin. If God did not punish sin He would not be just. "He is the Rock, His works are perfect, and all His ways are just. A faithful God who does no wrong, upright and just is He" (Deuteronomy 32:4). God never does anything wrong. That's one of the reasons I know He is God and I am not. Whatever judgment or disaster God brings upon a nation, a government, a business, a church, a family, or an individual is absolutely certain to be a just judgment.

## Sowing And Reaping

We reap what we sow. This principle is as true in farming or gardening as it is in everyday life. The Bible says, "Do not be deceived: God cannot be mocked. A man reaps what he sows. The one who sows to please his sinful nature, from that nature will reap destruction; the one who sows to please the Spirit, from the Spirit will reap eternal life" (Galatians 6:7-8). The problem with sowing wild oats is that it produces a wild crop. What we sow can come back to haunt us if we are not careful.

Dr. John MacArthur said, "Many have mocked God and His truth because of the sinful behavior of those who claim to be Christians. To be convinced that God can save from sin one needs to see someone who lives a holy life. When Christians claim to believe God's Word but do not obey it, the Word is dishonored."[91]

Joshua warned the Israelites of forsaking God and replacing Him with other gods. "If you forsake the Lord and serve foreign gods, He will turn and bring disaster on you and make an end of you, after He has been good to you" (Joshua 24:20).

If God has been so good to America, and He certainly has, would He purposely bring disaster upon America? Many people, including Christians, do not want to think like that. They cannot conceive of a God who would punish the sins of a nation by allowing it to experience a time of great suffering. Some may even say, "That's old-fashioned. You don't really believe that, do you? Get a life. We are living in the twenty-first century, not in the Dark Ages."

The Bible teaches that sin leads to death. If God chooses to take a person's life by either a disaster or natural means, the end is the same. Let God be God. Job lost his seven sons and three daughters in a terrible wind storm and he said, "The Lord gave and the Lord has taken away; may the name of the Lord be praised" (Job 1:21). The book of Proverbs declares, "There is a way that seems right to a man, but in the end it leads to death" (Proverbs 16:25). In the New Testament we read, "For the wages of sin is death, but the gift of God is eternal life in Christ Jesus our Lord" (Romans 6:23). Physical death will ultimately come upon all people some day in one way or another. Death is the result of sin. But those who are in Christ have the assurance of eternal life after physical death.

If our understanding of God is that He is a loving, kind, generous, benevolent grandfather-type who would never raise his voice or scold his children or grandchildren, then we are uninformed of what God reveals about Himself in Scripture. If we fail to acknowledge the true character of God and instead pick and choose which attributes of God we think He should have, we

---

[91] Queries and Answers." *New York Times* (30 August 1942), BR27

are not going to live a life that is pleasing to Him. As sinners, we are going to try to get away with a lot of things in our behavior and lifestyle. We've lost the concept of God's holiness. Because God is holy, He cannot tolerate sin. Because He is just, He cannot ignore sin. God hates sin and He must and will deal with it accordingly.

One of the greatest problems in America today is that people have lost any sense of the fear of God. Romans 3:14-18 declares, "Their mouths are full of cursing and bitterness. Their feet are swift to shed blood; ruin and misery mark their ways, and the way of peace they do not know. There is no fear of God before their eyes." This is surely descriptive of countless thousands of people in America today. Hebrews 10:31 contains some very solemn words: "It is a dreadful thing to fall into the hands of the living God." What do we do with verses like these? Do we try to ignore them, but to our own peril?

Jonathan Edwards was used mightily by God during the First Great Awakening in America during the 1740's. He preached a sermon entitled, "Sinners in the Hands of an Angry God," and scores of people turned to Jesus Christ for salvation. Some would accuse Edwards of scaring people into heaven. He simply preached the holy, inspired Word of God without compromising, being politically correct, or fearing man in any way. He feared God alone. Oh, that God would raise up many men today in America like Jonathan Edwards. Oh, that our pulpits would be aflame with Holy Spirit filled preaching of the true gospel of Jesus Christ including the message of repentance, brokenness, humility, righteousness and faith boldly and lovingly proclaimed without compromise of any kind.

Have we forsaken God and His Word as a nation? Are we reaping what we have sown? Is our immoral free fall into premarital sex, pornography, living together without being married, homosexuality, divorce, abortion, drug and alcohol abuse, child abuse, violent crime, gambling, and terrorism but symptoms of our departure from God? Would God be just in bringing judgment and disaster upon America? Someone said, "If God doesn't judge America He will have to apologize to Sodom and Gomorrah."

What kind of behavior can we expect from people who do not know God? They are only doing what comes naturally to them. What kind of behavior should we expect from God's people? Christians have the very presence of God Himself living within them. When a person receives Christ as Savior and Lord, the third person of the Trinity, the Holy Spirit, takes up residence in their heart. The Spirit gives them power over sin. Therefore, Christians should be living in ways that show that they belong to Christ. God calls Christians to be holy, which means to be set apart, as Christ followers. "Be holy, for I am holy" (1 Peter 1:16).

Was God trying to get our attention on 9/11? In spite of the sinful hatred in the hearts of the terrorists, what was God saying to us as a nation and especially to His people, Christians who claim Jesus Christ as their Savior and Lord?

Dr. Henry Blackaby said, "America is a reflection of God's people. I'm one along with Bill Bright who concluded that 9/11 was God's warning to God's people that He was beginning to remove the hedge of protection from the nation because of the sin of God's people, not the sin of the nation, because the sin of the nation is a reflection that the salt has lost its saltiness, and the light no longer dispenses the darkness."[92] Was God trying to get our attention through the events of 9/11? There were millions of Americans who attended prayer meetings and worship services in the days after the terrorist bombing of the World Trade Center Twin Towers on 9/11, but within a few weeks things returned to normal and the prayer meetings and worship services were no longer important to the vast majority of people who attended during the days of the crisis. Are there perhaps many other ways in which God is seeking to draw people to Himself by His invisible hand at work in America?

## Disasters

Would God remove His hand of protection from America and allow disasters to come upon our nation? Did God ever do

---

[92] Blackaby, Henry. "Why Revival Tarries" address. (The Cove, North Carolina: April 2004).

something like that before? Yes, God moved upon nations and individuals who had forsaken Him on numerous occasions in the past.

Israel rebelled against the Lord and suffered greatly. Would God purposely turn His own chosen people over to their enemies? When His people persisted in sin and refused to repent and return to the Lord He brought judgment upon them through their enemies. "Again the Israelites did evil in the eyes of the Lord, so the Lord delivered them into the hands of the Philistines for forty years" (Judges 13:1). Who delivered Israel into the hands of the Philistines? God did. Would God possibly turn America over to our enemies and let us be ruled by a foreign power? He did it before.

God spoke to Moses near the time of his death. He told him what the Israelites were going to do after he was gone. "And the Lord said to Moses: 'You are going to rest with your fathers and these people will soon prostitute themselves to the foreign gods of the land they are entering. They will forsake Me and break the covenant I made with them. On that day I will become angry with them and forsake them; I will hide My face from them, and they will be destroyed. Many disasters and difficulties will come upon them, and on that day they will ask, 'Have not these disasters come upon us because our God is not with us?'" (Deuteronomy 31:16-17). One of the first questions that is often asked when a disaster occurs is this: "Where was God when this disaster happened?"

If we have kicked God out of our elementary, middle, and high schools and colleges—wanting nothing to do with Him in our educational system, can we expect more disasters in our schools?

If we continue to rebel against God and take further steps to remove Him from our nation, will we have more terrorist attacks like 9/11 and the bombing in Boston in April 2013 during the Boston Marathon? Could God be lifting His hand of protection from us? It is extremely possible that we will have many more terrorists attacks in America that will make 9/11 pale in comparison. Will we seek the protection of Almighty God and even more so seek His forgiveness of our wicked ways before it is too late? Isaiah 65:2 clearly proclaims God's offer to rescue His people before it would be too late: "All day long I have held out My hands to an obstinate people, who walk in ways not good, pursuing their own imaginations." God's invisible hand was held out to His people but they refused to accept His merciful offer of protection, and, therefore, they had to face the severe consequences of their sins as the rest of Isaiah chapter sixty-five indicates. Will we as a nation humble ourselves under God's invisible hand and turn to Him as He reaches out to us? Listen to God's promise in I Peter 5:6: "Humble yourselves, therefore, under God's mighty hand, that He may lift you up in due time."

## Weather Conditions

Could God be bringing judgment upon America through adverse weather conditions? Does the invisible hand of God control the weather? When we have warm sunshine, gentle rains for our lawns, gardens and farmers' fields, and gentle breezes we want to thank the Lord for blessing us. Does not the same God send the hurricanes, tornadoes, violent thunder storms, snow storms, floods, droughts, and earthquakes? Some people would be quick to say, "God doesn't have anything to do with disastrous storms or earthquakes." What does the Bible say about these things?

"He (God) says to the snow, 'Fall on the earth,' and to the rain shower, 'Be a mighty downpour.' The tempest (violent storm) comes out from its chamber, the cold from the driving winds. The breath of God produces ice, and the broad waters become frozen. He loads the clouds with moisture; He scatters His lightning through them. At His direction they swirl around over the face of the whole earth to do whatever He commands them. He brings the clouds to punish men, or to water the earth and show His love" (Job 37:6,9-13).

Was it not God who sent the flood and destroyed all mankind except Noah, his wife, three sons, and their wives? Was it not God who rained fire and brimstone upon Sodom and Gomorrah and destroyed those cities completely?

Nahum 1:3-5 declares, "The Lord is slow to anger and great in power; the Lord will not leave the guilty unpunished. His way is in the whirlwinds (cyclone, tornado) and the storm, and clouds are the dust of His feet. He rebukes the sea and dries it up. Bashan and Carmel wither and the blossoms of Lebanon fade. The mountains quake before Him and the hills melt away. The earth trembles at His presence, the world and all who live in it." Do you recognize how intricately God is involved in the weather regardless of how pleasant or disastrous it may be?

Joel Rosenberg, in his book *Implosion: Can America Recover from Its Economic and Spiritual Challenges in Time?* reports startling statistics about historic and unprecedented weather conditions:

- Eight of the ten most expensive hurricanes in American history have happened since 9/11. The worst was Hurricane Katrina which nearly wiped out an American city and ended up costing more than $100 Billion.
- Hurricane Irene made 2011 the worst year in American history for natural disasters, with ten separate catastrophes costing $1 Billion or more.
- In 2011, America experienced the worst outbreak of tornadoes in nearly half a century.
- In 2011, Texas suffered the worst fires in the history of the state, amid the worst drought in Texas history.
- In 2011, Virginia — and much of the East Coast- experienced its biggest earthquake since 1875.[93]

### Earthquakes

Does God have anything to do with earthquakes? Numerous earthquakes are recorded in the Word of God. Could God use earthquakes to get our attention in America and turn our hearts back to Him? Isaiah, the prophet declared, "The Lord Almighty will come with thunder and earthquake and great noises, with windstorm and tempest (violent storms) and flames of a devouring fire" (Isaiah 29:6). Do we take seriously what God says

---

[93] Rosenberg, Joel, C., *Implosion: Can America Recover From It's Economic and Spiritual Challenges in Time?* (Carol Stream: Tyndale House PublishersI, 2012),167-168.

in His holy Word or do we try to ignore it and avoid thinking about it?

John Wesley delivered a sermon in the mid-1700's titled "The Cause and Cure of Earthquakes." In it he said, "Of all the judgments which the righteous God inflicts on sinners here, the most dreadful and destructive is an earthquake... Earthquakes are set forth by the inspired writers as God's proper judicial act, or the punishment of sin: sin is the cause, earthquakes the effect, of His anger... Now, that God is Himself the author, and sin the moral cause, of earthquakes...cannot be denied by any who believe the Scriptures."[94] God used earthquakes numerous times in biblical history to accomplish His purposes.

During a Sunday morning message in August 2011, I shared with our congregation that I feared the judgment of God upon our nation. I mentioned the storms, hurricanes, tornadoes, droughts, fires, and floods that much of our nation was experiencing in 2011, but it seemed like the East Coast of the U.S. hadn't had any of those things happen. Two weeks later on August 23, 2011, a 5.8 earthquake struck the East Coast. Four days after that, Hurricane Irene caused millions of dollars of damage. The East Coast was struck with an earthquake and a hurricane in the same week.

Jesus said before His return there would be earthquakes. "Nation will rise against nation, and kingdom against kingdom. There will be famines and earthquakes in various places" (Matthew 24:7). Jesus told us ahead of time that earthquakes will be happening before His return, but many people are absolutely convinced it will never happen where they live. Do you think God would be just if He brought major earthquakes to America? What do you think it will take to get the attention of the American people and turn our hearts to God?

## Economy

For many years I have wondered if some day God might bring an economic collapse upon our nation. We have become so materialistic and for many, money has become their god. Whatever is most important in a person's life is their god. "For

---

[94] Ibid, 171.

where your treasure is, there your heart will be also" (Matthew 6:21).

For millions of Americans, sports have become their god. They wouldn't think of missing a sporting event or spending any amount of money to attend sporting events. Many parents today are allowing their children to be involved in sports and other activities on Sunday mornings instead of attending church services with them. They're more concerned about their child's athletics than their spiritual life. Someone said, "We live in a culture that values fifteen minutes of fame and undervalues lifelong faithfulness." What kind of children are we raising for the future? Are we more concerned that our son can catch a football or that our daughter is captain of her soccer team than we are of their spiritual and moral development? Galatians 6:7 tells us clearly, "Do not be deceived: God cannot be mocked. A man (or woman or child) reaps what he (or she) sows." If all we want for our children is that they marry a nice person and acquire a good paying job, then we have missed out on the best that God has to offer us.

Paul Ryan, when he was Chairman of the House Budget Committee, warned in 2011 on ABC's "This Week" program, "We know we are going to have an economic collapse if we stay on the path we are on."[95] If we continue to spend and borrow more and more money as a nation, as families and individuals what will our future look like? What kind of a future will our children and grandchildren have to face?

Could God be lifting His hand from America? The invisible hand of God that blessed and guided this nation for so many years can become the hand of discipline and disaster. God is always just in His judgments. Those He loves He disciplines and always for their good and for His glory. Are we reaping what we have sown in this nation? Could the disasters, historic weather conditions, earthquakes and economic difficulties be God's way of drawing us back to Himself? Will we return to God before it's too late? Will our nation experience revival or complete ruin?

---

[95] Rosenberg, Joel C. *Implosion: Can America Recover From It's Economic and Spiritual Challenges in Time?* (Carol Stream: Tyndale House Publishers, 2012), 134.

## God's Hand Returned Upon A Nation

America is at a crossroads in our history. Will we continue to run away from God or will we run to Him? Will we repent of our sins and return to Him or will we end in ruin? Will God continue to lift His invisible hand from us, or will He return His hand of blessing upon us?

God had a message for Israel and Jeremiah was the prophet God called to deliver the message. This message could be applied to any nation, including America:

> "This is the word that came to Jeremiah from the Lord: 'Go down to the potter's house, and there I will give you My message.' So I went down to the potter's house, and I saw him working at the wheel. But the pot he was shaping from the clay was marred in his hands; so the potter formed it into another pot, shaping it as seemed best to him.
>
> "Then the word of the Lord came to me: 'O house of Israel, can I not do with you as this potter does?' declares the Lord. 'Like clay in the hand of the potter so are you in My hand, O house of Israel. If at any time I announce that a nation or kingdom is to be uprooted, torn down and destroyed, and if that nation I warned repents of its evil, then I will relent and not inflict on it the disaster I had planned. And if at another time I announce that a nation or kingdom is to be built up and planted, and if it does evil in My sight and does not obey Me, then I will reconsider the good I had intended to do for it.
>
> "Now therefore say to the people of Judah and those living in Jerusalem, 'This is what the Lord says: Look! I am preparing a disaster for you and devising a plan against you. So turn from your evil ways, each one of you, and reform your ways and your actions.' But they will reply, 'It's no use. We will continue with our own plans; each of us will

follow the stubbornness of his evil heart'"
(Jeremiah 18:1-12).

God does not want to bring disaster upon a nation, but if that nation continues on its sinful path and refuses to repent, then God will bring disaster upon it. God never fails to keep His Word. Whatever He says He will do. God's purpose in bringing disaster upon a nation is to lead that nation to Himself in genuine repentance. His purpose is not merely to punish that nation or individuals, but out of love He punishes those He created so they will learn to walk in His ways and be drawn to His Son Jesus Christ. Ephesians 2:3-5 declares: "All of us also lived among them (who followed the ways of the world, v.2) at one time, gratifying the cravings of our sinful nature and following its desires and thoughts. Like the rest, we were by nature objects of wrath. But because of His great love for us, God, who is rich in mercy, made us alive with Christ even when we were dead in transgressions –it is by grace you have been saved." When we receive Jesus Christ into our lives, our hearts are changed and we have a new nature in Christ and we want to obey Him. Those who do not know Jesus Christ by faith cannot obey God because His Spirit is not in them. General Douglas MacArthur said, "History fails to record a single precedent in which nations subject to moral decay have not passed into political and economic decline. There has been either a spiritual awakening to overcome the moral lapse or a progressive deterioration leading to ultimate national disaster."[96] America is in great political and economic decline. Without God's divine intervention, there is no hope of reversing the downward trends in America.

We need a mighty spiritual revival in America that will result in a spiritual awakening that will draw thousands of unbelievers to a personal relationship with Jesus Christ.

Revival has been defined in different ways. John Piper says, "Revival is the sovereign work of God to awaken His people with fresh intensity to the truth and glory of God, the ugliness of sin, the horror of hell, the preciousness of Christ's atoning work, the

---

[96]Imparato, Edward T. *General MacArthur Wisdom and Visions* (Paducah: Turner Publishing Co, 2000), 129.

wonder of salvation by grace through faith, the urgency of holiness and witness, and the sweetness of worship with God's people."[97]

Dr. Richard Owen Roberts, President of International Awakening Ministries, says: "Revival is nothing less than God manifesting Himself in the midst of His people. When God shows Himself to His people they experience holiness in their hearts, passionate love in their spirits, and spiritual fire in their bones that exceeds any spiritual experiences previously known. This is the greatest need of today's church. Millions of individuals and tens of thousands of churches need to make seeking God's face their primary endeavor and to persist in this labor of love until God comes and reigns righteousness upon us."[98] God is so anxious to revive His people and restore them to a vital and holy fellowship with Himself and with others in the body of Christ, His church. God wants to return His blessing upon America and restore our nation if we will only humble ourselves under His invisible hand and repent of our sinful ways and obey Him in all things.

Do you sense God's invisible hand upon your life personally drawing you into a closer fellowship and intimacy in your relationship with Him? When you cannot see His hand, trust His heart. Pause for a few minutes right now and turn to Him. Go ahead. He is calling you to Himself. His strong arms are open to you and His loving, invisible hands will embrace you. Don't make Him wait any longer. This could be a very special moment in your life. Tell Him you love Him and that you want to be fully restored to Him. You will be so glad you turned to Him. He will not turn you away.

## The First Great Awakening

God's invisible hand came upon America in revival a number of times in the past. During the First Great Awakening in the 1730s and 1740s, God used Jonathan Edwards as an instrument to

---

[97] Piper, John. *A Godward Life: Savoring the Supremacy of God in All of Life* (Sisters, Ore: Multnomah Books, 1997), 111.

[98] Roberts, Richard Owen. Preface in Nancy Leigh DeMoss, Tim Grisson, *Seeking Him: Experiencing the Joy of Person Revival* (Chicago: Moody Publishers, 2004).

spread revival. He was a pastor in Northampton, Massachusetts, who preached God's Holy Word fearlessly. In 1727, a great earthquake shook New England and many people were spiritually awakened and received Christ into their lives. People everywhere were talking about spiritual matters.

Jonathan Edwards wrote about the revival taking place in Northampton. It was amazing what God was doing:

> "The work of conversion was carried on in a most astonishing manner, and increased more and more; souls did as it were come by flocks to Jesus Christ....The number of true saints multiplied, soon made a glorious alteration in the town: so that in the spring and summer following, 1735, the town seemed to be full of the presence of God: it never was so full of love, nor of joy, and yet so full of distress, as it was then....It was a time of joy in families on account of salvation being brought to them; parents rejoicing over their children as new born, and husbands over their wives, and wives over their husbands. The doings of God were then seen in His sanctuary, God's day was a delight, and His tabernacles were amiable. Our public assemblies were then beautiful: the congregation was alive in God's service, every one earnestly intent on the public worship, every hearer eager to drink in the words of the minister as they came from his mouth; the assembly in general were, from time to time, in tears while the Word was preached; some weeping with sorrow and distress, others with joy and love, others with pity and concern for the souls of their neighbors."[99]

During the First Great Awakening in America, God also used George Whitefield (1714-1770), John Wesley (1703-1791) and Charles Wesley (1707-1788) and others to spread revival fires. The

---

[99] Edwards, Jonathan. *A Faithful Narrative of the Surprising Work of God.* (http://www.jonathan-edwards.org/Narrative.html).

mighty moving of God's invisible hand upon thousands of Americans in those days was just the beginning of more spiritual awakenings to come. God's manifest presence was revealed in the midst of His people as they turned to Him in genuine repentance and humbleness and they could not deny that this was a surprising work of God.

## The Second Great Awakening

The Second Great Awakening (1800-1850s) was marked by more revivals and spiritual awakenings in America. God used Francis Asbury (1745-1816), Timothy Dwight (1752-1817), a grandson of Jonathan Edwards and Charles Finney (1792-1875) as well as many other leaders to draw His people back to a restored fellowship with God and His people. These men preached the gospel with mighty power and boldness. "After they prayed, the place where they were meeting was shaken. And they were all filled with the Holy Spirit and spoke the word of God boldly" (Acts 4:31). These men were men of prayer and all experienced God's anointing upon them and the impact of their lives and ministries touched thousands of people throughout America. Revival fires often spread like wildfire.

## The 1857 Prayer Revival

In 1857 a layman's prayer revival began in New York City. Jeremiah Lanphier (1809-1890) was hired by the North Dutch Reformed Church on Fulton Street. He began a noontime prayer meeting on September 23, 1857. Only six men attended the first prayer meeting, but before long a hundred were attending and then thousands were gathering all over New York City seeking God at noontime.

Lloyd Turner wrote about this remarkable revival in his book, *Highways of Holiness*: "The Noon Prayer Meetings picked up intensity after the New York Stock Exchange crashed on October 13, 1857. Five months after the market crash, 10,000 people gathered for noon-prayer in New York City alone. Other churches and theaters began to sponsor prayer meetings, and all these rooms filled up almost as quickly as they opened. By now the prayer meetings had gained the attention of the popular press. The New York Herald and New York Tribune both devoted an entire issue to the prayer meetings early in 1858, and several widely circulated journals began publishing 'the Progress of the Revival' as a featured column."[100] It is estimated that about one million converts were added to the churches of America within two years of this prayer revival. When we work, we work—but when we pray, God works. Oh, that God would stir our hearts to pray like this again. United prayer is the spark of revival. If God shows up in amazing ways when His people unite together in prayer, why do we not make corporate prayer a greater priority in our lives?

In Matthew 18:20 Jesus spoke these powerful words: "For where two or three come together in My name, there am I with them." If Jesus shows up at a prayer meeting of just two or three of His children who gather in His name, we can only imagine what could happen if whole congregations, with hundreds, and even thousands of His people would unite in prayer.

Is God calling you to join a corporate prayer gathering? You will be pleasantly surprised as to what will happen as you join with others in united prayer. Ask God to lead you to a corporate prayer group if you are not presently attending one. Remain faithful and invite others to join you.

### The 1904 Revival In Wales

In 1904 in the little country of Wales, God brought revival and the ripple effects of it touched thousands of people in America. Evan Roberts, who was a young coal miner, was the instrument God used in this revival. Prayer meetings began to spring up all over Wales. Matthew Henry said, "When God wishes to bless His people, He first sets them a-praying."[101] When God's people sense

---

[100] Turner, Lloyd. *Highways of Holiness* (San Jose: Transformational Publications, 2006), 124.

[101] Billy Graham, et al. *Revival in Our Time: The Story of the Billy Graham Evangelistic Campaigns* (Wheaton: 1950), pg 35.

His invisible hand drawing them to pray they want to pray. They discover renewed power and victory as they pray.

A.T. Pierson declared, "There has never been a spiritual awakening in any country or locality that did not begin in united prayer."[102] Jonathan Edwards agreed that prayer was essential to revival. He wrote, "When God has something great for His church, it is His will that there should precede it the extraordinary prayers of His people."[103] It is estimated that five million people were converted to Christ by 1906 in many parts of the world as a result of this revival.

The front page of the Denver Post on January 20, 1905 had the headlines, "ENTIRE CITY PAUSES FOR PRAYER EVEN AT THE HIGH TIDE OF BUSINESS AS THE SOUL RISES ABOVE SORDID THOUGHTS."[104] All over Denver and many other cities in America, prayer meetings were held at noontime as businesses closed so employees and customers could turn to God in prayer. I can only imagine what could happen in America today if God's people again became serious about prayer.

## The 1970 Asbury Revival

In February 1970, Asbury College and Seminary in Wilmore, Kentucky was visited by God as His invisible hand touched the lives of hundreds of students, faculty, and people across our nation. This revival affected me personally when a team of students from Asbury College visited Houghton College in New York. I was a senior at Houghton when Asbury students shared testimonies of what God was doing in revival at their college. As the students simply shared the wonderful works of God that were happening at Asbury, suddenly the presence of God seemed to fill Wesley Chapel at Houghton. This was one of the most memorable and amazing experiences of my life.

---

[102] Orr, J Edwin. *Prayer and Revival, The Role of Prayer in Spiritual Awakening* (http://www.jedwinorr.com/resources/articles/prayandrevival.pdf).

[103] Edwards, Jonathan. *The Works of President Edwards, Vol 3* (Bedford: Applewood Books, 1808), 336.

[104] De Moss, Nancy Leigh. "The Presence of God." Revive Our Hearts Radio. (https://www.reviveourhearts.com/radio/revive-our-hearts/thepresence-of-god/: 05 Jan. 2005).

One Asbury student, a petite young girl, smiled at the students who filled the seats in Wesley Chapel that day and with a very weak voice said, "I just want to love you with the love of Jesus." Her face was glowing with the presence of Jesus Christ shining through her. Psalm 34:5 says, "Those who look to Him are radiant; their faces are never covered with shame." She looked to the Lord and I saw the beauty of the Lord radiating through her. When she made eye contact with students in the audience, many of them came under deep conviction of sin and began to weep. God's invisible hand was moving profoundly in many lives in Wesley Chapel that day. I will never forget what I experienced in that chapel service at Houghton College that cold winter day in February 1970.

I personally experienced two examples of the convicting power of the Holy Spirit during the chapel service. The first example happened with the girl who sat beside me. She turned to me and confessed that she had had a bad attitude toward me and asked if I would please forgive her. I had no idea she felt that way toward me. I forgave her and we were both overjoyed as we recognized that God immediately restored Christian fellowship between us.

The second example of God's Spirit at work in that service took place when I felt the need to go forward and kneel in prayer at the kneeling rail at the front of the chapel. As I prayed, my history professor knelt beside me, and I was suddenly convicted by the Holy Spirit that I had been harboring a bad attitude in my heart toward him. Now it was my turn to ask him to forgive me. He graciously forgave me and prayed with me. Only God could have led my professor, out of the hundreds of students and staff in chapel that day, to come and kneel beside me so I could be reconciled to him. I will always be grateful to God for what I experienced of the manifest presence of God that cold winter day in 1970.

It has been the prayer and longing of my heart over the past forty-six years since I left the Houghton College campus that I would once again have the privilege of experiencing the invisible hand of God at work in spiritual revival. Would you please join me in praying that God would send a mighty spiritual revival into the hearts of millions of Americans who know Him, but need a fresh touch from His invisible hand upon their lives? (Please pause right now and pray.)

If God chooses to send revival among His people, throughout our nation, it will result in the spiritual awakening of multitudes of unbelievers who will come to know Jesus Christ as their Savior and Lord. Can you think of anything more wonderful that could happen in America than spiritual revival among God's people and a spiritual awakening among lost people who desperately need Jesus Christ in their lives?

When the invisible hand of God is moving in revival, people want to get right with God and with one another. Someone said, "When you have been in the fire of revival, the smell of smoke never leaves you." Oh, that the fragrant smell of His smoke would be evident in our lives today!

## The 1995 Convocation On Revival

In February 1995, I attended a Convocation on Revival in Little Rock, Arkansas. Two other pastors, Harvey Copperwheat from Bethlehem, Pennsylvania, and Charles McConnell from Allentown, Pennsylvania, attended the conference with me. All three of us were deeply burdened for revival in the Lehigh Valley area of Pennsylvania where God had called us to minister as pastors. One night during the revival conference the three of us went forward and knelt in prayer at the front of the sanctuary in the church where the conference was held. Our united prayer was "Lord, use us in revival regardless of the cost or the consequences." We had no idea what our future held, but we knew Who held our future. Corrie Ten Boom said, "Never be afraid to commit an unknown future to a known God."[105]

Thirty-two days after we arrived home from the Convocation on Revival Harvey Copperwheat, my close friend and weekly prayer partner, died suddenly at the age of fifty-two from a blood clot. I was in shock when Harvey died. I was asked to preach at his funeral a few days later. That was one of the most difficult assignments I have ever had in my ministry. I wasn't sure I could

---

[105] Ten Boom, Corrie. *Clippings from My Notebook* (Minneapolis: World Wide Publications, 1982), 27.

do it, but by God's grace He enabled me to preach at my friend's funeral.

A lady in my congregation knew about my close relationship with Harvey and how difficult it would be for me to handle his death and to speak at his funeral, so she interceded in prayer for me during those very difficult days in my life. A few days after the funeral she sent a note to me and indicated she was praying that the Lord would lift me up with His "everlasting arms" as Deuteronomy 33:27 speaks about. That was exactly what I experienced as I spoke at Harvey's funeral. In the first few minutes when I began speaking I was overcome with emotion, but suddenly I felt like someone put their hands under my arms and lifted me up and I began to preach with God's power and anointing. I can only explain what happened that day as the invisible hand of God at work in my life.

Nine months after Harvey died I was diagnosed with prostate cancer in December 1995. In February 1996, Charles McConnell and I planned to attend the Convocation on Revival in Little Rock for the second time. Two weeks before we were to begin our long drive from Pennsylvania to Arkansas, Charles called to discuss our travel plans. He said, "Larry, I have been thinking about what has happened since we went to the Convocation on Revival last year. Harvey died and you have been diagnosed with prostate cancer. I've been wondering if something may happen to me."

Five days before Charles and I were to leave for the Convocation on Revival, he had a brain seizure and was diagnosed with malignant brain cancer. Thirty-two months after we buried Harvey, my dear friend Charles McConnell also passed. For some unknown reason, and I do not question God's wisdom and perfect plan, my two brothers in Christ went to be with the Lord, while I survived cancer and have continued in the ministry.

God called me to Calvary Baptist Church in Bethlehem, Pennsylvania, in 1983. In September 2016, Lord willing, I will complete thirty-three years of ministry at Calvary and in the Lehigh Valley of Pennsylvania. My heart continues to burn with the desire to be used of God in whatever ministry opportunities He has planned for me in the future. I pray daily that I will live to see the revival and spiritual awakening I have longed for throughout the years of my ministry.

## A Call For Revival Today

I continue to believe the main elements of revival are found in II Chronicles 7:14. "If My people, who are called by My name, will humble themselves and pray and seek My face and turn from their wicked ways, then will I hear from heaven and will forgive their sin and heal their land." God will bring a mighty healing to America and to any nation that will obey what He says in this powerful verse of Scripture written hundreds of years ago, but still just as relevant today as ever before.

Revival is not for unbelievers. They do not need revival. They simply need life in Christ through being born again as John 3:1-8 indicates. Revival is for God's people who know Him and confess Jesus Christ as their Savior and Lord, but they have grown cold in their fellowship with Him. In Revelation 2:4 the Spirit of God is speaking to the church at Ephesus. This is what the Spirit said: "You have forsaken your first love." The Spirit then calls on the church to "Remember the height from which you have fallen! Repent and do the things you did at first" (Revelation 2:5).

God is calling His church today to genuine repentance and to return to Him, their first love. Will the church in America repent and return to God and experience a spiritual revival that will lead to a great awakening among those who do not yet know Jesus Christ as Savior and Lord? In Psalm 85:6 the Psalmist cried out to God in prayer for revival. "Will You not revive us again, that Your people may rejoice in You?" God's people will only be able to rejoice in Him when they are in close fellowship with Him and when there is no unconfessed sin in their lives. Let us commit our lives to seeking God and praying that He will use each one of us to spread genuine Christ-centered and Word-centered revival in America before it is too late.

There are many pastors and Christian leaders who are involved in corporate prayer groups in the Lehigh Valley like Share the Power, One Voice Pastors Network and Pray Lehigh Valley that are seeing God unite Christians in fervent prayer for revival and spiritual awakening. There are also many national prayer groups like OneCry.org that are calling America to pray for revival.

God has used a wonderful Bible study in many churches in the Lehigh Valley called "Becoming One," written by Jack Jacobs and Ed Rodgers. The purpose of the Bible study is to show the importance of Jews and Gentiles becoming one in the Messiah, Yeshua ("Jesus"). Unity among believers of both Jews and Gentiles who confess Jesus as the Messiah will help to bring forth the revival that God desires to birth in our nation and around the world.

In His high priestly prayer in John 17:20-23, Jesus prayed for unity among His people. "My prayer is not for them alone. I pray also for those who will believe in Me through their message, that all of them may be one, Father, just as You are in Me and I am in You. May they also be in Us so that the world may believe that You have sent Me. I have given them the glory that You gave Me, that they may be one as We are one. I in them and You in Me. May they be brought to complete unity to let the world know that You sent Me and have loved them even as You have loved Me."

When the church of Jesus Christ takes seriously the unity that Jesus prayed for, then revival cannot be far away. Let us as followers of Jesus Christ, the Messiah, do all we can to repent, return and be united in Him.

G. Campbell Morgan said, "We cannot send revival, but we can set our sails to catch the wind when God chooses to blow upon His people."[106] Please join me as we set our sails together.

In 1993 I wrote in the front of my Bible a Mission Statement for my life. *My mission in life is to fulfill God's calling to help lead the body of Christ, His Church, in intercessory prayer, revival, world-evangelization and missionary service to the glory of God, today, tomorrow and always.* This is what I have committed my life to the past twenty-three years and this is what I plan, by God's grace and strength, to commit my life to until He takes me home to heaven someday.

---

[106] Olford, Stephen F. Heart Cry for Revival Conference message. (Lancaster: May 26-29, 1998, http://www.heraldofhiscoming.com/Past%20Issues/1998/September/the_pattern_for_revival.htm).

Writing this book has been on my heart for at least the past fifteen years. I am so grateful to God for the strength and time He gave me to write it. In God's divine plan and timing, He gave me twelve weeks to recuperate from back surgery in 2013 and the elders of Calvary Baptist Church gave me an additional four weeks of sabbatical during which time the first draft of this book was written.

It is the prayer of my heart that as a result of reading, *The Invisible Hand of God at Work–An Extraordinary God Experienced in an Ordinary Life*, that you will desire to experience more and more evidence of the invisible hand of God at work in your own life. As that happens, "To God Be the Glory."

## Think About It

- What evidence of God's invisible hand at work have you experienced in your personal life?
- What evidence of God's invisible hand at work do you believe happened in the founding of America?
- In what ways do you see America becoming more godly or more godless?
- If God chooses to bring judgment upon America, how do you think that may happen?
- Are you seeking to repent of anything God reveals to you that is not right in your life? Are you doing your part to help turn America to God before it is too late?

# TEN TIPS ON HOW TO REMEMBER NAMES

Dale Carnegie in his book, *How to Win Friends and Influence People,* wrote: "Remember that a man's name is to him the sweetest and most important sound in any language."[107] The Bible tells us that Jesus "calls His own sheep by name" (John 10:3). If He places great value on a person's name then we should as well. Remembering someone's name is a skill you can learn if you apply some simple principles. I have developed and used these ten tips on how to remember names. I hope they will help you as well.

1. *YOU MUST WANT TO REMEMBER SOMEONE'S NAME.* If you do not really want to remember a person's name, you won't. If you care about a person, you will make a genuine effort to remember his name.

2. *YOU MUST CONCENTRATE ON REMEMBERING SOMEONE'S NAME.* When you know you are going to be meeting someone for the first time, be ready. Focus on the person you are meeting and not on yourself. If you did not catch the person's name, immediately say, "I'm sorry I didn't catch your name. What did you say your name was?" Here is where many people fail in learning to remember names. If they did not catch the person's name, they are embarrassed to ask the person to repeat it. Actually, people feel honored that you are making a genuine effort to remember their names, so go ahead and politely ask them to please repeat their name.

3. **SILENTLY REPEAT THE PERSON'S NAME SEVERAL TIMES IN YOUR MIND.** This will help you remember the name much better.

---

[107] Carnegie, Dale, *How to Win Friends and Influence People* (New York: Pocket Books, Inc. 1936), 83.

**4. IF THE PERSON HAS AN UNUSUAL NAME, ASK HOW HE SPELLS IT.** This will also give you a little more time to concentrate on his name before you move on and talk about other things.

**5. IMMEDIATELY REPEAT THE PERSON'S NAME SEVERAL TIMES IN YOUR CONVERSATION.** "Where do you live, John?" "Do you have a family, Mary?" By repeating the person's name several times, you will be able to remember it more easily, but do not repeat it too many times.

**6. TRY TO ASSOCIATE THE PERSON'S NAME WITH SOMEONE ELSE YOU KNOW.** If the person's name is "Betty", quickly think of someone else you know whose name is Betty. Picture in your mind the two Betty's as cousins. If you can form this mental picture of the two Betty's standing together you will be amazed how easily you can remember the person's name. If perhaps the person's name you just met reminds you of a famous person who has the same name, take a mental picture of those two people standing together.

**7. *IF YOU ARE IN A SOCIAL GATHERING AND YOU FORGET SOMEONE'S NAME, DISCREETLY ASK SOMEONE ELSE WHO HOPEFULLY KNOWS THE PERSON'S NAME TO TELL YOU WHAT IT IS.*** Never point to the person you are inquiring about.

**8. *IMMEDIATELY AFTER LEAVING THE PERSON YOU JUST MET, WRITE HIS NAME DOWN ON A PIECE OF PAPER.*** Transfer his name to a permanent list of people you have met. You may also want to record a fact or two about the person that will help you remember his name better. If you can get the person's business card, that will prove to be exceptionally helpful to you in remembering his name.

**9. *OCCASIONALLY REVIEW THE LIST OF PEOPLE YOU HAVE MET, ESPECIALLY IF YOU KNOW YOU WILL BE SEEING THEM AGAIN SOON.*** For instance, if you are going to call on a client, attend a business meeting or social gathering, or attend a church service or some other function, be sure to review the names on your list before you see those people again.

**10. *IMMEDIATELY UPON MEETING A PERSON AGAIN, CALL THE PERSON BY NAME.*** If perhaps you call the person by the wrong name, simply humble yourself and ask him to please forgive you. Politely ask him to tell you his name again. Now you will make a much greater effort to remember the person's name. Be sure to record the correct name on your list of names and review that person's name regularly so you don't make the same mistake again.

Don't convince yourself that you cannot remember people's names. Yes, you CAN remember names if you really want to and make the effort to do so. The time invested in remembering names pays great dividends.

# TEN VALUABLE THINGS MY DAD TAUGHT ME

### 1. *ALWAYS PUT THE LORD FIRST IN EVERY AREA OF YOUR LIFE*
"But seek first His kingdom and His righteousness, and all these things (the necessities of life) will be given to you as well" (Matthew 6:33).

### 2. *SERVE THE LORD WITH ALL YOUR HEART*
"Whoever serves Me must follow Me; and where I am, My servant will also be. My Father will honor the one who serves Me" (John 12:26).

### 3. *HONOR THE LORD WITH ALL HE GIVES YOU—YOUR TIME, TALENTS AND TREASURES*
"Remember how short my time is" (Psalm 89:47). "Honor the Lord with your wealth, and with the firstfruits of all your crops; then your barns will be filled to overflowing, and your vats will brim over with new wine" (Proverbs 3:9-10).

### 4. *EXPRESS LOVE AND AFFECTION*
"Dear friends, let us love one another, for love comes from God. Everyone who loves has been born of God and knows God" (I John 4:7).

### 5. *SPEND QUALITY TIME WITH YOUR FAMILY AND FRIENDS*
"Redeeming the time, because the days are evil" (I Thessalonians 5:16).

### 6. *LIVE A GODLY LIFE AND SET A GOOD EXAMPLE FOR OTHERS TO FOLLOW*
"Follow my example, as I follow the example of Christ" (I Corinthians 11:1).

### 7. *BE FRIENDLY AND KIND AND MAKE EVERYONE FEEL SPECIAL*
"He who has friends must show himself friendly" (Proverbs 18:24).

### 8. *TAKE A GENUINE INTEREST IN PEOPLE OF ALL AGES*
"Each of you should look not only to your own interests, but also to the interests of others" (Philippians 2:4).

### 9. *GET TO KNOW PEOPLE BY NAME*
"He calls His own sheep by name and leads them out" (John 10:3).

### 10. *GIVE MORE THAN WHAT IS EXPECTED AND WORK HARD*
"If someone forces you to go one mile, go with him two miles" (Matthew 5:41)

# TWENTY-FIVE CHALLENGES FOR A MAN OF GOD

"Tell Archippus: 'See to it that you complete the work you have received in the Lord'" (Colossians 4:17).

### 1. *MAJOR ON YOUR PERSONAL RELATIONSHIP WITH JESUS CHRIST*
Let other things go if necessary, but don't neglect the Lord. Psalm 27:4, Matthew 6:33, Luke 10:42

### 2. *GET A GOOD GRIP ON GOD'S WORD BY DAILY READING, HEARING, STUDYING, MEDITATING AND MEMORIZING IT*
Psalm 119:9-11, Matthew 4:4, Romans 10:17, Colossians 3:16, I Timothy 4:15, II Timothy 2:15, Revelation 1:3

### 3. *BE A MAN OF PRAYER*
Strive for the goal of at least one hour a day in prayer. Matthew 26:40, Mark 1:35, Colossians 4:12

### 4. *BE A MAN OF FAITH*
Mark 11:24, Matthew 13:58, Romans 4:20-21, Hebrews 11:6 "Attempt great things for God; expect great things from God." (Missionary William Carey)

### 5. *BE A MAN OF PATIENCE*
Hebrews 10:36, 12:1, James 5:7-8 Remember: "Rome wasn't built in one day."

### 6. *BE A MAN ON FIRE FOR GOD*
Jeremiah 20:9, Psalm 104:4, John 5:35

### 7. *BE A MAN CONTINUALLY FILLED WITH THE HOLY SPIRIT*

Acts 4:31, 13:52, Ephesians 5:18
8.   *BE A MAN IN PURSUIT OF HOLINESS*
Isaiah 6:1-8, Hebrews 12:14, I Peter 1:15,16

9.   *BE A MAN OF HUMILITY*
Proverbs 16:18,19, Psalm 115:1, Isaiah 57:15, John 3:30

10.   *BE A MAN OF CHRISTLIKE CHARACTER*
Romans 8:29, II Corinthians 3:18, I John 3:2

11.   *BE A MAN WITH A BURDEN FOR LOST PEOPLE*
Matthew 9:36-38, Luke 19:10, Romans 9:1-3, 10:1

12.   *BE A MAN WHO DISCIPLES OTHERS*
Matthew 28:18-20, Colossians 1:28,29, II Timothy 2:2

13.   *SPEND QUALITY TIME WITH YOUR FAMILY*
Deuteronomy 6:7, Psalm 127, Ephesians 5:25

14.   *HAVE FAMILY DEVOTIONS*
Deuteronomy 6:6-7, Joshua 24:15, Ephesians 6:4, Remember: K.I.S.S.= Keep it short and simple.

15.   *LOVE THE PEOPLE GOD HAS CALLED YOU TO SERVE*
John 13:34,35, I John 4:7-8

16.   *PREACH THE GOSPEL*
Mark 16:15, I Corinthians 2:1-5, 15:3-4, II Timothy 4:2

17.   *CALL PEOPLE TO COMMITMENT TO FOLLOW JESUS CHRIST*
Matthew 4:19, 22, 9:9, 10:32,33

18.   *REMAIN COMMITTED TO JESUS CHRIST REGARDLESS OF THE COST OR CONSEQUENCES*
Luke 9:23, I Corinthians 11:23-28, 15:58, II Timothy 2:3,4

19. *SEEK TO OBEY GOD IN ALL THINGS*
I Samuel 15:22, Luke 6:46, John 14:21, James 1:22

20. *GET OUT OF DEBT AND STAY OUT OF DEBT*
II Kings 4:1-7, Proverbs 22:7, Romans 13:8

21. *HONOR GOD THROUGH GIVING TITHES, OFFERINGS AND LOVE GIFTS*
Genesis 28:22, Proverbs 3:9-10, Malachi 3:9-10, I Corinthians 16:2, II Corinthians 9:6,7

22. *BE A FAITHFUL OVERSEER OF THE MINISTRY TO WHICH GOD HAS CALLED YOU*
Acts 20:28, I Peter 5:1-4

23. *LOVINGLY CARE FOR THE FLOCK GOD HAS GIVEN YOU*
Jeremiah 23:1,2, Ezekiel 34:1-11, John 21:15-17

24. *SEEK RECONCILIATION QUICKLY WITH GOD AND WITH OTHERS*
Matthew 5:23,24, 18:15-17, II Corinthians 5:18,19, I John 1:9

25. *SEEK TO BE A GODLY EXAMPLE IN ALL YOU DO AND SAY*
Matthew 5:16, John 13:15, I Corinthians 11:1

# FORTY-TWO OF MY FAVORITE JOKES

The Bible says, "A cheerful heart is good medicine, but a crushed spirit dries up the bones" (Proverbs 17:22). In Ecclesiastes 3:4 Solomon said there is " a time to laugh." When the Lord delivered His people from their captivity Psalm 126:2 tells us they declared, "Our mouths are filled with laughter, our tongues with songs of joy." Laughter is a good medicine. Good clean jokes can lift our spirits, give us a cheerful heart and a joyful countenance. Here are some of my favorite jokes. I hope at least some of them will make you laugh.

## THREE HUSBANDS

Three husbands were patiently waiting for their wives to give birth. The delivery room nurse came to the first husband and announced, "Your wife just gave birth to twins." He said, "That's amazing. I'm a baseball player with the Minnesota Twins baseball team." A few minutes later the nurse spoke to the second husband, "I can't believe what's happening in the delivery room today. Your wife just gave birth to triplets." He responded, "What a coincidence. I work for the Three M Corporation." Upon hearing this the third husband got up and started racing toward the door. The nurse said to him, "Where are you going?" He replied, "I'm getting out of here. I work for 7 UP."

## FOUR HUSBANDS

A lady married a banker, but he died. Then she went to an outdoor theater and fell in love with an actor and married him, but he died. Her third husband was a pastor, but he also died. Her last husband was a funeral director, but before long he died as well. Someone asked the lady why she married four different professional men. "Was there some reason why you married a banker, actor, pastor and funeral director?" "Oh, yes", she said, "I wanted one for the money, two for the show, three to get me ready, and four to go."

## *MARRIAGE*

A man and woman just got married. The man said to his wife, "Now in this new corporation we have just formed, would you like to be the President or the Vice President?" She replied, "Oh, honey, you can be both." He said, "But what role will you play?" She quickly responded, "I'll just be the treasurer."

A husband asked his wife if they could handle their checkbook of a 50/50 basis. She was delighted with the idea and said, "That's a great idea. You put the money in and I'll take it out."

When they got married a man and his wife decided that he would make all the major decisions and she would make all the minor decisions. After being married for 37 years the man said, "We've been married all these years and we have never had a major decision come up."

Bob and Betty were not speaking to each other. It was a whole week since they said a word to one another. Bob decided he would take Betty for a ride in the country on Sunday afternoon. As they rode along Bob saw an old mule in a farmer's field. He thought he'd break the silence and said to his wife, "Is that one of your relatives out there in the field?" Betty replied, "Yes, on my husband's side of the family."

Herman and Hilda were now in their nineties, but they loved each other dearly. As they sat on the front porch one summer evening Herman said, "Hilda, would you like a little ice cream tonight? That sounds so good to me." Hilda said, "Yes, I would like some ice cream, but Herman you know we are getting forgetful so please write it down." Herman got up out of his rocking chair and said, "Hilda, I don't need to write it down. I can remember." As Herman walked toward the screen door Hilda said, "Herman, could you put some chocolate syrup on the ice cream for me, but please write it down 'cause you know we are getting forgetful." Herman said, " I can remember that and I don't need to write it down." As Herman reached the kitchen Hilda called out to him again in a loud voice, "Herman, could you put some peanuts on the ice cream, that sounds so good to me, but PLEASE write it down." Herman shouted back, "Yes, Hilda, but I'm not writing it down." About an hour later Herman came out of the house with a large platter in his hand. On the platter were scrambled eggs and toast. As Hilda looked at the platter she said, "Herman, I told you we are getting forgetful. You should have written it down. You forgot the bacon."

Herman and Hilda were not getting along so they decided to go to a counselor. For the entire hour in the counselor's office they bickered back and forth with one another. When the hour was over the counselor got up and walked over to Hilda and gave her a little hug. He then said to her husband, "Herman, this is what Hilda needs at least three times a week." Herman responded, "Ok, I'll bring her in on Monday, Wednesday and Friday."

On the way home from the counselor's office Herman and Hilda were still bickering with one another. Hilda said, "Herman, I've had it. All these years of bickering have got to stop. I'm going to tell you how I have been praying. I've been praying that the Lord will take one of us home. And when He does I'm moving to Florida."

They say you're incomplete until you're married, and then you're finished.

I have a friend who is now in his eighties. He never got married. When asked why he never married he said, "I would rather go through life wishing for something I don't have, than having something I wish I didn't."

A man said he discovered that there are three rings involved in a marriage. There is the engagement ring, the wedding ring and the suffering.

A man and his wife were not getting along and she insisted that he go the doctor and get a physical. When he went to the doctor the doctor asked him, "What seems to be your problem?" The man said, "I'm irritable, tired and not getting along with my wife." The doctor asked him if he gets any exercise. "No," he replied, "I don't like to exercise." Then the doctor asked him if he eats green vegetables. Again, he said, "No, I don't like green vegetables." The doctor said, "Here's what I want you to do. I want you to start walking ten miles a day, eat green vegetables every day and call me at the end of the week." The man wasn't the sharpest knife in the drawer, but he told the doctor he would do what he said. At the end of the week he called the doctor. The doctor asked, "Did you walk ten miles each day this past week?" The man replied, "Yes, I did." The doctor then asked, "Did you eat green vegetables every day this past week?" Again the man responded, "Yes, I did." The doctor said, "Well then, how are you getting along with your wife?" The man replied, "Just great, I'm seventy miles from home."

## PASTORS AND THEIR PEOPLE

One Sunday a pastor had an exceptionally long sermon. A young man who was sitting in the front row got up and started to walk toward the door. The pastor asked him, "Where are you going?" The man replied, "I'm going to get a haircut." The pastor said, "Why didn't you get a haircut before you came to church?" The man said, "I didn't need one then."

A little girl was sitting in church with her grandmother when her grandmother fell asleep. The pastor stopped his sermon and said to the little girl, "Honey, would you please wake your grandmother." The little girl was quite sharp and replied, "Pastor, you put her to sleep. Let's see if you can get her awake."

A little boy was sitting in church with his grandmother, but he was really bored. He kept looking all around the room until he spotted a plaque on the wall. "Grandma, what's that plaque on the wall all about?" The grandmother answered, "That plaque has the names of all those who died in the service." The boy asked, "Grandma, was that the early service or the later service?"

A little boy spoke to the pastor as he shook hands with him after the worship service. The boy said, "Pastor, when I grow up and get a good job I'm going to give you money." The pastor asked, "Why would you want to give me money?" The boy replied, "Because my daddy says you are the poorest pastor we have ever had at our church."

A mother and her little girl greeted the pastor after the morning service. The mother was so appreciative of the message the pastor gave that Sunday and she said, "Pastor, you really fed us today. I feel so full." Her little girl added, "Pastor, I'm fed up too."

A family invited relatives, friends and people from their church to a picnic one summer afternoon. The father of the family asked his young son Georgie if he would pray before they began to eat. Georgie was shy and said, "Daddy, I don't know what to pray." His father said, "Georgie, just pray what you hear your mother praying." Georgie bowed his head and prayed, "Dear Lord, why did we invite all these people on such a hot day?"

One Sunday afternoon a group of people from the church gathered around the swimming pool at the home of one of the deacons. As they were talking one of the men dropped his car keys and they fell into the deep end of the pool. They were debating about who should jump into the pool and get the keys. Should it be the man who owned the pool? Should it be the man who dropped the keys? When the pastor arrived at the gathering they said he should jump into the pool and get the keys. When the pastor asked why he should be the one to get the keys someone replied, "Pastor, we don't know anyone who can go down deeper, stay down longer and come up drier than you."

As the pastor drove down the lane to the farmhouse the farmer's wife said to her husband, "I'm going to hide that crazy parrot in the closet and hope it keeps quiet when the pastor is here." As the pastor was visiting with the farmer and his wife, suddenly a little voice was heard coming out of the closet: "Give me a kiss. Give me a kiss." The farmer's wife was so embarrassed as she said, "Pastor, we bought this crazy parrot at the pet store and all day long it says, 'Give me a kiss. Give me a kiss.'" The pastor commented, "That's interesting. I have a parrot and all day long my bird says, 'Let's pray. Let's pray.'" I'll bring my parrot over some day and let's see what happens when we put them together. So they put the two parrots in the closet and closed the door. A few minutes later a little voice said, "Give me a kiss. Give me a kiss." Then the pastor's parrot said, "My prayer's been answered. My prayer's been answered."

The pastor's wife was going out of town to visit her sister. Before she left she asked her husband to promise that he would not look under the bed while she was away. He promised his wife that he wouldn't, but after about three days his curiosity got the best of him and he looked under the bed. He was surprised to find a shoe box filled with cash and two eggs. When his wife returned she asked him if he looked under the bed when she was away. He said, "I tried my best not to look under the bed, but I did. But what is that shoe box filled with cash and two eggs all about?" She said, "Every time you had a bad sermon I put an egg in the box." He replied, "Well, I guess I haven't had too many bad sermons." She responded, "Whenever I got a dozen eggs I sold them and put the cash in the box."

A little boy was sitting beside his older sister during a worship service. The girl said to her little brother, "You must be quiet in church or the hushers will make you to leave."

The pastor came to church one Sunday with a Band-Aid on his cheek. He told the congregation that he was thinking about his sermon when he was shaving and he cut his cheek. After the service a lady said to the pastor, "Next week maybe you should think about your cheek and cut your sermon."

A rather critical lady said to her pastor, "Pastor, I have decided you need to do one of two things with your sermons. You either need to put more fire into your sermons, or more of your sermons into the fire."

A man was sitting in a church service, but was very bored. During the announcements he heard the pastor say he wanted to meet with the church board in his office following the service. The man went to the pastor's office following the service. The pastor said, "Sir, I need to meet with the church board." The man replied, "If anyone is more bored than I am I want to meet them."

## PROFESSORS

A professor, who was a nuclear scientist, traveled across the country giving the same speech night after night. One day his chauffeur said to him, "Boss, I have heard your speech so many times that I think I could give it word perfectly." The professor said, "Alright, tonight you put on my tuxedo and get up and give the speech. I will put on your chauffeur's uniform and sit in the back of the auditorium." The chauffeur gave the speech without a flaw and received a standing ovation. As he was walking off the stage a student asked if he could answer a question for him. He replied, "What is your question?" The student said, "If you mixed two quarts of hydrogen peroxide with forty tons of potassium what effect would that have on Einstein's theory of relativity in a vacuum over a period of two years?" The man looked at the student and said, "That's a dumb question. If fact, it is so dumb that I am going to ask my chauffeur to answer that one."

A university professor gave strict instructions to his class of 150 students before they took their final exam. He said, "When I say begin you must begin writing your essay questions in your blue books and when I say stop you must stop immediately. You will have exactly one hour for your exam. When the hour is up I want you to take your blue books and place them on my desk and then you may be dismissed. If you do not follow my instructions exactly as I have stated, I will disqualify your exam. Begin writing." At the end of an hour the professor told the students to stop writing. The students pilled their blue books on the professor's desk and left the auditorium. One student in the back of the auditorium continued writing. About forty-five minutes later he finished writing and walked toward the professor's desk. The professor said, "You did not follow my instructions exactly as I said so I am disqualifying your exam." The student looked at the professor and said, "Do you know WHO I am?" The professor said, "Well, not really." The student replied, "Good" as he picked up a pile of the blue books and shoved his under the pile.

An absentminded professor came home one night and his wife said, "Where is the car?" He replied with a puzzled look on his face, "The last thing I remember is that I stopped on Center Street to pick up a hitch hiker. I then got out of the car and thanked him for the ride."

### *BIBLE JOKES*

Where is the first baseball game recorded in the Bible? Genesis 1:1 says, "In the big inning God created the heavens and the earth."

What happened in the first baseball game? Eve stole first. Adam stole second. Then the Lord threw them both out and they raised Cain, as they were Able.

Who had the fastest car in the Bible? David, because the roar of his Triumph was heard throughout the desert.

Are there any other cars mentioned in the Bible? Yes, the Honda is mentioned in Acts 1:14. They were all together in one Accord.

Is Santa Claus mentioned in the Bible? Zechariah 2:6 ( KJV )says, "Ho, Ho, come forth and flee from the land of the north."

Could the apostle Paul have had a job as a baker? In one of his letters he said he went to fill a pie (Philippi).

Who was the best tennis player in the Bible? It was probably Moses. He served in Pharaoh's court.

Who was the smallest man in the Bible? Many people think it was Zacchaeus because he was "little of stature." Others think the smallest man was KNEE-HIGH MIAH (Nehemiah), or Bildad the SHOE-HEIGHT (Shuhite). But what about the two men who fell asleep on their watch? Wouldn't they be the smallest?

Who was the best actor in the Bible? It was Samson. He brought the house down.

### LITTLE BILLY'S PHYSICAL

A little boy went to the doctor for a physical. The doctor put the stethoscope on his heart, patted his chest, and said, "Billy, your heart sounds really good." Billy replied, "That's not my heart." The doctor then put the stethoscope on Billy's ears and let him listen to his heart, but Billy said, "That is not my heart." The doctor was really confused by now and said, "Billy, where is your heart?" Billy pointed to his little back-side and said, "This is my heart." The doctor asked Billy why he thought that was his heart? Billy replied, as he patted his back-side, "Whenever grandma comes to see us she always pats me on my back-side and says, 'Bless your little heart, Billy.'"

A man ordered a pizza at a pizza shop. When he arrived to pick up the pizza the owner of the pizza shop said, "Do you want me to cut your pizza into eight pieces or ten?" The man replied, "Oh my, cut it into eight pieces, I could never eat ten."

### HEAVEN

Two ladies died and went to heaven. One day they were talking about how wonderful heaven was and one lady said to the other: "Just think about it. If we hadn't eaten so much oat bran we could have been here two years sooner."

Two mice died and went to heaven. After a few weeks Saint Peter asked the mice how they liked heaven. The mice said, "We love it here in heaven, but we have a problem." Saint Peter replied, "This is heaven. What kind of a problem could you possibly have?" The mice said, "Heaven is so big and we can't get around to see it all." Then Saint Peter told the mice that he had a solution to their problem. He strapped a little pair or roller skates to their feet and they went racing off through heaven. About a month later an old tom cat died and went to heaven. Saint Peter asked the tom cat what he liked about heaven. The tom cat remarked, "I just love those meals on wheels."

## *CONTACT INFORMATION*

If God used this book in any way to bless your life please give God the praise and glory. I would be delighted to hear from you if you would like to contact me by writing to: Larry E. Burd, 7481 Township Line Road, Nazareth, Pa. USA 18064 or by email at lburd@calvarybaptistpa.org.

If I can be of service to you as a guest speaker in your church, ministry, or organization, please feel free to contact me. I am also available for consulting services.

# ABOUT THE AUTHOR

Larry Burd is a native of Pennsylvania. He is a graduate of Houghton College and Gordon-Conwell Theological Seminary. He has pastored churches in the Boston, Buffalo and Bethlehem area over the past forty-three years. He has been the senior pastor of Calvary Baptist Church in Easton, Pennsylvania for the past thirty-three years. He is the host of the weekly TV program Living Truth broadcast in Eastern Pennsylvania, New Jersey and parts of Delaware. Larry is a part time Regional Minister with the Atlantic Association of the North American Baptist Conference of churches. He is the chairman of Share the Power, a ministry to pastors and Christian leaders. He has traveled and ministered the gospel in churches and on mission fields on six continents. He is married to his wife Sharon and they have four married children and nine grandchildren. Larry lives with his wife in Nazareth, Pennsylvania. He enjoys hunting, fishing and gardening.

Made in the USA
Middletown, DE
23 June 2016